Criminal Investigation
Essays and Cases

James N. Gilbert

Merrill Publishing Company
Columbus   London   Toronto   Melbourne

For Susan, Bennett, Robert, and Blake
—a fine group of siblings.

Published by Merrill Publishing Company
Columbus, Ohio 43216

This book was set in Garamond.

Administrative Editor: Stephen Helba
Production Editor: Sharon Rudd
Art Coordinator: Ruth Ann Kimpel
Cover Designer: Russ Masselli

Library of Congress Catalog Card Number: 89–64197
International Standard Book Number: 0–675–21200–6
Printed in the United States of America
1 2 3 4 5 6 7 8 9—94 93 92 91 90

Preface

It would be a pleasure to report to today's student of criminal justice that the need for effective criminal investigation has decreased. However, just the opposite is true, as documented by a myriad of sources indicating a continuing increase in serious crime. The investigative challenge of the 1990s is the most difficult ever to face law enforcement investigators. Serious felony crime, aided substantially by our outrageous national drug problem, threatens the tranquillity of most urban cities and is of concern to all Americans everywhere.

The readings and case studies within this volume are presented with several objectives in mind. They should develop an awareness of certain investigative concerns that are newly emerging areas of focus. Topics such as genetic identification, rural investigations, youth drug gangs, serial homicides, crack-cocaine, and the rural production of marijuana were not generally of primary interest to criminal investigators just a decade ago. Now they are of vital importance to all investigators and will continue to be so for many years to come.

Other topics within this text detail new information and/or changing trends in more traditional areas of criminal investigation. The use of informants, courtroom testimony, legal shifts affecting investigators, child abuse, death inquiries, and white collar crime—all have traditionally interested criminal investigators but now are dramatically affected by new techniques and research data.

A third focus of this book is exploration of nontraditional areas that are not commonly encountered in similar texts but that help prepare students for work within the criminal justice system. Two readings detail managerial concerns;

another aids the development of an ethical consciousness, as a safeguard against corruption in the field. Also presented is a first-person account of the pressures of undercover assignments. The final chapter explores the fascinating future of criminal investigation.

In addition to these eighteen original readings, four specific case studies are offered. The studies were selected for their overall timeliness and importance to criminal investigation. Each study details an actual felony inquiry that had significant impact on the criminal justice system at large.

Criminal Investigation: Readings and Cases is designed to fill an instructional void, serving as a supplemental text to expand the traditional body of knowledge generally included in primary textbooks. The readings and case studies are highly readable and relevant and are arranged to complement the order of presentation found in most standard texts. Although intended for introductory criminal justice students, this text is equally suitable for in-service practitioners.

I would like to thank David Stock of Chadron State College for his suggestions regarding this manuscript.

Contents

1

Criminal Investigation from a Small Town or Rural Perspective

Vic Sims
Lamar University

Criminal investigation presents unique challenges, puzzles, stressors, opportunities, and personal rewards for small town or rural police officers. The
absence of bureaucratic limitations and requirements, coupled with the presence of
increased police-community interaction and citizen-officer communication, results
in a different atmosphere for criminal investigators in small towns and rural communities. A spirit of self-policing supports the methods and techniques utilized by
small town and rural criminal investigators.

Rediscovery and application of small-group dynamics in recent years has
labeled such practices new. In reality, interpersonal communication among police
officers and between individual officers and citizens, as well as a greater degree of
citizen trust in officers, existed in U.S. policing long before the impersonality of
bureaucracies and specialization arrived on the scene.

Definition of Small Town and Rural Police

Small town and rural police are best identified as those police officers employed by
a department with a total strength of fifteen or fewer officers. Beyond that number,
specialization and bureaucratization blossom. Small town and rural police are
generalists. They police without clearly defined roles or sharply outlined responsibilities, authority, or expectations. The least-experienced officer in the department
may act as the principal investigator in a felony case, and the twenty-year chief may
retrieve the proverbial cat from the tree top. Beyond such differences in organization, however, research fails to show any correlation between the size of a police

agency and the types of crimes committed within its jurisdiction. This variance remains best explained by the chemistry of those policed.

In small town and rural policing, the terms *police officer* and *criminal investigator* seem interchangeable more often than they appear anywhere else in police science. Some departments employing nine to fifteen officers designate one person as a full-time detective, but such a situation seems the exception nationwide. More often, the title of detective or investigator describes a position, rather than duties. Virtually all small town and rural police officers serve as criminal investigators, investigating the total spectrum of criminal activity.

The Process of Criminal Investigation

Investigating and solving crimes in any location involve nothing more than processing information—that is, locating, identifying, collecting, analyzing, sorting, evaluating, recording, and storing it effectively. Experience shows that the probability of solving any individual case increases as the investigator increases the volume of collected data related to it. Some law enforcement officers fight crime with increased arrests, even though such tactics remain totally ineffective.[1] Persuasive evidence indicates that effective criminal investigators increase indictments by processing information.[2]

The sources of information available to criminal investigators appear limited only by their imagination and the law. The most successful investigators seem the most imaginative. However, five major sources account for the vast majority of information used in solving crimes: crime scene processing, neighborhood canvassing, file searches, informants, and follow-ups. Some investigators favor one or two of these sources, and many reach a final disposition in a case without using all five. But no wise criminal investigator continuously ignores any one of the five sources.

To oversimplify a complex process, criminal investigators detect and solve crimes as follows. They collect data from the five sources, constantly expanding and broadening the scope and focus of the investigation until they exhaust all information sources or the available time or both. Then they reverse the process and begin to narrow the focus of the investigation by evaluating and culling data until only one suspect remains or neither time nor energy remains, whichever comes first. In essence, investigators develop suspects until none remain unidentified, and then they eliminate suspects until only one remains. Experienced investigators resist the temptation to lock onto the first outstanding suspect and rush to judgment.

Criminal investigation requires certain traits—intelligence, good reasoning ability, imagination, curiosity, intuition, observational skills, legal knowledge, good reading and studying habits, organizational ability, refined and well-developed interpersonal communication skills, and perhaps most importantly, persistence.[3] It also requires time and money, and these two elements highlight major differences in the work of criminal investigators in small town and rural settings as opposed to urban bureaucracies. Police bureaucracies generally possess adequate money but limited time, whereas the smaller groups possess limited money but adequate time.

These conditions translate into less-than-optimum effectiveness for all criminal investigators.

Crime Scene Processing

Crime scene processing refers to all of a criminal investigator's activities associated with a crime scene. These activities include protecting the scene from deterioration; searching for, recognizing, recording, identifying, photographing, documenting, collecting, preserving, handling, and transporting evidence; taking notes; sketching, diagraming, and photographing the scene; locating and interviewing witnesses; and gaining a general feel for the crime scene.[4] This last task requires intuition and use of the senses in assessing atmosphere, mood, and countless seemingly insignificant and often unnoticed aspects of the situation. Such a feel remains essential to successful crime investigation and helps explain why police officers in the field account for as much as 90 percent of all solved crime.[5]

Successful criminal investigators bear in mind that the crime scene may not exist when a jury needs to visit it. Therefore, these investigators strive with measurements, diagrams, photographs, and video recorders to collect sufficient data to enable other investigators years later to reconstruct the scene with charts, illustrations, models, dioramas, and videotapes. Serial murderers Bianchi and Buono committed numerous unspeakable acts of sexual perversion and murder in a small upholstery shop, which was bulldozed and paved over soon after their arrests.[6] However, superb crime scene processing contributed to the successful prosecution of the two culprits.

Beginning investigators too frequently forget to work in volume and collect less evidence than is needed. If in doubt, an investigator should collect as much evidence as possible. Discarding surplus evidence remains a pleasure in contrast to the agony of permitting a criminal to evade justice because of insufficient evidence. Investigators should be constantly mindful of possible defense tactics and should counteract any potential for juror doubt.[7] In the well-publicized case against Charles Manson, the failure to collect blood samples from each of the many puddles at the murder scene subsequently created unnecessary difficulties for the prosecution.[8]

Crime scene processing requires considerable time. Because the ratio of officers in the field to citizens in the jurisdiction remains significantly greater in small towns and rural communities and because those residents have grown accustomed to more police attention, small town and rural investigators appear to spend more time processing crime scenes than do investigators in larger police departments. Conversely, residents of densely populated cities seem resigned to less police attention. Police department bureaucracies prevent many investigators from spending the needed time in crime scene processing.

Burglary investigation is just one example. Generally speaking, small town and rural police officers investigate burglaries in a scrupulous manner, whereas an increasing number of large police departments refuse to dispatch officers to investigate burglary reports. These departments ask victims to give a telephone report, and a few advanced bureaucracies boldly require victims to go to the police department to make a burglary report.

Until less than a decade ago, criminal investigators relied more on testimony and witnesses than on physical evidence. However, a few recent cases have underscored the power of modern forensics and crime labs in solving crimes consistently and reliably. Now, a growing trend seems to exist to invest more effort in the physical evidence of a case. The importance of witnesses and testimony—and the parallel need for good interpersonal communication skills—remains strong. But when investigators cannot secure both witnesses and testimony and physical evidence, the latter takes precedence.

Those aspects of crime scene processing that require expensive equipment typically receive more attention in larger police departments: video cameras, fumigation tents, mobile crime labs, portable generators, and even relatively inexpensive vacuum cleaners with removable paper bags. However, those aspects of crime scene processing that require significant periods of time often receive far greater attention in small town and rural departments: searches for evidence of questionable value, searches of large areas, repeated searches of the same area, detailed measurements, searches extending to the fringes of the crime scene, and searches of any approach and escape routes. Small town and rural police usually tackle crime scene processing with great vigor and attention to detail.

All criminal investigators must protect the chain of evidence, which is the written account of the location of and person responsible for the evidence, from its finding until its admission in court. A continuous chain of evidence convinces a jury that no one has tampered with the evidence, and sharp defense attorneys frequently check the chain of evidence before anything else. Large police departments generate special forms, but legally any writing or testimony that explains the location of the evidence at all times will suffice. Each bit of independent evidence must be linked to a chain of evidence.

With a pellet pistol Prosenjit Poddar shot attractive Tanya Tarasoff several times in her living room, followed her into the kitchen, attacked her with a butcher knife, and then chased her into the front yard, where he savagely and fatally stabbed her.[9] Tarasoff's bloody footprints led across the street, where she collapsed and died. Small knots of curious onlookers suddenly emerged from nowhere as two patrol officers investigated. The murderer seemed secure, arrested and handcuffed in a police car.

Crime scene deterioration began before the ambulance's siren had faded. Possible witnesses mingled with each other while youngsters on bikes delighted in riding back and forth through the thick blood. A forced choice immediately emerged: the two officers could rely on witnesses or evidence or an inadequate sampling of both, but two officers could not secure both. The investigators knew the importance of locating and identifying witnesses, but gathering physical evidence claims top priority in a forced choice situation.

The pellets, blood, gun, and knife required undivided attention and detailed diagrams. Consequently, one of the officers, designated as the finder, assumed responsibility for handling all physical evidence, noting the location of each piece and establishing a chain of evidence. This approach keeps the chain of evidence confined to a minimum number of people and helps prevents costly gaps.

In the Tarasoff murder the finder of the butcher knife needed to mark it for later identification. Since the knife bore no serial number, the finder scratched his initials into the blade, enabling him to testify under oath that the knife in question was the same knife found at the crime scene. Properly identified evidence and a flawless chain of custody offer convincing proof to a jury.

Modern crime scene investigation requires such attention to detail that even microscopic evidence must not escape examination. Because of the costs involved, investigators in large departments generally outperform their small town and rural counterparts in this area. All types of trace evidence—dust, lint, hair, fibers, dirt, and other microscopic particles—should be collected,[10] for they possess identifying characteristics that associate them with a certain class or group.

Criminal investigators vacuum areas that might yield trace evidence. They then remove the paper bags from the cleaners and label each bag with the case number, date, and precise location of collection. Thus begins the chain of evidence. In a complex case an investigator may divide each room into halves or quadrants with a separate bag for each part. With help from a crime lab, such attention to detail frequently solves crime.

Criminal investigators process vehicles just like any other crime scene. They check all surfaces, not just the obvious, for prints. They also vacuum the floor and carpet, as well as the cracks and crevices of automobile upholstery, which remain valuable sources of information. They remove an entire ashtray, if possible, and deliver it undisturbed to the crime lab. They even examine wheel wells, carefully and diligently scraping into a bag all caked and accumulated debris from underneath each wheel housing. Each bag is precisely labeled and identified as coming from a particular wheel well.

Once an investigator identifies a vehicle for crime scene processing, the vehicle becomes fragile evidence and must be moved out of the weather to retard deterioration. When properly done, workers winch the vehicle onto a trailer or a truck, the floor of which has been covered with a large sheet of plastic to catch any particles that drop from the vehicle. As with any crime scene an effective investigator remains constantly alert. Evidence of mechanical work performed on a vehicle may lead to information. Nonfactory work, custom installations, or modifications may jog a mechanic's memory. An investigator seeks always to expand the available information.

Neighborhood Canvassing

Small town and rural criminal investigators use the technique of neighborhood canvassing quite often. In a neighborhood canvass an investigator searches along the avenues of approach to and escape from a crime scene and in other selected locations for persons with some knowledge about a particular crime. The canvassing investigator contacts people in homes, workplaces, supermarkets; he or she contacts joggers, juveniles, winos. Again, the most successful investigators appear the most imaginative and determined. They are also prompt, since a lapse of time after the commission of a crime decreases the probability of a fruitful neighborhood canvass.[11]

Neighborhood canvassing assumes that information related to a particular crime does exist in the community. Additionally, neighborhood canvassing assumes that persons with needed information do not always realize the value of their information or are not always ready to come forward. If citizens delivered unsolicited information to the police on a regular basis, neighborhood canvassing would become unnecessary. However, all too often the unused telephone sits conveniently nearby, covered with emergency police numbers.

Neighborhood canvassing is effective because it hinges on personal interaction—a face-to-face, one-on-one give and take. Since as much as 80 percent or more of our communication involves nonverbal messages, it's small wonder that some seem to accomplish so little over the phone.[12]

Neighborhood canvassing requires a great investment of time but no money. Consequently, small town and rural criminal investigators can take full advantage of this information source.

Using proven interviewing techniques, effective canvassers make many contacts and process massive volumes of information. They face many rejections and unmeasured discouragement, but the race goes to the persistent.

Neighborhood canvassing generates at least two important side effects: it reinforces police-community relations, and it may close other cases. Citizens with absolutely no information to contribute appreciate the personalized attention of the police officers soliciting their help. In addition, some will later call the police with other information, which may prove to be significant. In any event, neighborhood canvassing promotes communication between the citizenry and the police, and that in itself is beneficial.

Neighborhood canvassing also serves to remind the police that they cannot solve crimes alone. They must interact with people whom they would never meet otherwise. And that contact helps investigators maintain a healthy perspective, avoiding the cynicism that would result from associating too long with only the criminal community.

File Searches

File searches are the most misunderstood and least used of the five major information sources.[13] Police officers seem action oriented, not given to poring over volumes of forgotten lore. Of the major information sources only file searches involve no activity in the field and no interaction with people. Files seem boring, not like real police work.

Nonetheless, criminal investigators who consistently close cases are the same ones who spend countless hours, both paid and unpaid, perusing the files, frequently unsure of exactly what they're seeking. Successful investigators make maximum use of file searches, haunted by the possibility that the files conceal not only the name and identity of a suspect they seek, but the total solution to the crime as well. Once beginning investigators reach this understanding, they reach a milestone in developing their full potential for solving crimes.

File searches, like the other information sources, offer valuable information and helpful clues; the challenge lies in locating and retrieving the data needed. In sharp contrast to the information available in neighborhood canvassing, virtually all information stored in files correlates directly or indirectly with crime, criminals, or criminal activity. File searches are similar to a child's Easter egg hunt, with countless varieties of candy and eggs hidden in a very small area. The investigator must find the one very special prize.

In most larger police agencies master files, arrest files, and case files remained the primary sources of stored information on crimes until the late 1960s.[14] The implementation of the National Crime Information Center (NCIC) at that time probably did more to improve overall criminal investigation in the United States than did any other single event. NCIC eliminated much of the fragmentation and duplication occurring among investigators working for different agencies.[15] NCIC also served to greatly improve communications among investigators. Investigators unafraid of file searches have benefited the most from the information explosion. Files have expanded and accessibility has grown until many street officers in more affluent jurisdictions today drive cars equipped with terminals and printers.

Master, or alpha (alphabetical), files remain the most fundamental and general source of information for investigators.[16] In theory, an alpha file contains every name of every person coming to police attention since a given department started filing. In reality, alpha files contain many names and leads and provide investigators with an invaluable starting point. Alpha files, like all others, reference case numbers, which link the different files.

Case files are the only pure files; technically, other files exist as indices, not files. The cases themselves constitute the case files and fill entire rooms in some larger police departments. Each case file contains original copies of all the work done on that particular case. The cases may range from a nearly blank 5-by-8 card to scores of thick file folders filling yards of shelf space.

Arrest files contain the names, charges, dispositions, case numbers, arrest numbers, and FBI rap sheet numbers of all persons arrested in a given jurisdiction—an important limitation. Likewise, both case files and, to a lesser degree, alpha files focus narrowly and selectively on individuals and crimes long associated with an immediate area. These limitations cause investigators greater difficulty in small town and rural police departments.

Other files commonly utilized by investigators have included chronological police bulletins, modus operandi (MO) or crime files, arrest books, field interrogation cards, street address files, jail visitors logs, auto accident files, missing persons files, runaway juvenile files, stolen property files, nickname files, other cross references, mug shots, high school yearbooks, vehicle model books, National Auto Theft Bureau publications, other juvenile files, intelligence files, social security numbers index, and the sometimes overlooked telephone directories. A county clerk's office contains many volumes of personal records that are accessible and free. In addition, every county courthouse maintains a free public law library, and local libraries offer city directories.

Files provide investigators with tools. Again, only an investigator's imagination and persistence limit the generation of leads in most file searches. An investigator typically enters a file search with what appears to be insufficient data. For example, with nothing more than a nickname for a clue, an experienced investigator might quickly retrieve all entries matching that name in the nickname file. Those entries would lead to names, addresses, dates of birth, social security numbers, and possibly other information. Another investigator, with nothing more than a particular offense—a burglary perhaps—and a general time frame, might search the field interrogation card file. That file could yield the names of drivers, passengers, pedestrians, and people on the street when the burglary occurred, as well as vehicle license plate numbers and other information. That same investigator might also check a crime file or an address file and be led directly to a suspect in the case files.

Wise investigators multiply information by making the files do the work. As they evaluate, sort, save, and eliminate leads, the process then gradually changes from multiplication to division. Seasoned investigators all tell favorite stories of solving difficult cases without leaving the records division. Retired investigators also tell of disappointment, frustration, and injustice from knowing that the identity of a sought-after criminal remained hidden in the files.

Often, small town and rural police departments fail to maintain adequate records and crime files. Departments with fewer than five or six officers may claim no files, whereas many departments with ten to fifteen officers have deficient systems. Small town and rural police officers tend to interact more with people in the field and hence to deemphasize record keeping. As police officers they may manage superbly; as record keepers they typically manage poorly or not at all. Unfortunately, the lost opportunities resulting from insufficient records pose a severe handicap.

The most important and profound contribution that some small town and rural criminal investigators can make to solving crime is the establishment of a record-keeping system. Starting a system often proves to be the hardest part because it requires change. However, even in small town and rural departments with crime files in place, investigators must not grow complacent. Criminal investigators everywhere must ensure that the files they utilize have unlimited room for expansion.

Computers

Today an ever-increasing number of investigators depend on computers to search files and generate suspects. Because computers process volumes of data with lightning speed and exhaust unthinkable numbers of possibilities, they supply criminal investigators with unprecedented advantages. The most progressive investigators now conduct file searches in seconds instead of hours, scan records in ways never before possible, and even direct computers to identify and rank order suspects.

Before computers, investigators could scan records only by file titles. Now investigators can scan records using any field or combination of fields, such as height, weight, race, sex, hair color, or clothing description. They can even look for a particular entry, such as a missing finger, a nervous habit like teeth clenching, or chronic sniffling. They can search certain files or certain records or fields in certain files. Yesterday's larger police departments relied on pin maps, which held great potential but presented too much data for the human mind to search and cross-reference. Today's computers can quickly and easily unlock that potential. Computers are solving crimes with never-before-imagined speed, consistency, and reliability.

A few pioneers in criminal investigation also use computers for profiling and crime prediction. When properly programmed, computers can quickly spot trends and patterns. For example, the best single predictor of future criminal behavior is past criminal behavior. However, nothing limits the computer to using only one predictor. And the more variables the computer utilizes, the greater the accuracy of the prediction. We know that a great majority of all homicides occurring in a residence involve alcohol, firearms, and a record of at least five previous police interventions.[17] We also know that the best single predictor of a man's killing his wife, lover, or girlfriend is his beating of that woman. And we know that police officers have accurately predicted murder after dealing with certain family disturbances. Police files currently contain these variables and hundreds more in a proliferation of raw data begging for the attention of police computer programmers.

Thus, computers are verifying what the police have known all along: crime is predictable and therefore preventable. Crime prevention must be the absolute goal in criminal investigation since crime itself is an injustice. The purest justice imaginable will always be no crime and no victim. With computers tomorrow's criminal investigators will investigate and solve crimes more efficiently and effectively, and they will prevent more crime.

A strong positive correlation exists between the size of a police department and its use of computers in identifying suspects and solving crimes. Since the overwhelming majority of police departments are small town and rural agencies, most police departments do not own a computer. Start-up costs, lack of expertise, paralyzing conservatism, resistance to change, and outdated views of the goals of policing and criminal investigation stand in the way. Of these factors, start-up costs are probably the greatest hurdle for small town and rural investigators to overcome. But without computers and adequate files criminal investigators will struggle and stumble.

The success of criminal investigators using computers will relegate other investigators to a distinctive subspecies, causing the first major division in the history of investigation. The NCIC system brought all criminal investigators closer together; the absence of computers in small town and rural departments threatens to alienate these investigators from their big city counterparts to a far greater extent than was ever experienced previously.

Informants

Without doubt informants remain the oldest information source. They may also be the most universal and most consistently used source. Absolutely anyone can serve as an informant, regardless of age, gender, race, or political persuasion. Proximity to criminal activity or to crime-related information and a willingness to inform are the necessary ingredients. Informants serve as extensions of an investigator's eyes and ears; and since most informants receive no money for their revelations, small town and rural investigators can benefit fully from their involvement.

There are three general categories of informants: well-placed citizens, persons on the fringes of crime, and criminals themselves.[18] Well-placed citizens often hold valuable information for conscientious criminal investigators, and this source is most frequently tapped by small town and rural investigators. This category of informants includes waitresses and waiters, barbers and cosmetologists, janitors, and many others. Any person who meets or rubs shoulders with the public is positioned to absorb information. Postal carriers, especially in small towns and rural settings, frequently remember faces as well as names. In addition, route drivers, delivery persons, sanitation workers, and others whose jobs place them repeatedly on the street may possess valuable knowledge.

Persons on the fringes of crime often yield information that may be at the heart of a case. Cab drivers and bartenders are representative of this category. Bartenders work in perhaps the best of all capacities to overhear conversations thought private by the participants. However, wise investigators must understand that good informants require cultivation and careful handling over a period of time, sometimes a long time. For example, few bartenders want their customers seeing them talking to the police. Consequently, effective investigators wait until after closing hours or until no customers are around before approaching a bartender. Investigators must work hard to build a trusting relationship with an informant but must never trust the informant with more information than they can afford to lose.

Criminals themselves form the third pool of potential informants. Because of their location inside the criminal world, they possess information unobtainable from any other source. Because of their life-styles and experiences, however, criminal informants also pose the greatest danger to investigators. An investigator's personal safety must remain a top priority at all times; an opportunity for valuable information must never overshadow concern for safe investigation practices.

Department policy and tradition serve as major determinants in the use of informants. Larger departments seem to use paid informants with greater frequency; small town and rural investigators seem more likely to benefit from gossip and volunteered information. Community-based policing, more common in small towns and rural neighborhoods, encourages informants, especially well-placed citizens and those on the fringes of crime. And self-policing, a virtually exclusive hallmark of small towns and rural communities, tends to establish a more tolerant atmosphere for informants than that found in big cities, where the police bureaucracy is often expected to operate without citizen assistance.

Follow-up

During follow-up an investigator reviews the total case, recontacts each significant party, rechecks each information source, and rethinks the investigation. Like the other major information sources, follow-ups solve crime. And like neighborhood canvassing, follow-ups serve a powerful police-community relations function, which may in itself help solve or prevent future crimes.

Follow-ups require considerable time and practically no money. Consequently, small town and rural investigators usually complete follow-ups regularly in all criminal cases and in some other areas of public service. In contrast, investigators in larger departments thoroughly follow up only the most serious criminal cases. Small town and rural investigators remain better able to conduct repeat follow-ups also, since they have the time and encounter many reminders. When they see a recent victim, for example, they can intervene and follow up. And face-to-face follow-ups generally yield far better results than those produced by telephone calls.

Any procedure that incorporates citizen involvement in the criminal investigation process is apt to result in some degree of success. Follow-ups solve crimes chiefly because affected parties spend time contemplating, reviewing, reliving, recounting, and resolving the crimes. And most people delight in playing criminal investigator, welcoming any opportunity. In addition, some crimes require a certain amount of aging for the solution to surface.

Follow-ups also play an important therapeutic role for both individual victims and the community as a whole. Such contact offers the much-needed assurance that society cares about the welfare of victims and they remain necessary parts of the whole. In addition, follow-ups give victims closure even when investigators feel only frustration and failure.

Anniversary observations, a type of follow-up, require time but little or no money and thus remain the domain of small town and rural criminal investigators. An anniversary observation returns an investigator to a crime scene at the same hour the crime occurred to restudy conditions and search for witnesses or individuals with information related to the crime. Anniversary observations may occur the next day, one week later, one month later, and so on.

Anniversary observations do not assume that criminals return to the scene of the crime, simply that people remain victims of habits and routines. Commuters, workers, street people, alcoholics, professors, and even suspects travel in certain patterns, and investigators hope to intervene in these patterns on anniversary observations.

A police officer, my friend and locker partner, was murdered during a traffic stop late one night in Berkeley, California. A roadblock at the exact time of the occurrence the following three nights produced many leads but nothing monumental. Then an officer boarded a bus exactly one week—to the minute—after the slaying. A request for information produced nothing until the next day, when the driver phoned the police department with information. He was a relief driver who drove that route only once a week. He didn't want others to know that he had given information to the police, and he would not have initiated the interaction but he responded to an anniversary observation with important information.

Interviewing

Successful criminal investigators owe much to the techniques and attitudes they employ in interviews. Effective investigators practice cognitive interviewing, which uses certain methods to jog and guide the memory of a victim or a witness.

Memory consists of numerous elements in a collection. Each remembered element has multiple access paths so that information not responding to one retrieval device may emerge with another. The more effective the recall aid, the more elements it shares in common with the particular memory.[19] However, even a slight stimulus can excite the recall of a memory long forgotten.

In actual interview situations investigators should first put interviewees at ease and gain their confidence. When the interviewer and the interviewee are of different genders, investigators may find that the presence of a third person of the same sex as the interviewee adds comfort and security even when the subject matter does not appear sensitive. Before the interviewee begins the narrative, the investigator should briefly outline the entire interview and explain the four major memory retrieval methods: reconstructing the circumstances, reporting everything, recalling the events in different order, and changing the perspective.

In reconstructing the circumstances, an interviewee should try to rethink and rebuild the entire incident—the locations, positions, and appearances of all people and things. Mental reconstruction is a form of revisiting the crime scene, and reliving personal emotions frequently provides usable data. An interviewee should be instructed to withhold absolutely nothing. One remembered detail may engage another by association, and evaluating evidence must remain the task of the interviewer.

The interviewer should also encourage the interviewee to recall the events in a different order, perhaps starting with the most impressive or discussing the incident in reverse chronological order. The interviewee might also try following the order of time required for each event, from the longest to the shortest. Recalling events in different order programs the memory to scan all record markers.[20] In addition, the investigator should ask the interviewee to change perspectives, assuming the role of another person involved in the incident and considering what that person observed or thought. Changing perspectives helps fill in details otherwise overlooked.

Productive interviewers also tease out information with prompters, searching for the unusual or the unique. Did the suspect remind the witness of a friend or acquaintance? How? If the suspect spoke a name, can the witness recall the first letter? How many syllables? Did the case involve any numbers? Large or small? How many digits? What colors were on the license plates? Dark on light or light on dark? Did the suspect's voice remind the victim of anyone else's voice? How? A dialect or speech pattern? Slang, idioms, or colloquialisms?

In a television detective series, actor Peter Falk, playing Columbo, has superbly demonstrated cognitive interviewing. Feigning a slow, dense mind, Columbo motivates others to explain how a crime occurred. He takes advantage of most people's unconscious desire to play criminal investigator, and his style prompts others to talk.

Like Columbo, the most successful interviewers are the best listeners. While listening for the facts, good listeners hear innuendos and suggestions that encourage additional conversation. The model interviewer says little but enables the subject to do the talking. Once again, wise criminal investigators simply gather and manage other people's information.

The Crime Laboratory

Thorough knowledge of the potential of crime labs, criminalistics, and physical evidence remains as crucial to the criminal investigator as proper use of information sources. It seems impossible to overemphasize the importance of physical evidence.[21] Working with heavy caseloads and limited time, successful investigators should concentrate their energy and resources on physical evidence, for it seems to solve crimes and convince juries with a power and consistency not found in any other single aspect of criminal investigation. The triangle of interaction among criminal investigators, computer scientists, and forensic scientists appears ready to demolish all obstacles to the advancement of criminal investigation, and physical evidence remains the cornerstone of that triangle.

More than three hundred crime laboratories exist in the United States today, appearing at local, county, regional, state, and federal levels. Many remain limited in the tests and processes they can perform, and none of the labs possess unlimited resources. Thus, criminal investigators must determine which crime lab services they can use most wisely, because the overworked labs have been forced to restrict their activities. Wise investigators must work within the restraints of this unavoidable injustice.

The FBI maintains the largest and most complete crime laboratory in the world, and any police department in the United States can use its services free. Small town and rural investigators should never hesitate to learn the simple procedures for preparation of evidence to submit to the FBI crime lab. Bashfulness is inconsistent with superior criminal investigation.

The terms *forensic science* and *criminalistics* sometimes appear to be interchangeable. Forensic science, the broader term, includes criminalistics, as well as all sciences applied to answering legal questions. Criminalists uses the natural sciences to recognize, identify, individualize, and evaluate physical evidence in legal matters. Although they may never meet face-to-face, criminal investigators and criminalists are interdependent, sharing equally critical roles in many major cases.

Physical evidence is classified into two groups—evidence that is linked to a certain class or category and evidence that is linked to a particular individual or single source.[22] Some evidence, such as shoe prints, may be classified in either group. Common examples of evidence that criminalists might associate beyond a reasonable doubt with a class or category include hair, drugs, paint chips, soil, safe insulation, tags from explosives, tire and shoe prints, fibers, dust and floor sweepings or vacuumed debris, glass fragments too small to piece together, and evidence of a serological nature—blood, semen, vaginal secretions, urine, perspiration, saliva, feces, and vomitus. Evidence that might be linked beyond a reasonable doubt to a particular source or single individual includes fingerprints, footprints, lip prints, teeth marks, firearms evidence, handwriting, tire and shoe prints, tool marks, typewritten copy, voice prints, photocopies, and fingernail clippings.

DNA fingerprinting, or genetic identification, holds great promise for unprecedented breakthroughs in criminal investigation and criminalistics. The possibility increases steadily that DNA fingerprinting will elevate serological evidence from categorical to individualized status.[23] DNA fingerprinting has proved successful in Great Britain's court system in both paternity and criminal cases. Another technological breakthrough permits criminal investigators to lift footprints from carpets and incriminating smudges from floors, drapes, and walls.[24] A company in England currently markets this process, which British investigators say frequently enhances invisible evidence enough to identify criminals.

The potential of unlocking convincing and convicting evidence offers inspiration for all criminal investigators, regardless of the size of their employing departments. This potential also reminds all investigators of the need to perfect skills associated with the collection of invisible evidence.

Future Directions

Examination of the most recent Uniform Crime Reports reveals a negative correlation between the population of a jurisdiction and the crime clearance rate[25]: the greater the population, the lower the clearance rate. A formal, scientific study of small town and rural criminal investigation offers more promise than does any other research area for the identification and isolation of variables related to success or failure in the detection, solving, and prevention of crime. Scholarly study of small town and rural criminal investigators may lead to profound principles of crime prevention, from which we all would benefit.

Until then, we may all take comfort in the knowledge that criminal investigators, regardless of the size of the department or the population of the jurisdiction, perform in a conscientious and competent manner in the vast majority of settings and situations. The greatest contribution that each of us can make to improved criminal investigation is to seize every opportunity to help the investigators. Our information may make a difference.

Notes

[1] U.S. Department of Justice, National Institute of Justice, *Perspectives on Policing* (Washington, DC: Government Printing Office, 1988–1989).

[2] J. Mills, *The Underground Empire: Where Crime and Governments Embrace* (Garden City, NY: Doubleday, 1986).

[3] J.N. Gilbert, *Criminal Investigation,* 2d ed. (Columbus: Merrill, 1986); R. Nelson, *The Cop Who Wouldn't Quit* (New York: Bantam Books, 1984).

[4] J.L. Dowling,*Criminal Investigation* (New York: Harcourt Brace Jovanovich, 1979).

[5] P.W. Greenwood, J.M. Chaiken, and J. Petersilia, *The Criminal Investigative Process* (Lexington, MA: D.C. Heath, 1977).

[6] T. Schwarz, *The Hillside Strangler* (New York: Signet Books, 1982).

[7] P.B. Weston and K.M. Wells, *Criminal Investigation Basic Perspectives,* 4th ed. (Englewood Cliffs, NJ: Prentice-Hall, 1986).

[8] V. Bugliosi and C. Gentry, *Helter Skelter* (New York: Bantam Books, 1974).

[9] D. Blum, *Bad Karma* (New York: Jove Books, 1986).

[10] R. Saferstein, ed., *Forensic Science Handbook,* Vol. 2 (Englewood Cliffs, NJ: Prentice-Hall, 1988).

[11] C.R. Swanson, Jr., N.C. Chamelin, and L. Territo, *Criminal Investigation,* 3d ed. (New York: Random House, 1984).

[12] H.A. Bosmajian, *The Rhetoric of Nonverbal Communication* (Glenview, IL: Scott, Foresman, 1971).

[13] Gilbert, *Criminal Investigation.*

[14] Ibid.

[15] Dowling, *Criminal Investigation.*

[16] Gilbert, *Criminal Investigation.*

[17] J. Godwin, *Murder U.S.A.* (New York: Ballantine Books, 1978); D.T. Lunde, *Murder and Madness* (Stanford, CA: Stanford Alumni Association, 1975).

[18] Swanson, Chamelin, and Territo, *Criminal Investigation.*

[19] R.E. Geiselman and R.P. Fisher, Interviewing victims and witnesses of crime, *Research in Brief* (Washington, DC: National Institute of Justice, December 1985).

[20] Ibid.

[21] Saferstein, *Forensic Science Handbook.*

[22] Dowling, *Criminal Investigation.*

[23] DNA fingerprinting. Brochure published by Cellmark Diagnostics, 20271 Goldenrod Lane, P.O. Box 1000, Germantown, MD 20874.

[24] "Crime-Fighting Invention Lifts Footprints," *USA Today,* 10 December 1984, 3B.

[25] U.S. Department of Justice, Federal Bureau of Investigation. *Crime in the United States* (Washington, DC: Government Printing Office, 1986).

2
Marijuana as a Cash Crop:
Drugs and Crime on the Farm

Ralph A. Weisheit
Illinois State University

For many years the drug problem in the United States was largely fueled by drugs smuggled in from other countries. In the 1980s, however, the United States became the fastest-growing source of marijuana. The increase was sudden and dramatic. In fact, a 1982 Drug Enforcement Administration (DEA) report admitted that in the previous year 38 percent more domestic marijuana was seized than was previously believed to exist.[1] In 1984 the police destroyed more than 13 million marijuana plants in the United States, and in 1985 the U.S. Justice Department sponsored Operation Delta 9, a coordinated national effort to eradicate marijuana. In the first three days of this operation 342,635 marijuana plants were destroyed.[2]

The sharp rise in domestic marijuana production can be directly traced to the success of efforts to make it more difficult to smuggle marijuana into the United States. In 1969 the United States began a large-scale effort to intercept marijuana smuggled in from Mexico, a major producer of marijuana for U.S. consumption. Then, in 1978, the United States and Mexico entered into a cooperative arrangement to spray Mexican marijuana fields with the herbicide paraquat. Interdiction efforts made smuggling from Mexico more difficult, and concerns about the harmful effects of smoking marijuana treated with paraquat caused some traffickers to look elsewhere for a stable and safe supply of marijuana. One way to ensure the purity and

This research project was partially supported by a grant from the National Institute of Justice (No. 88–IJCX–0016).

availability of marijuana was to become more directly involved in its cultivation. It has been argued that these federal efforts have provided the major impetus for increased domestic production.[3]

The profit motive has also influenced the situation. Since the penalties are harsh for smuggling drugs of any sort and since marijuana is quite bulky (per dollar of profit), smugglers have found cocaine and heroin to be better investments. Consequently, the supply of available marijuana has decreased, thus raising its street price and the potential for profits. Growers can make more than $1500 per plant on a crop that can be turned over three times a year and that will grow with little cultivation in many types of soil. A small warehouse equipped with grow lights to raise 400 plants can yield a gross profit of $1,800,000 a year.[4]

Although there has been much research on drug smuggling and drug dealing, relatively little has been done on domestic marijuana production.[5] The research that is available focuses on adventuresome individuals who live on the edge of the law.[6] What has not been examined is the rise of a new type of marijuana grower—the upstanding citizen who begins growing marijuana to supplement legitimate income. As early as 1981 some had predicted that farmers would begin growing marijuana for profit, and in the past few years such individuals have been identified by the police with regularity.[7]

Although precise estimates of illicit marijuana production are suspect, the National Organization for the Reform of Marijuana Laws (NORML) estimated that in 1985 marijuana production reached $18.6 billion, surpassing corn as America's biggest cash crop. Their 1986 estimate was $26.7 billion, a 44 percent increase over 1985. The U.S. Drug Enforcement Administration more conservatively estimated 1985 production at about half the $18.6 billion amount, which still made marijuana one of America's top five cash crops.[8]

One of the unfortunate ironies of the battle against drugs is that some short-term solutions have led to other long-term problems. For example, efforts to stop the use of marijuana among soldiers in Vietnam did lead some to stop but also led others to switch to heroin, which was easier to conceal.[9] Similarly, there is some indication that in Wisconsin restricting the availability of marijuana and cocaine has been partly responsible for an increased use of LSD by teenagers.[10]

In addition, domestic detection efforts may have unintended consequences for marijuana cultivation patterns. For example, aerial detection has been among the most common methods used to locate marijuana production. One response by growers has been to use warehouses or empty barns to grow marijuana indoors under controlled light, humidity, and temperature. The increasing popularity of this method of production is partly reflected in the September 1987 issue of *High Times* magazine, devoted entirely to their "Second Annual Indoor Growing Guide." The immediate consequence of indoor cultivation has been a year-round growing season. In the short run this shift means that even more marijuana can be produced each year from the same amount of space and that production will be even more difficult for police to detect. A likely long-term consequence will be the development of more potent varieties of marijuana to most effectively use the space and equipment required.

Characteristics of Marijuana

Marijuana, also known as the hemp plant, was given its scientific name—*cannabis sativa,* which is Latin for "cultivated hemp"—in 1753 by Linnaeus, a great Swedish naturalist and classifier.[11] Out of respect for Linnaeus, it is sometimes referred to as *cannabis sativa L.* It is also referred to as *cannabis indica,* which tacks on the country of origin,[12] or by its common name Indian hemp. The word *marijuana* (also spelled *marihuana*) is derived from the Spanish word *maraguango,* referring to any substance producing intoxication. In South America this word has been broadly used to describe a variety of intoxicating plants.[13]

Marijuana has been cultivated throughout recorded history and probably much earlier. The plant produces not only a drug but also a strong fiber that has long been used in the manufacture of fine linen, canvas, and rope. The oil of the plant resembles linseed oil and has value in making paints dry quickly. In addition, the seeds have been used as birdseed, and the leaves, flowering tops, and resin have been used for a variety of religious and medical purposes.

Marijuana is a fibrous plant that grows as male and female plants ranging from 30 inches to almost 20 feet tall. The male plants usually grow somewhat taller, and both plants secrete resins that can be used as hashish. These resins are used by the plant to slow water loss in hot and dry environments. Generally, the hotter and drier the climate, the more resin that is produced.[14] The female plants, which produce the most resin, slow down production once they are fertilized; consequently, people who grow hemp for its intoxicating effects often separate the male and female plants before pollination occurs. It is not true, as some believe, that female marijuana plants yield more potent leaves. The leaves are similar in their concentration of THC, even though female plants do produce more resin, which can be made into hashish.[15]

Marijuana is very hearty, preferring cpen areas and warm weather. The plant needs very little water, except during germination and the establishment of its main root. It can grow in a variety of temperature and moisture conditions but grows best in areas with hot summers. Interestingly, the plants that grow around marijuana can influence the hemp's growth. For example, if it is grown next to spinach or rye, those plants will do very well, but the hemp will do poorly. In contrast, the hemp plant does very well if grown next to corn or turnips.[16]

> Marijuana grows best under the same conditions of soil and climate that favor corn: lots of water, especially in the early seedling stage; lots of light; and a soil or loam that is high in nitrogen and potash, moderate in phosphorous and containing little or no clay.[17]

At one time there was a large hemp industry in the United States, particularly during World War II, when sources of sisal rope had been cut off by the Japanese invasion of the Philippines.[18] Today much of this hemp still grows wild, particularly in the Midwest. As an intoxicant, however, this wild marijuana is of such low potency that law enforcement officers refer to it separately as ditchweed. The 1986 figures for the Domestic Cannabis Eradication/Suppression Program reported that 4.7

million cultivated plants had been destroyed and more than 125 million ditchweed plants had been eradicated.[19]

From the beginning the intoxicating effects of marijuana were recognized, and it has been described as "one of the oldest and most widely disseminated hallucinogens."[20] The active ingredient by which the potency of marijuana is measured is THC (tetrahydrocannabinol). There are more than 200 varieties of marijuana plant, and the concentration of THC differs among them. Importantly, the potency of marijuana can be easily increased through plant breeding:

> ... with modern plant-breeding technology, it should be possible to produce strains of grass that are more potent than anything hitherto known and to make the common weedlike strains that grow wild over the Midwest into powerfully hallucinogenic drugs.[21]

At present, one of the most potent forms of marijuana is *sinsemilla* (a Spanish word meaning "without seeds"), which in 1986 was about 8 percent THC. According to the National Narcotics Intelligence Consumers Committee (NNICC), that level is about double the concentration of THC in commercial grade marijuana and is far higher than the 1.5 percent THC level reported in a 1970 study of Mexican marijuana.[22] Sinsemilla potency has even increased in the short span between 1983 and 1986, and as potency increases, so do the profits for growers.[23] In 1986 commercial grade marijuana was selling wholesale for $350 to $700 a pound whereas sinsemilla was selling for $800 to $2,000 a pound. A typical plant yields between one-half and one pound of marijuana, depending on the size of the plant.

History of Marijuana

The precise origins of marijuana are unknown but are believed to have been in western China or central Asia.[24] One of the earliest references to marijuana is in a Chinese document dated 2737 B.C., in which marijuana was described as a medicine. Other documents place it in India as early as 2000 B.C. and in the Middle East as early as 650 B.C. Marijuana was well established in the Islamic world by A.D. 1000, and in later years Arabs spread its use to Africa and the Mediterranean.

The Greeks preferred alcohol to marijuana, but they were aware of marijuana. It is likely that the drug written about by Homer was marijuana. There also appear to be several references to marijuana in the Old Testament of the Bible, although some dispute this.[25] From the beginning, people have apparently recognized marijuana for both its intoxicating effects and its use in making cloth and rope. Oil from marijuana seeds was also in early use for making soap and for illumination. The residues created by the extraction of oil were used as fishbait and as fertilizer.[26]

Although most Americans today think of marijuana as something to be smoked, the practice of smoking marijuana did not begin until the 1500s and 1600s, after the introduction of tobacco to Europe. Before that time marijuana was eaten or added to foods. In some very early societies (e.g., 2500 B.C.) groups of people burned marijuana in a tent or other small enclosure and spent time breathing in the fumes. Still other groups threw piles of it onto a campfire and stood nearby to inhale the fumes. More commonly, particularly in India and the Middle East, the resin from female marijuana plants was used as an intoxicant, rather than smoking or burning the leaves directly.

Marijuana has a long history of use in Africa. It was probably introduced by Arab traders many years before Europeans ever settled there. In Africa, marijuana was smoked by most of the races and for a variety of reasons; it functioned as a painkiller for women during childbirth and was used during coffee breaks by men working in mines. One study even found a tribe that used marijuana as a punishment. When tribesmen wanted to punish a troublesome member of the group, they made that person smoke until he or she passed out.[27]

Marijuana in South America

From Africa marijuana was introduced to South America through the slave trade, probably in the 1600s. The first South American country in which it was commonly used was Brazil, where smoking marijuana became popular in the 1700s. All of the Brazilian names for marijuana (for example, *maconha, macumba, diamba, liamba,* and *pungo*) are African words borrowed from the various languages and dialects of the original slaves. Some of the most potent marijuana grown in this hemisphere comes from Brazil.[28]

Marijuana soon moved its way up the South American continent to Mexico, where it was commonly used. Soldiers in the Mexican army were reportedly large consumers of marijuana, and many in Pancho Villa's army of peasants were said to have been stoned most of the time, a condition recalled in the song "La Cucaracha."[29] In addition, marijuana was commonly used to subdue fighting animals in Mexico, particularly the cocks used in fights.[30]

Latin American cultures demonstrate the extent to which the effects of a drug are shaped by the circumstances under which it is taken. In the United States we associate marijuana smoking with passivity and a reluctance to engage in violence, whereas in many Latin American countries marijuana is associated with violence, just as alcohol is in this country.[31]

Marijuana in the United States

It is unclear how marijuana first came into this country. There is no record that the Pilgrims brought it with them, but settlers did bring it to Jamestown in 1611 and cultivated it for its fiber. Its importance for cloth and rope had long been recognized in England, and King James I ordered the settlers to produce it for export to England.[32] From the early 1600s until after the Civil War, marijuana was a major crop in North America, and by the 1700s it was important to the economy of many states. Some states even offered rewards for high production and penalized those who did not produce.[33] It has been estimated that by 1630 half of all winter clothing and nearly all summer clothing of the American colonists was made from hemp fibers.[34]

In 1765 George Washington was growing hemp at Mount Vernon. Even though it seems that he was primarily interested in its fiber, there is also evidence that he was concerned with separating male and female plants before pollination and in increasing the potency of the plants. These factors suggest that he had medical uses in mind for marijuana.[35]

By the 1800s the center of hemp production was Kentucky, where roads were built and slaves were traded as part of the hemp industry, which was almost entirely devoted to the manufacture of cloth and rope. Following the Civil War, production declined as cheaper imported hemp was available and as the invention of the cotton gin and cotton and wool machinery made these fabrics cheaper alternatives.[36]

Early Americans also recognized the medicinal value of marijuana. In the 1850s its recommended uses included the treatment of gout, rheumatism, tetanus, opiate withdrawal symptoms, menstrual cramps, convulsions, depression, delirium tremens, insanity, and asthma. In fact, marijuana was officially recognized as a medicine in the *U.S. Pharmacopoeia* and could be prescribed by doctors for a variety of ailments until 1937, when Congress passed the Marijuana Tax Act.[37]

Although people were well aware of its intoxicating effects, marijuana was not generally used as a recreational drug in the United States until the early 1900s. Even then its use was centered in Mexican laborers, who brought it across the border, and in certain fringe groups, such as jazz musicians. Much of the pressure for federal legislation regulating marijuana arose not from the Federal Bureau of Narcotics (FBN), but from local law enforcement agencies in the South and Southwest that saw it as directly linked to violent crime and to problems with Mexican immigrants.[38] Thus, early on the recreational use of marijuana was associated with Mexican workers in Texas, and eventually throughout the West and Southwest, and efforts to control the drug often had strong racial overtones.[39]

Beginning in the late 1920s, there was a growing campaign to educate Americans about the evils of marijuana. The common belief that it was a highly addictive narcotic found support even in the medical community, which argued that marijuana addiction was more sinister in many ways than addiction to the opiates.[40] Marijuana was blamed for increases in violent crime, sexual promiscuity, and even insanity. When it was believed that marijuana use was spilling over into the white population, it was perceived as a national menace.[41]

In the early 1900s the center for the importation and use of marijuana was New Orleans, where sailors brought the drug from South America and the West Indies and where Mexican immigrants brought the drug through the Gulf. In 1917, during the first World War, the Navy frequently used the port of New Orleans and was concerned about its sailors being corrupted on leave. With the help of local authorities the Navy closed down the largest red light district in New Orleans. The jazz musicians who were driven from this area took their music and their marijuana up the Mississippi to Chicago.[42]

During the early 1900s, America's favorite drug, alcohol, was on its way to being banned and was already seen by many as evil and harmful. Ironically, prohibition of alcohol may have played a significant role in the discovery of marijuana as a recreational drug. For some, particularly in the jazz world, alcohol was evil but marijuana was good for the user. Louis Armstrong, for example, the king of jazz in both New Orleans and Chicago, was a heavy user of marijuana until he died. He believed that alcohol was evil but that marijuana improved his performance.[43] Until the 1960s, marijuana was seen by the public as an exotic drug used only by artists, musicians, and movie stars—and this perception had an element of truth in it.

Marijuana was never a widely used recreational drug until the late 1960s and early 1970s. For example, the first Gallup Poll on marijuana was done in 1969 and found that 4 percent of the American people had used the drug at least once. By 1977, 24 percent had used it at least once.[44] The widespread use of marijuana was not limited to college students but had been adopted by a broad range of citizens, including as many as 69 percent of the soldiers serving in Vietnam.[45]

Ambiguity About Marijuana

Much as they reacted to alcohol, Americans have exhibited ambiguous feelings about the evils of marijuana. Some view it as little different from heroin, whereas others see it as no more harmful than tobacco. These ambiguous views have been reflected in changing social policies toward marijuana. In the mid-1930s the federal government, under the guidance of Harry Anslinger, led an all-out campaign against marijuana to convince the public that it was highly dangerous and to push for legislation to outlaw the drug. Numerous stories were told about ax murderers under the influence of a single marijuana cigarette and women who became prostitutes as a result of marijuana use. Most of the public at that time equated marijuana use with low-status or deviant groups—such as Mexican laborers, jazz musicians, and poor blacks.

"Between the mid-30s until the mid-1960s there was a strong public consensus that marijuana was a dangerous drug and that moderate use was impossible."[46] All marijuana use was considered dangerous, and government hearings described it as more dangerous than heroin or cocaine.[47] In many states the criminal penalties for marijuana were identical to those for heroin.

By 1940 all states and the federal government had outlawed marijuana; in the 1950s state and federal penalties were increased. By 1965, typical marijuana laws included penalties of two years in prison for the first conviction of simple possession, five years for the second offense, and ten years for the third. Except for first offenders, persons convicted of possession had mandatory sentences with no opportunity for parole or probation. Penalties for selling were even harsher. By current standards some states had unusually harsh penalties. In Alabama, for example, simple possession carried a mandatory minimum sentence of five years; in Missouri a second conviction for possession could have brought a life sentence; in Georgia a second conviction for sale to minors could have been punishable by death.[48]

All of this began to change after the mid-1960s, however. The 1970 Comprehensive Drug Abuse Prevention and Control Act rewrote the federal law and separated marijuana from narcotic drugs. At the federal level both simple possession and nonprofit distribution of small amounts were changed from felonies to misdemeanors.[49] In addition, first offenders were able to have their criminal records expunged. Many states copied these federal efforts, and within a few years all but Nevada had reduced simple possession of marijuana to a misdemeanor.[50]

In 1972 the National Commission on Marijuana and Drug Abuse recommended decriminalization or partial prohibition, keeping penalties for selling but removing them for personal use and nonprofit distribution of small amounts. Although there was some criticism, decriminalization drew support from a wide range of groups—both liberal and conservative. The conservative William F. Buckley, Jr., for example, openly supported decriminalization.[51] By 1978 eleven states, representing one third of the U.S. population, had decriminalized marijuana use. Thirty others had provisions for conditional discharge (with charges dropped or no penalty attached), and twelve states provided for the expungement of records for first-possession offenders. Even President Carter was recommending decriminalization at the federal level.[52]

Two primary factors brought about a more relaxed government approach to the control of marijuana.[53] First, federal agencies that were not oriented toward law enforcement (as the DEA was) were brought into the debate—including the National Institute on Drug Abuse. These agencies made possible an open discussion of the topic from differing points of view.

Second, and more importantly, marijuana was being used more and more by middle-class youth. Nebraska, for example, reduced marijuana possession to a misdemeanor in 1969, as the result of a case in which the sons of a prominent county prosecutor and a university professor were charged with possession. In addition, the son of a U.S. senator spent time in jail for simple possession.

The rise of middle- and upper-class users not only exerted political pressure to change the law but also began the process of reidentifying the typical marijuana user. People began to think that marijuana users were not all crazed monsters who would murder without a moment's hesitation. Such changes in perception raised questions about the extent to which marijuana is harmful, and people began to distinguish among experimentation, occasional use, and heavy use.

Nonetheless, marijuana was still illegal, and arrests continued throughout the 1970s at about 400,000 per year, with about 90 percent of those being for simple possession.[54] In addition, even though penalties had been reduced, people were still being penalized. For example, in 1961 the average length of imprisonment for those convicted in the federal courts of marijuana violations was just over seventy months. By 1975 the average had dropped to about thirty months, but that was still a relatively serious penalty.[55]

Then in 1978 the backlash began. The federal government completely reversed its stance on marijuana; the New Right became a powerful political force and made an antimarijuana stance part of its program; and parents' groups formed to deal with the issue of marijuana use by children.

Federal Government Reversal

In 1977, publications of the DEA de-emphasized the importance of the marijuana problem and argued that enforcement was a matter best left to the states. The agency also suggested that decriminalization might be an option worth considering. However, by 1980 the DEA was portraying marijuana as the most serious drug problem facing the country, requiring a coordinated federal and state effort. The White House also shifted its position on marijuana. In 1977 a presidential advisor was urging Congress to decriminalize marijuana in federal laws. By 1979 that advisor's replacement was stressing the growing problem of marijuana use and the importance of federal action.[56] At the same time the average penalty for marijuana users convicted in federal courts rose from about thirty months in 1975 to more than fifty months in 1982.[57] And some of the extreme penalties of the past were once again being applied. In 1982, for example, the Supreme Court upheld a forty-year sentence for the possession of nine ounces of marijuana.[58]

Rise of the New Right

Some conservatives, such as Buckley, shared the libertarian view that the criminalization of marijuana was an unnecessary intrusion of government into the lives of citizens. More vocal, however, were the conservatives who moved into power in the late 1970s. Those individuals were more concerned with the use of marijuana for simple hedonistic pleasure and with its possible harmful effects.[59] In 1986 the White House drug adviser to Ronald Reagan stated publicly that smoking marijuana caused individuals to become homosexual.[60]

Rise of Parent Groups

Hundreds of antidrug parent groups arose during this time and included marijuana among their targets. Such groups have focused on antidrug education, stricter policing of schools, and legislation outlawing drug paraphernalia shops. Part of their concern was a response to national surveys reporting that drug use among adolescents was increasing. And even though research did not generally support the idea that marijuana causes any long-term physical damage, much of the research was inconclusive, and parents were particularly concerned about its effects on growing children.[61]

Public Perceptions

The impact of the backlash has been considerable. There has been a crackdown on the sale of drug paraphernalia as well as a major effort to eradicate domestic production.[62] There has also been a reduction in public support for decriminalization—since 1977 no additional states have decriminalized marijuana—and an increase in the percentage of people who believe that the regular use of marijuana is harmful.[63] In 1969 only 12 percent of Americans thought marijuana should be legalized. By 1977 this number had risen to 28 percent, but by 1985 it had fallen to 23 percent.[64]

Such figures illustrate that there is still no widespread public consensus about the proper legal response to marijuana use and production. There has not been a return to the view that anyone who uses marijuana will become a crazed killer, and there is still a distinction between occasional and heavy use. Also, most states have kept their reduced penalties. The resulting ambiguity is apparent even among law enforcement officials. A 1988 survey of state and local prosecutors found that 25 percent thought marijuana should be decriminalized, and 73 percent rejected the zero tolerance program of the federal government.[65] It is within this context of cultural ambiguity and stepped up interdiction of foreign marijuana that domestic marijuana production has increased.

Domestic Production

Domestic production of marijuana did not become an important factor until the 1970s. In the 1980s the popularity of domestic cultivation continued at an accelerated pace. The National Narcotics Intelligence Consumers Committee (NNICC) estimated that in 1984 domestic marijuana comprised about 12 percent of the total U.S. supply. By 1987 this figure had risen to 24 percent, and some have suggested that this figure underestimates domestic marijuana production by as much as one-half.[66]

Two factors in the late 1960s appear to have hastened the increase in domestic production. These were the United States-Mexican border interdiction program known as Operation Intercept and the U.S. government's cooperative agreement with Mexico to spray marijuana plants there with the herbicide paraquat.

Operation Intercept

Operation Intercept began on Sunday, September 21, 1969, at 2:30 P.M. in an effort to halt the flow of drugs across the Mexican border. The operation was aimed at stopping all drugs, including heroin, but was aimed mainly at marijuana and was timed to stop shipment of the fall harvest of marijuana.[67]

The project was enormous, covering the entire 2,500-mile-long border between the United States and Mexico and including all thirty-one border-crossing stations, where individuals and vehicles were searched for drugs. It was the largest peacetime search-and-seizure operation by civil authorities in history and used the services of more than two thousand agents. Even so, they simply did not have the manpower to do the job. Within an hour after the operation began, traffic was backed up for more than 2 1/2 miles. Before the operation a normal vehicle inspection required one minute per vehicle. During the operation the time was expanded to an average of two to three minutes per vehicle.

In the first week of the operation, 1,824 border crossers were strip searched, resulting in only thirty-three arrests and leaving some 1,987,000 people to cross with little or no search. It is impossible to know how many shipments were never made because of fear of detection. We do know, however, that before the operation an average of 150 pounds of marijuana were seized per day and that figure was unchanged during the operation.

Just twenty days after it began, Operation Intercept ended. The precise reasons for its termination have not been revealed, but they are likely a combination of (1) the urging of the Mexican government, (2) the small quantities of drugs seized, and (3) pressures from businessmen on both sides of the border. The precise impact of Operation Intercept may never be known. On the positive side it may have deterred smugglers from even trying to bring drugs across the border. Even though there were no large seizures of marijuana, there were reports of diminished supplies in some cities. However, it must be noted that Mexico had been in a drought and less marijuana had been produced and also that the demand for marijuana had increased dramatically within a short time.

On the negative side Operation Intercept appears to have had several unintended consequences.

1. Legitimate businesses in the thirty border towns were hurt by as much as 50 percent. Further, for the many Mexicans with permits to live in Mexico but work in the United States, absenteeism from work was common because of the difficulty of going through the checkpoints.

2. Smugglers learned the advantages of bringing their shipments across the border in airplanes. Although the government had set up sophisticated radar, pilots could simply fly low through the mountains separating Mexico and Texas and avoid the radar. Many flights were made at night by moonlight.

3. Although in many cities marijuana was as available as it was before the operation, the shortages that did occur prompted many users to switch to other drugs, often LSD or other hallucinogens. The greatest increase of all was in the importation of hashish from North Africa.

4. Some of the shortages of Mexican marijuana were made up for by increased shipments of marijuana from other countries, such as Vietnam. Thus, the base broadened from which marijuana could be obtained and as a result guaranteed a more stable market in the future.

5. The marijuana shortage (or rumors of it) induced many in the United States to begin growing their own marijuana. One immediate response was to begin locating and harvesting the marijuana growing wild in many states.

Paraquat

In 1975 the U.S. government entered into an agreement with Mexico to spray the herbicide paraquat on fields of Mexican marijuana, a cheap low-potency variety that constituted most of the marijuana being smuggled into the United States. The program received a great deal of attention and did wipe out substantial portions of the Mexican crop. However, the marijuana that survived was still shipped north, "where it caused widespread concern among marijuana smokers and public-health officials."[68]

An immediate impact of this program was a shift to Jamaican and Colombian marijuana, both of which were much more potent than the Mexican variety. Columbia is still an important source of marijuana today, jockeying with Mexico as the single largest source for American consumption. In 1984 Columbia was estimated to have provided approximately 48 percent of the marijuana consumed in the United States, as compared with only 24 percent coming from Mexico.[69] In 1985, however, Mexico came back as the number one producer (about 40 percent), suggesting that the long-term impact of eradication programs may be slight. "Despite aerial spraying, it has been estimated that about 1,300 tons of Mexican marijuana was available for distribution in the United States in 1983, compared to 750 tons in 1982."[70]

A second impact of the paraquat program was to increase domestic production.

> The spraying of foreign marijuana fields with paraquat and other herbicides meant a bonanza for California growers, for U.S. marijuana smokers who had long preferred imported marijuana now demanded domestic marijuana to avoid the adverse effects of herbicide residues. Thus, the foreign herbicide spraying program became in effect a kind of farm-aid program, helping U.S. marijuana growers capture a larger share of the market.[71]

Even though domestic production first started in California, it quickly spread throughout the United States as a result of a spraying program in California modeled after the one in Mexico.[72]

Marijuana Growers

Less glamorous than smugglers, less visible than street addicts, marijuana growers have received relatively little attention in the professional and popular literature. The federal government estimates that there are between 90,000 and 150,000 commercial growers in the United States and more than one million people who grow for personal use.[73] NORML estimates the number of growers by combining overall crop production estimates with estimates of the amounts that typical growers produce in a year (five pounds for personal-use growers and thirteen pounds for commercial growers). Using this approach, NORML estimated that there were approximately 250,000 commercial growers and more than two million personal-use growers in 1986.[74] If the latter figures are correct, the arrest and imprisonment of all commercial growers alone would result in a 50 percent increase in state and federal prison populations, assuming no increase in the number of commercial growers since 1986.

Not much is known about the characteristics of marijuana growers. It appears, however, that growers are drawn from all walks of life and do not fit the media image of drug dealers. According to a 1984 DEA report on domestic marijuana growers,

> All types of individuals are involved in domestic marijuana cultivation, ranging from seasoned drug traffickers to white collar business executives. Farmers, who generally are economically hard pressed, are cultivating marijuana in addition to corn or wheat to meet financial obligations and satisfy debts. Persons who are unemployed or senior citizens who can't live off retirement benefits are selling marijuana as an alternative source of income. Successful business executives are financing marijuana cultivation as another form of investment. Domestic marijuana cultivation has become an integral part of the economy in depressed areas of southeastern Oklahoma and northern California.[75]

One exception to the general lack of knowledge about growers has been the attention focused on growers in Humboldt County, California. Aside from coverage by the popular press, this group is discussed in some detail by Raphael

(1985) and Warner (1986).[76] Raphael depicts marijuana growers as modern day moonshiners. Some of the first growers in the Humboldt County area had the strong libertarian belief that government should stay out of the lives of citizens, preferred a simple life-style away from the complexities of modern society, and grew marijuana primarily for their own consumption. As the price and quality of marijuana increased, they saw that easy money could be made by engaging in an activity that was consistent with their life-style. People in the area then began growing for the explicit purpose of making a profit, and consequently the scale of production increased. Raphael notes that, ironically, large profits often drew people back into the very patterns of conspicuous consumption they had sought to escape by moving to Humboldt County.

Although most of Warner's efforts were directed at marijuana smugglers, he did spend time among the Humboldt County growers and provides rather detailed descriptions of several individuals. As he notes, the very nature of marijuana growing involves a different type of individual from that found in marijuana smuggling.

> Marijuana growing is land-bound. It is an ample but slow buck, dependent on a plant cycle. People don't drift in and out of growing marijuana as much as they do in smuggling. If they make money from their first crop without being traumatized, they tend to stay with it for a few years, changing their garden sites, changing their techniques and their partners, but still enmeshed in the cycle of putting seeds in the ground and waiting for the harvest.
>
> Like smuggling, something resembling an 80-20 rule seems to hold for marijuana growing. That is, the majority, maybe 80 percent of the growers, produce a minority of the domestically grown marijuana, maybe 20 percent, using ballpark figures.[77]

Although none of the growers described by Raphael or Warner also earned their livelihood from legitimate crops, it is worth noting that growing marijuana requires no commitment to a criminal life-style. Many contemporary marijuana growers come from conventional backgrounds and hold conventional values, even more so today than in the 1960s or 1970s.

> In the early '70s marijuana was cultivated by die-hard hippies who bought land in the backwoods of Humboldt County so they could escape Los Angeles or San Francisco, and the trappings of middle-class life. But now, housewives, businessmen, pensioners, and unemployed loggers alike have been known to grow a few plants. It gives working people a much needed second income; the unemployed their only income.[78]

While Raphael and Warner refer to specific individuals and make no effort to develop broad categories, three types of growers can be identified from their illustrations, from the popular literature, and from this author's ongoing research.

The Communal Grower. This kind of grower purchases land as part of a larger life-style of retreat from the rest of society. For many of these growers, growing marijuana also makes a social statement. Some specifically intend to grow marijuana when they purchase land, whereas others drift into growing it as part of their general life-style. These individuals have little interest in growing marijuana as a business or for the accumulation of money, although the money may help them through short-term financial problems. Some communal growers are holdovers from the late 1960s and early 1970s. One case discussed by Warner involved a grower who shared his land with others in exchange for a share of their crops, although little attention was paid to the amount each tenant owed. Proceeds were used to construct a religious meditation tower, and the tenants lived much like a large extended family.

Although some of these individuals gradually drift into large-scale production, most have more modest goals.

> Many of them are motivated as much by ideas of self-sufficiency (the satisfaction of growing their own) or thrift (not having to buy pot) as by making money selling their extra ounces or pounds. What money they make seems to go to a few purchases they could not afford otherwise, and to good times.[79]

When production is approached in this way, other growers are seen as kindred spirits rather than as threatening competitors. This group is also less likely to engage in the violence sometimes associated with marijuana growing, such as setting booby traps and guarding crops with automatic weapons or dogs.[80] Raphael quotes a woman who says,

> I think my motives then were pretty much economic. And also it made perfect sense. . . . So the dope was perfect. It was like, what could be better? You get to stay home. You get to have some money. You get to basically do something you enjoy. It causes zero destruction. . . . I liked the independence. I liked the activity. It was nice to be outside. It was nice to be nurturing these living things.[81]

The Hustler. This type of marijuana grower is an entrepreneur by instinct. He or she may have used marijuana and may have engaged in some dealing for the challenge of it, although neither activity is a necessary prerequisite for involvement in growing. Some of these growers utilize farmland that they already own, others purchase or rent farmland for the explicit purpose of growing marijuana, and still others enlist the aid of landowners who are having financial problems. For some, the risks associated with growing are part of its appeal. Although the money they make may serve as some indication of success, these individuals are generally less motivated by the money than by the challenge of being a successful entrepreneur. They could just as easily have set up business in any one of a dozen legitimate or illegitimate enterprises, and they are likely to move out of marijuana growing as soon as the thrill of the chase wears off.

A 1985 Texas case illustrates this type of grower. The grower was a sixty-three-year-old farmer who was arrested with six hundred pounds of processed marijuana, two hundred pounds of seeds, and 22,284 marijuana plants growing in a barn equipped with grow lights. He was among the best-known businessmen in his small Texas town and had a reputation for hard work. In addition to owning almost five thousand acres of land, he owned a local feed store, a chemical company, and a company that sold satellite dishes, hog pellets, and sheep manure.[82]

The Pragmatist. This type of grower is driven to marijuana production by economic necessity. Such individuals approach marijuana with no moral or philosophical righteousness. They often see what they are doing as both legally and morally wrong but feel they have few options because of the profits involved. One of Warner's marijuana growers described himself and his wife as staunch Republicans who had never even tried marijuana. He had punched out his son for smoking marijuana six or seven years earlier but later used his son's help in growing marijuana. He described his feelings about marijuana and himself as a grower in these terms:

> I don't even consider [smoking] it. I'm not going to fry my brains . . . I'm just involved in producing a saleable product. I'm just trying to make money . . . I'm antimarijuana. . . . I feel that marijuana is destroying young people by changing their attitudes about working. I feel so strongly about that I'm almost ashamed of growing it.[83]

This third type of grower is particularly interesting because it demonstrates that growing requires no commitment to a drug life-style or even a liberal or tolerant attitude toward drugs in general. Two other case summaries from the popular press help to illustrate the types of individuals involved in marijuana growing.

> A farmer was arrested for growing approximately two acres of marijuana on his three-hundred-acre farm. The forty-year-old man was a lifelong resident of the community of 1,300. He was also a veteran who "was called upon to deliver patriotic addresses on the 4th of July, Armistice Day and meetings of the local VFW." Working with the farmer were two police officers who were boyhood friends of his and a local tavern owner. The town was shocked, and the mayor was quoted as saying, "Next you'll be telling me they've got the minister and the bank president."[84]

> A thirty-year-old farmer was arrested for growing 1,400 marijuana plants among rows of corns and soybeans. The plants were started indoors in a windowless growing room and then transplanted outdoors in the spring, where they were watered through an elaborate irrigation system. He had apparently been growing marijuana for several years and may have used banks in the Bahamas to launder the drug money. He pled guilty but requested that he be released prior to sentencing because "I'm a farmer, your honor, I have crops in the fields to get out."[85]

Including farmers in the study of marijuana production adds a new dimension to our understanding of that activity. Existing studies have focused on people whose life-styles exposed them to marijuana use and whose social networks validated or accepted their involvement in marijuana cultivation. For farmers the situation may be quite different. The people in their social world often strongly oppose drugs. Further, although they are well versed in the general principles involved in growing plants, technical information specific to marijuana production or distribution may not be readily available to farmers. And finally, because they are not involved in a social world that looks favorably on drugs and because they may lose their farms if arrested (through drug forfeiture laws), farmers risk much more than many other marijuana producers.

These differences between farmers and other growers have important implications that extend beyond marijuana production. Understanding these farmers can help us understand the process by which people move from the legitimate to the illegitimate world. Thus, there are implications for areas such as white collar and political crime.

Notes

[1] Cited in R. Warner, *Invisible Hand: The Marijuana Business* (New York: Beech Tree, 1986), 30.

[2] "Crackdown on Grass Farmers," *Time,* 19 Aug. 1987, 21.

[3] J.S. Lang, "Marijuana: A U.S. Farm Crop That's Booming," *U.S. News and World Report,* 12 Oct. 1981, 63–64; E.M. Brecher, "Drug Laws and Drug Law Enforcement: A Review and Evaluation Based on 111 Years of Experience," *Drugs and Society* 1, no. 1 (1986): 1–27.

[4] Brecher, "Drug Laws," 23.

[5] Works addressing drug smuggling include J.A. Inciardi, *The War on Drugs: Heroin, Cocaine, Crime, and Public Policy* (Palo Alto, CA: Mayfield, 1986); R.E. Long, ed., *Drugs and American Society* (New York: Wilson, 1986); and Warner, *Invisible Hand.* Works addressing drug dealing include P.A. Adler, *Wheeling and Dealing: An Ethnography of an Upper-Level Drug Dealing and Smuggling Community* (New York: Columbia University Press, 1985); P.A. Adler and P. Adler, "Criminal Commitment among Drug Dealers," *Deviant Behavior* 3 (1982): 117–35; idem, "Relations Between Dealers: The Social Organization of Illicit Drug Transactions," *Sociology and Social Research* 67, no. 3 (1983): 260–78; idem, "Shifts and Oscillations in Deviant Careers: The Case of Upper-Level Drug Dealers," *Social Problems* 31, no. 2 (1983): 195–207; T. Mieczkowski, "Geeking Up and Throwing Down: Heroin Street Life in Detroit," *Criminology* 24, no. 4 (1986): 645–66; and J. Mandel, "Myths and Realities of Marijuana Pushing," in *Marijuana: Myths and Realities,* ed. J.L. Simmons (North Hollywood, CA: Brandon House, 1967), 58–110.

[6] For instance, R. Raphael, *Cash Crop: An American Dream* (Mendocino, CA: Ridge Times Press, 1985); Warner, *Invisible Hand.*

[7] Lang, "Marijuana," 63–64.

[8] J.B. Gettman, *Marijuana in America—1986* (Washington, DC: National Organization for the Reform of Marijuana Laws, 1987).

[9] E.M. Brecher, "Marijuana and Hashish," in *Licit and Illicit Drugs,* ed. E.M. Brecher (Boston: Little, Brown, 1972), 395–472.

[10] "Wisconsin Teens Using More LSD," *Chicago Tribune,* 14 May 1987, 3.

[11] M.D. Merlin, *Man and Marijuana: Some Aspects of Their Ancient Relationship* (Rutherford, NJ: Fairleigh Dickinson University Press, 1972); L. Grinspoon, *Marijuana Reconsidered,* 2d ed. (Cambridge; Harvard University Press, 1977).

[12] A. Goldman, *Grass Roots: Marijuana in America Today* (New York: Harper and Row, 1979).

[13] R.P. Walton, *Marijuana: America's New Drug Problem* (Philadelphia: Lippincott, 1938; New York: Arno, 1976).

[14] Merlin, *Man and Marijuana.*

[15] Brecher, "Marijuana and Hashish," 395–472.

[16] Merlin, *Man and Marijuana.*

[17] Goldman, *Grass Roots,* 34.

[18] D. Solomon, "The Marijuana Myths," in *The Marijuana Papers,* ed. D. Solomon (Indianapolis: Bobbs-Merrill, 1966), xiii–xxi.

[19] National Narcotics Intelligence Consumers Committee, *The NNICC Report 1987: The Supply of Illicit Drugs to the United States from Foreign and Domestic Sources in 1987* (Washington, DC: US. Government Printing Office, 1988).

[20] Merlin, *Man and Marijuana,* 50.

[21] Goldman, *Grass Roots,* 34.

[22] NNICC, *The NNICC Report 1985–1986: The Supply of Illicit Drugs to the United States from Foreign and Domestic Sources in 1985 .and 1986* (Washington, DC: U.S. Government Printing Office, 1985–1986); R.C. Pillard, "Medical Progress: Marijuana," *New England Journal of Medicine* 283 (1970): 294–95.

[23] NNICC, *NNICC Report 1985–1986.*

[24] Merlin, *Man and Marijuana.*

[25] Brecher, "Marijuana and Hashish," 395–472; Walton, *Marijuana.*

[26] W. Reininger, "Historical Notes," in *The Marijuana Papers,* ed. D. Solomon, 100–101.

[27] Ibid.

[28] Goldman, *Grass Roots.*

[29] R.J. Bonnie and C.H. Whitebread II, *The Marijuana Conviction: A History of Marijuana Prohibition in the United States* (Charlottesville: University Press of Virginia, 1974); Goldman, *Grass Roots.*

[30] Walton, *Marijuana.*

[31] Goldman, *Grass Roots.*

[32] L. Grinspoon, *Marijuana Reconsidered.*

[33] Brecher, "Marijuana and Hashish," 395–472.

[34] J. Rosevar, *Pot: A Handbook of Marijuana* (New York: University Books, 1967)

[35] G. Andrews and S. Vinkenoog, eds. *The Book of Grass: An Anthology of American Hemp* (New York: Grove Press, 1967).

[36] Brecher, "Marijuana and Hashish," 395–472.

[37] Grinspoon, *Marijuana Reconsidered*; J.L. Himmelstein, *The Strange Career of Marijuana: Politics and Ideology of Drug Control in America* (Westport, CT: Greenwood Press, 1983).

[38] Walton, *Marijuana.*

[39] D. Musto, *The American Disease: Origins of Narcotic Control* (New Haven: Yale University Press, 1973); Himmelstein, *Strange Career.*

[40] Bonnie and Whitebread, *Marijuana Conviction.*

[41] Ibid.

[42] Himmelstein, *Strange Career*; Goldman, *Grass Roots.*

[43] Goldman, *Grass Roots.*

[44] Brecher, "Marijuana and Hashish," 395–472.

[45] L.N. Robins, J.E. Helzer, and D.H. Davis, "Narcotic Use in Southeast Asia and Afterwards," *Archives and General Psychiatry* 32, no. 8 (1975): 955–61.

[46] J.L. Himmelstein, "The Continuing Career of Marijuana: Backlash Within Limits," *Contemporary Drug Problems* 13, no. 1 (1986): 4.

[47] Bonnie and Whitebread, *Marijuana Conviction.*

[48] Himmelstein, "The Continuing Career," 1–21; J. Inciardi, "Marijuana Decriminalization Research," *Criminology* 19, no. 1 (1981): 145–59.

[49] Himmelstein, "The Continuing Career," 1–21.

[50] See J.F. Galliher and J.R. Cross, "Symbolic Severity in the Land of Easy Virtue: Nevada's High Marijuana Penalty," *Social Problems* 29, no. 4 (1982): 380–86 for a discussion of marijuana laws in Nevada.

[51] Himmelstein, "The Continuing Career," 1–21.

[52] Ibid.

[53] Ibid.

[54] Ibid.

[55] E.J. Brown, T.J. Flanagan, and M. McLeod, eds., *Sourcebook of Criminal Justice Statistics—1983* (Washington, DC: U.S. Government Printing Office, 1984).

[56] Himmelstein, "The Continuing Career," 1–21; P.R. Koski and D.L. Eckberg, "Bureaucratic Legitimation: Marijuana and the Drug Enforcement Administration," *Sociological Focus* 16, no. 4 (1983): 255–73.

[57] Brown, Flanagan, and McLeod, *Sourcebook of Criminal Justice Statistics—1983.*

[58] Cited in T. Szasz, *The Therapeutic State: Psychiatry in the Mirror of Current Events* (Buffalo: Prometheus Books, 1984).

[59] Himmelstein, "The Continuing Career," 1–21.

[60] T.E. Johnson, M.G. Warner, and G. Raine, "Reagan Aide: Pot Can Make You Gay," *Newsweek,* 27 Oct. 1986, 95.

[61] Himmelstein, "The Continuing Career," 1–21.

[62] Ibid.

[63] L.D. Johnson, P.M. O'Malley, and J.G. Bachman, *Drug Use Among American High School Students, College Students, and Other Young Adults: National Trends Through 1985* (Washington, DC: U.S. Government Printing Office, 1986).

[64] G. Gallup, Jr., *The Gallup Poll,* (Princeton: Gallup, 1985).

[65] M. Coyle, "Prosecutors Admit: No Victory in Sight," *The National Law Journal,* 8 Aug. 1988, S2–S3.

[66] NNICC, *NNICC Report 1987.*

[67] L.A. Gooberman, *Operation Intercept: The Multiple Consequences of Public Policy* (New York: Pergamon Press, 1974); Brecher, "Marijuana and Hashish," 395–472.

[68] M. Falco, "The Big Business of Illicit Drugs," *New York Times Magazine,* 11 Dec. 1983, 108–12.

[69] NNICC, *NNICC Report 1985–86.*

[70] Brecher, "Drug Laws," 20.

[71] Ibid., 21–22.

[72] Ibid., 1–27.

[73] Cited in Gettman, *Marijuana in America—1986.*

[74] Ibid.

[75] Cited in J.B. Slaughter, "Marijuana Prohibition in the United States: History and Analysis of a Failed Policy," *Columbia Journal of Law and Social Problems* 51, no. 4 (1988): 460.

[76] R. Edwards, "The Modern Moonshiner," *Newsweek,* 27 Oct. 1986, 8; Raphael, *Cash Crop*; Warner, *Invisible Hand.*

[77] Warner, *Invisible Hand,* 200.

[78] Edwards, "The Modern Moonshiner," 8.

[79] Warner, *Invisible Hand,* 200.

[80] B. Lawren, "Killer Weed," *Omni* 7, no. 12 (1985): 16, 106; Warner, *Invisible Hand*; Raphael, *Cash Crop.*

[81] Raphael, *Cash Crop,* 48–49.

[82] P. Applebome, "What Was Farmer Brown Doing with All That Pot?" *Texas Monthly* 13(1985): 10–11.

[83] Warner, *Invisible Hand,* 229.

[84] W. Smith, "Marijuana Seized Down on Farm," *Chicago Tribune,* 10 Sept. 1987, 3.

[85] "Knox Farmer Pleads Guilty to Marijuana-Growing Charge," *Peoria Journal-Star,* 28 Aug. 1987, p. A5; S. Williams, "Raid Uncovers Giant Marijuana Farm," *Peoria Journal-Star,* 19 Aug. 1987, pp. A1–A2; S. Williams, "Drug Agent Says Tipster Told Him of Pot Farm," *Peoria Journal-Star,* 21 Aug. 1987, p. C6.

3

The Investigation of Youth Drug Gangs

James N. Gilbert
Kearney State College

Gangs involving juveniles and young adults have followed a cyclical pattern in the United States. Gangs flourished during the late 1700s and early 1800s and then again during the late 1950s.[1] An increase in juvenile crime and considerable media attention during the 1950s brought about intense public awareness of youth gangs. Primarily a white or Hispanic urban phenomenon, the gangs of that decade were involved in limited criminal activity, such as robbery and extortion and fought mainly among themselves.

The gangs that emerged during the late 1980s were a unique development with little similarity to previous gangs. In fact, certain youth gangs of today may be considered examples of organized crime, differing primarily in the age of the members and the criminal focus of their activities. Gang members are rarely older adults but are more likely to range in age from their early teens to late twenties. The most distinguishing factor of today's gangs is the drug connection—specifically the using and selling of crack-cocaine. The flood of crack now posing such a tremendous problem in the United States is distributed mainly by violent youth gangs. Although there are literally hundreds of violent criminal gangs of varying racial and ethnic composition in the United States, two specific black gangs have emerged to dominate the crack-cocaine market—the Crips and the Bloods.[2]

Two Southern California Gangs

Both of these gangs were originally formed in Southern California during the late 1960s. They are closely associated with colors that identify membership and allegiance: blue for the Crips and red for the Bloods. Initially, gang members were black Los Angeles–based high school youths who patterned themselves after the 1950s gang model of territorial warfare and small-time theft, robbery, and extortion. However, as the drug demand began and continued without abatement throughout the 1970s and 1980s, the West Coast gangs began to sell narcotics and dangerous drugs. The Crips and the Bloods first distributed primarily marijuana and PCP in various minority neighborhoods within Los Angeles County. Then about 1972 the gangs began selling cocaine. When the popularity of crack-cocaine created an even greater demand among ghetto youth, the membership of the two gangs swelled to the present estimate of 30,000.

By 1986 law enforcement efforts had successfully constricted the old drug routes through south Florida, and drug smugglers shifted to Mexico and southern California. As California became the central distribution point for cocaine, the Crips and the Bloods naturally came to dominate much of that drug market. It is currently estimated that one-third of all drugs reaching the rest of the nation flow through California.[3]

Because of the tremendous amount of cocaine within California, a glut of the narcotic occurred and caused the street price to fall. The gangs then expanded their distribution efforts to reap the higher profits obtainable in the Midwestern and Eastern markets. For example, in Los Angeles one ounce of cocaine currently sells for $600 to $800, whereas the average price in the Midwest is $1,000 to $1,200 per ounce. To take advantage of this profit potential, the California-based gangs have dispatched many members into previously gang-free regions to establish drug operations. Both the Crips and the Bloods now regularly transport crack-cocaine from California to various Midwestern and Eastern cities.

Identification of Drug Gangs

Before criminal investigators can successfully terminate drug dealing by organized gangs, they must be able to recognize the presence of gang members. As the gangs have come under intense police and media scrutiny, they have been much more discreet in displaying their colors, particularly when they are engaged in transporting and/or selling narcotics. Whereas members originally displayed red or blue clothing openly, they now may wear only a red belt or use a blue comb, or they may engage in no display whatsoever. Even the display of mirrored sunglasses and heavy gold jewelry so favored by members of both gangs may be absent or subdued when they are engaged in drug activities.

Members of both gangs (and of most other organized gangs) can also be identified by their means of communication. Two particular forms are commonly found among organized drug gangs—nonverbal hand signs and graffiti. Hand signs, or flashing as the gang members call it, date to the early 1970s for most black and Hispanic gangs. Gang members may use hand signs as a means of greeting each other, or the flashing may precede violent confrontations between rival gangs. The hand signs may involve one or both hands and will vary greatly among various subsets of each gang organization. Criminal investigators and patrol officers should be alert for youths who are flashing hand signs of any sort.[4]

The use of gang graffiti is a much older form of gang communication, dating to the early 1940s, when Hispanic gangs used highly stylized script-type letters to designate their territorial boundaries. Black and Hispanic gangs still use considerable graffiti, although black graffiti is less stylized and requires less artistic skill and time to complete. Consequently, graffiti used by the Crips and the Bloods generally lacks the flair and attention to detail that characterizes the Hispanic gangs of California and the Southwest. Black gang graffiti is apt to contain profanity, expressions of individual power, and illustrations of weapons. Generally found on the walls of buildings, billboards, fences, and bridges, graffiti may be located on any smooth surface. Although any type of writing material can be used, marking pen and spray paint are the most commonly encountered.[5]

Criminal investigators should make every effort to interpret the meaning of graffiti. Varied information can be determined from the inscription, including which particular gang is in control of a given area, whether the area is being contested by other gangs, and what the identity of individual gang members. When a gang's territory is not being disputed and the gang is in full control, the graffiti will remain free of any cross-out. Cross-outs are the attempts by rival gangs to mark through the graffiti and write their own messages or challenges.

Although the Bloods and the Crips and similar gangs lack the more precise hierarchy of adult organized crime groups, the general elements of a social hierarchy can often be identified.

☐ *Original gangsters* are the oldest members of the gang. Typically in their thirties or forties, they supply the cocaine and crack to the younger gang members and are held in high esteem because of their experience and the material possessions acquired through years of drug dealing.

☐ *Hard-core members* are generally sixteen to twenty-four years of age and are totally dedicated to gang enterprises and activities. These individuals wear the gang colors and direct most street-level sales of cocaine.

☐ *Baby gangsters* are younger gang members, usually from twelve to sixteen years of age. These juveniles are frequently used as couriers and often sell small quantities of crack on the street. Most are not formal gang members but aspire to membership.

☐ *Tiny gangsters* represent the youngest level and generally serve as messengers and lookouts for older gang members.[6]

Another indicator of gang activity is a drive-by shooting, in which a gang member fires from a moving vehicle at a rival gang member. Such indiscriminate shootings have wounded and killed a large number of nongang victims, since the shooters do not hesitate to fire into large crowds. Although any type of firearms may be used, fully automatic weapons are common.

Additionally, investigators may observe juveniles wearing waistband beepers. Each beeper is connected to mobile phones used by older gang members who are dealing in narcotics. A common routine is to order the juvenile through his beeper to report back to the older gang member. When contact is made, the juvenile is instructed to deliver the crack to the buyer and collect the money from the drug sale. Juveniles (typically the baby gangsters mentioned earlier) are purposely used in this capacity since they will not be seriously incarcerated if arrested.

Combatting the Spread of Gangs

Law enforcement officials are particularly concerned as the Crips and the Bloods organizations move farther away from their Los Angeles base. Gang-related activity, once thought to be confined to the West and East coasts, is now considered to be alarmingly on the rise in the Midwest. Police officials in large urban areas once gang free—such as Omaha, Nebraska, and Seattle, Washington—are experiencing considerable gang-related violence. For example, Seattle police reported contact with more than 350 Los Angeles gang members during 1988, and from January 1988 to June 1989, Omaha reported forty woundings and five deaths by shooting determined to be related to Crips and Bloods violence.[7]

The general pattern of operation is for a West Coast gang or occasionally an East Coast gang to send senior members to an area previously unoccupied by gang activity. The members begin crack distribution by either absorbing existing local gangs or eliminating the resistance of small local drug dealers. Once the distribution network is in place, crack-cocaine is transported from Los Angeles to the new area. Originally, the cocaine was delivered via airports, bus depots, and train stations. However, police surveillance has forced the gangs to turn to transportation by vans, cars, and pickup trucks. Numerous arrests of gang members operating vehicles on interstate highways between California and the Midwest have documented the shift to this method of operation.

Investigative strategies include the use of specialized gang units or squads. For example, the New York Police Department and the county district attorney's office operate one gang unit that investigates and prosecutes only gang-related narcotics homicides. This unit has existed since 1984 and has succeeded in bringing about twenty-four murder convictions. The gang unit was organized specifically because of the increasing number of criminal homicides connected to gang sale of crack-cocaine. Even smaller cities such as Sioux City and Waterloo, Iowa, and Lincoln and Omaha, Nebraska, have experienced serious increases in violence connected to the appearance of outside drug gangs. Accordingly, specialized units, as well as multi-agency task forces are being formed within smaller police organizations to effectively react to the problem.[8]

Another approach, which is quite controversial, involves placing criminal responsibility on parents for the gang-related activities of their children. A new California law allowed the 1989 prosecution of a Los Angeles mother who was accused of failing her parental duties by allowing her teenage son to participate in the Crips gang. Two days after the arrest of her son for the gang rape of a twelve-year-old girl, the mother was arrested when investigators found the boy's bedroom covered with gang graffiti and found two photo albums showing the mother posing with members of the Crips gang, flashing hand signs. The misdemeanor charges against the mother were dismissed prior to the trial.[9]

It is important to note that the distribution and sale of cocaine and crack are not confined solely to the Crips and the Bloods organizations. Although these two gangs are responsible for a large portion of the crack-cocaine sold in the United States, many other ethnic and racial gangs are involved, as are thousands of independent street dealers. However, the magnitude of crack dealing connected to these specific groups is so great that a significant reduction in the crack-cocaine problem could be obtained through successful prosecution of the Crips and the Bloods gangs.

As with most major investigative challenges of the 1990s, eradication of drug-dealing youth gangs will not be a simple task for the police. Because of the long-standing entrenchment and large memberships of the southern California gangs, it is unlikely that the Crips and the Bloods can be eliminated from Los Angeles. However, combatting the spread of gang activity into new areas offers a greater opportunity to negatively impact gang-related drug sales. Since outsiders are apt to be recognized and identified by police and informants, criminal investigators may be able to use traditional techniques to eliminate the gangs before they become established. By becoming familiar with the identifying characteristics of the major drug-dealing gangs, investigators can be ready to react quickly when and if the problem presents itself.

Notes

[1] Gerald Leinwand, ed., *The Police* (New York: Pocket Books, 1972), 71–88.

[2] "The Drug Gangs," *Newsweek,* 28 Mar. 1988, 20–27.

[3] David Thompson, "Gang Colors Hidden, Anti-Drug Officer Says," *Omaha World-Herald,* 9 June 1989, 17–18.

[4] Robert K. Jackson and Wesley D. McBride, *Understanding Street Gangs* (Los Angeles: Custom Publishing, 1985), 80–83.

[5] Jackson, *Understanding Street Gangs,* 61–62.

[6] Jacob V. Lamar, "Kids Who Sell Crack," *Time,* 9 May 1988, 20–33; David Thompson, "Midlands Lawmen Polled to Be Alert for Gang Activities," *Omaha World-Herald,* 11 June 1989.

[7] C. David Kotok, "Rise in Shooting Deaths Appears Linked to Gangs," *Omaha World-Herald,* 30 June 1989, 1, 9.

[8] "Police-Prosecutor Teams," *NIJ Reports,* May/June 1989, 5–7.

[9] "Gang Mom Shows Concern: Case Dropped," *Omaha World-Herald,* 11 June 1989, 17.

4

The Cocaine-Crack Explosion: Investigative Solutions

James N. Gilbert*
Kearney State College*

Amerian crime patterns often seem to emerge in decade cycles. The 1950s focused on juvenile delinquency and organized crime, the 1960s brought widespread marijuana and hallucinogenic experimentation, and the 1970s demanded investigation of white-collar crime and sex offenses. The 1980s and 1990s have and will center on a single, overriding concern—drug and narcotic abuse and addiction.

Specifically cocaine and its potent derivative crack have so alarmed our criminal justice system that a succession of American presidents have declared war on this particular area of criminal behavior. Cocaine poses the most serious drug problem for the United States for many reasons, and the magnitude of alarm is well justified, given the drug's widespread availability and use and significant health consequences. According to a recent federal survey, approximately 5.8 million Americans used cocaine at least once in the month just prior to the survey. This figure represented a 38 percent increase over a three-year period. Additionally, on the National Drug Abuse Institute's annual survey of high school seniors, one senior in six reported trying cocaine.[1] And as presented in Table 4-1, cocaine-related hospital emergencies (one way authorities gauge the use of a drug), have steadily escalated from 4,277 in 1982 to 24,237 in the first half of 1988.

Even though the estimated 72 metric tons (158,760 pounds) of cocaine imported into the United States each year is used by a wide variety of people, a significant amount of abuse can be directly linked to active criminality. The National Institute of Justice has developed a drug forecasting system, which tests arrested males for cocaine at the time of their arrests. This program has confirmed what many

TABLE 4–1
Cocaine-related hospital emergencies

Year	Number of Emergencies
1983	5,223
1984	7,865
1985	9,750
1986	21,249
1987	37,535
1988 (Jan.-June)	24,237

Source: National Institute on Drug Abuse, data from the Drug Abuse Warning Network (DAWN) (Rockville, MD: U.S. Department of Health and Human Services, 1989), Series G, no. 22.

experienced criminal investigators have long suspected: a strong linkage exists between drug abuse and criminal activity. The program documents that 54 to 90 percent of male arrestees tested used drugs such as cocaine, PCP, heroin, marijuana, or amphetamines. In specific regard to cocaine, as illustrated in Figure 4–1, twelve of the twenty-one surveyed cities showed over 50 percent of the arrestees testing positive.[2]

Other research studies confirm the continued association between drug use and crime. About 35 percent of the state prison inmates in the United States were under the influence of an illegal drug at the time they committed the crimes for which they were incarcerated. Twelve years earlier, that figure was not quite 25 percent. Several studies have indicated that one-quarter or more of criminal homicides are related to drug trafficking or the attempt to purchase illegal drugs. Finally, research has documented that 75 percent of robberies and 50 percent of felony assaults by youthful perpetrators are committed by less than 3 percent of the offenders, a small but highly active criminal group characterized principally by their use of illegal pills or cocaine and heroin.[3]

Research of this nature is highly important to criminal investigators. It effectively puts to rest the myth that the only victims of drug abuse are the abusers themselves. It reveals that many addicts are more violent than was previously believed and, most importantly, suggests that targeting enforcement and treatment efforts against regular narcotics abusers will reduce serious crime.

As research such as this has become accessible to the police and the general public, enforcement efforts against drugs have expanded to a multifront attack. Federal efforts have involved many law enforcement and military units. Strategies that attempt to eliminate the raw materials used to produce drugs have been repeatedly used, with mixed success. In addition, interdiction efforts that seek to halt illicit drugs at the U.S. borders are constantly utilized. However, when one realizes that law enforcement officers must place more than 12,000 miles of international boundary under surveillance, with more than 270 million people and 420 billion tons of goods crossing these borders, the near impossibility of success with

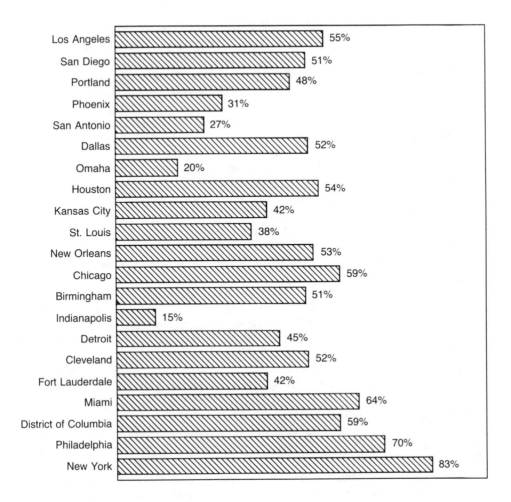

FIGURE 4-1

Percentage of male arrestees testing positive for cocaine in the most recent quarter of 1988 for which data are available.

Source: National Institute of Justice, *NIJ Reports*, March/April 1989, 7.

this approach becomes apparent. Public and private efforts at changing the attitudes and behavior of current and potential youthful abusers show hopeful signs of aiding the problem, yet such attempts are far from a complete solution to the problem.

Local Enforcement Strategies

Because of the limited success of these traditional tactics, enforcement attention has begun to center once again on local police efforts. In a practical sense, local law enforcement can attack the drug problem only on two possible fronts—high-level enforcement and street-level enforcement. High-level enforcement involves criminal investigations aimed at the organizations responsible for producing, importing, and distributing drugs. With this approach, which has been the traditional law enforcement approach for the last half-century, investigators seek to immobilize or eradicate the trafficking networks.

Unfortunately, law enforcement is not certain that this strategy can succeed in the 1990s. The difficulty stems from many factors, one of which is that criminal drug organizations are less dependent on single top leaders. In addition, the tremendous cost of this approach is limiting. Continuous efforts to recruit and pay informants, to conduct regular and electronic surveillances, and to use undercover criminal investigators require large sums of money.

As a result, greater attention is now being concentrated on the street-level approach. In the past, street-level enforcement, which targeted the minor figures in the drug world, was given a low priority by criminal investigators. However, there is encouraging evidence that intensive street enforcement can rid communities of drug dealers and users.

The most commonly encountered addictive street drug in the United States is crack (also known as rock on the West Coast), which is processed by converting cocaine hydrochloride (HCl) back to a cocaine base. Because crack is smoked, its effects are more intense and more rapidly obtained than those from cocaine, which is ingested nasally. Crack is readily available in most urban areas of the country and is spreading rapidly into suburban and rural America.[4] It is typically sold by retail-type drug dealers on the street or by dealers operating out of crack houses. Generally, for as little as five to ten dollars, addicts can purchase vials containing 60 to 100 milligrams of the rocklike cocaine.

Crack's popularity is relatively new but has been building in a steady fashion for the last five years. For example, during the last three years in Washington, DC, crack-cocaine use among arrestees has more than tripled.[5] Recently, this type of drug distribution has been closely associated with various street gang organizations, such as the California-based Crips and Bloods and the East Coast Jamaican posses.

Because of the visibility and prevalence of crack drug dealing and the resulting ripple effect such criminal activity inevitably brings to a given neighborhood, local police must act at once to resolve this contemporary problem. As mentioned earlier, reliance on federal authorities cannot be the only approach. The problem is simply too large and too immediate in its linkage to violent crime. With a focus on street sales, the investigative strategies being used can be categorized as street enforcement, data analysis, and citizen-oriented enforcement.[6]

Street Enforcement

Street enforcement is aimed primarily at those who sell drugs directly to drug abusers and at the street buyer of drugs. Even though street enforcement is increasingly focused on crack, the following enforcement procedures are commonly used to combat a wide variety of illegal street drugs. To obtain information about drug sellers and sales locations, police make frequent use of surveillance, informant tips, and drug hotlines. When information leads to street sales, which are more common than other drug sales methods, the police frequently conduct saturation patrols, or large-scale arrests of both dealers and buyers. Additionally, investigators often work in an undercover capacity, posing as drug dealers and arresting abusers who attempt to purchase narcotics from them. Although this "reverse sting" approach is highly successful in apprehending large numbers of buyers and is a powerful deterrent to potential drug buyers, its use is somewhat limited by legal and citizen concerns with entrapment and the propriety of police posing as drug sellers.

Another method, asset seizure, involves the civil seizure of property that has been used as an integral part of a completed criminal offense. Although it has been a fairly common tool in federal cases involving drugs and income tax evasion, it has rarely been used in local street enforcement operations. Nonetheless, asset seizure can be effective locally, especially when homes are being used as crack houses. In such cases the police can notify the legal owners that illegal activity is taking place. If the owners, who may or may not be involved in the actual selling of narcotics, fail to take action to stop the illegal activity, civil seizure of their property can take place, with the property then being forfeited or even destroyed by the authorities. Legal seizure can also involve automobiles, boats, or other valuable commodities and can be directed at drug buyers as well as drug sellers.

Data Analysis

Data analysis—commonly referred to as problem-oriented policing—emphasizes the collection and analysis of information. With this approach criminal investigators utilize data on individuals, past and present incidents, and police responses to criminal incidents and then develop specific prevention and/or enforcement strategies based on that data. Although data analysis can be used in any type of criminal investigation, it is quite applicable to narcotics investigation. By examining drug arrest information, for example, investigators can determine what specific age group they should be targeting. Or they can pinpoint conditions that encourage or support continued drug sales, such as abandoned buildings or unsupervised public parks.

Citizen-Oriented Enforcement

This method operates on the concept that no crime problem is the sole responsibility of the police force. Police in a democratic society must join with the community not only in controlling present crime problems, but in preventing future offenses. Thus, local citizens may form support groups to aid the police in eliminating the conditions that contribute to the drug problem. For example, citizens might conduct neighborhood cleanup projects and pressure absent landlords to renovate abandoned homes used as crack houses into homes that could be rented in a legitimate fashion. Citizens might also establish drug hotlines and anonymous reward programs to aid investigators in identifying drug sellers and users.

Contemporary Drug Enforcement

The combination of empirical evidence linking drugs with the commission of other serious crimes and the intolerable effect of drug dealing on community tranquility has placed much of the immediate responsibility for drug eradication on local police. In response to this pressure, local police investigators have begun to employ a wide range of tactics, all of which are aimed primarily at destroying drug markets by intensifying the risk of arrest for dealers and users. The National Institute of Justice (NIJ) recently reported the following illustration of such strategies:

> In Lynn, Massachusetts, a vigorous street-level enforcement program attacked an open, active heroin trade in the city. Six state troopers and a detective from the Lynn Police Department were assigned to a drug task force to crack down on street sales by making such transactions more difficult. By using undercover operations, surveillance, and information gathered from a drug hotline, police made more arrests and executed more search warrants in the targeted area. Following this crack-down, heroin consumption appeared to decline, robberies and burglaries decreased sharply, and the very visible street sales disappeared with no evidence of displacement into substitute markets in the city.[7]

New York City police also recently developed street-level strategies that utilize both street enforcement and data analysis to combat a crack-cocaine problem. As reported by the NIJ, Operation Pressure Point involved a vigorous street-level enforcement effort in Manhattan.

> During the operation's initial phase, narcotics enforcement was strengthened, and highly visible saturation patrol was initiated, leading to a substantial increase in narcotics and misdemeanor arrests. Traffic and parking enforcement efforts in the area were also stepped up. The results resembled Lynn's: many open markets were closed and crime was reduced.[8]

Other enforcement and investigation programs are currently being evaluated by criminal justice researchers to gauge their effectiveness. In Oakland, California, drug investigators implemented a door-to-door campaign to stimulate police-citizen interaction to combat a local drug problem. In other areas of the country citizen-enacted drug hotlines and neighborhood watch programs are active.

Thus, as local law enforcement responds to its increased role in combatting drugs, innovative strategies are complementing the traditional enforcement methods of the past (Table 4–2). Criminal investigation in the 1990s must continue to be adaptive, always identifying new approaches to address developing problems. At the same time criminal justice research must attempt to answer certain questions that have great bearing on investigative methods.

1. How can the link between drug use and crime be further documented, and what are the specific drug-related crimes?
2. How can a specific police agency or criminal investigative unit determine the exact nature and extent of the drug problem within its jurisdiction?

TABLE 4–2
Enforcement strategies.

	Traditional	Innovative
User-targeted	Possession arrest	Reverse stings Street enforcement Asset seizure

Dealer-targeted	Undercover
	   surveillance
	Buy arrests
	Possession arrests
		Crack enforcement
		Street enforcement
		Asset seizure
		Problem-oriented
		   policing
		Citizen-oriented
		   policing

Source: National Institute of Justice, *NIJ Reports*, March/April 1989, 5.

3. How effective are the innovative methods of drug enforcement in comparison with traditional methods?

4. How do innovative enforcement programs compare in cost and effectiveness with more traditional approaches?

5. Do innovative strategies really reduce cocaine and heroin street sales or merely disperse them to other locations?

Research data to answer these questions will greatly enhance the funding and operational decisions necessary to achieve truly effective local drug investigation.

Notes

[1] National Narcotics Intelligence Consumers Committee, *The NNICC Report 1985–1986: The Supply of Illicit Drugs to the United States from Foreign and Domestic Sources in 1985 and 1986* (Washington, DC: U.S. Government Printing Office, 1987), 26.

[2] David W. Hayeslip, Jr., "Local-Level Drug Enforcement: New Strategies," *NIJ Reports,* Mar./Apr. 1989, 7.

[3] "Probing the Links Between Drugs and Crime," *NIJ Reports,* Feb. 1985, 1–5.

[4] "The Drug Gangs," 28 Mar. 1988, 24–25.

[5] Eric D. Wish, "Drug Use Forecasting," *NIJ Research in Action,* Feb. 1987, 4.

[6] Hayeslip, "Local-Level Drug Enforcement," 3.

[7] Ibid., 5.

[8] Ibid.

CASE STUDY

Mexico, Drugs, and the Death of KiKi Camarena

James N. Gilbert
Kearney State College

On February 7, 1985, Enrique Camarena, an agent of the U.S. Drug Enforcement Administration (DEA), was abducted in Guadalajara, Mexico. Shortly after his kidnapping, he was murdered. The killing of any law enforcement officer is tragic and infuriating, but this particular murder had serious international consequences. It demonstrated to the world that the corrupting power of drug profits can reach even the highest levels of government.

In 1980, when Camarena, known as KiKi to his fellow investigators, was first assigned to the DEA regional office in Guadalajara, Mexico was a booming drug import and export center. It was then and remains now the largest national source of heroin and marijuana entering the United States, as well as a major transit route for U.S. cocaine imports.

The heroin produced in Mexico accounts for more than 40 percent of all the heroin consumed in the United States. Recently, a type of Mexican heroin known as black tar has become quite common in this country, particularly in the West and Southwest. Black tar heroin is chemically processed in a shorter time period than that required for traditional brown powder heroin, leaving several impurities in the narcotic and coloring it dark brown to black. The sheer quantity of Mexican heroin has increased dramatically, as is evidenced by the drug's falling price. At the same time, average purity levels have increased. Currently, Mexican heroin sells for 40 percent less than it did eight years ago, but the average purity has climbed from 20 percent in 1981 to a current level of 55 percent.

In addition to heroin, half of all the marijuana used in the United States comes from Mexico. In 1982 only 6 percent of the marijuana imported into the United

States originated in Mexico, a figure that increased to 11 percent in 1983, 24 percent in 1984, and 40 percent in 1985. These rapid increases are attributed to expanding cultivation, reduced eradication efforts, and a reduction in government seizures. The sizes of the various shipments across our border range from a few pounds to multiton quantities. Transportation methods include aircraft, campers, trucks, autos, and pedestrians.

Although there is no known cultivation of the coca plant in Mexico, the country has nevertheless become a major route by which bulk quantities of South American cocaine travel to the United States. Largely because of increased enforcement pressure in the southeastern United States, particularly in south Florida, cocaine traffickers in South America have been increasingly routing multi-hundred-kilogram shipments of cocaine through Mexico.

Because of the expanding Mexican drug scene in the early 1980s, the DEA supervisor in Guadalajara requested additional investigative assistance, specifically KiKi Camarena. The agent was a former police officer who was particularly well-suited to being a federal narcotics agent. Bilingual and streetwise as a result of a rough childhood spent in poor border towns, Camarena had become an excellent criminal investigator with natural undercover abilities.

For the next four years Camarena was exposed to a narcotics world far beyond his previous experience. He saw firsthand the tremendous quantity of drugs destined for the United States. Additionally, he saw the extent to which drug money had corrupted Mexican government officials. Time after time Mexican judicial, law enforcement, and military officials appeared to sabotage the DEA's plans to arrest drug operators and destroy their products.

Camarena became convinced that corrupt officials in the Mexican attorney general's office were purposely destroying the country's aerial spraying program and diverting millions of dollars provided by the U.S. State Department for its operation. He first became aware of government corruption when he and other DEA agents raided a vast marijuana farm in the middle of the central Mexican desert. It was an extensive growing operation in which thousands of plants were irrigated by underground wells. Because the fields were clearly visible from the air for twenty miles in any direction and because the Mexican government allegedly flew antidrug patrols throughout this area, it was obvious to Camarena that many government officials must have been aware of the marijuana farm. Numerous additional incidents proved to the agent that Guadalajara's drug situation was totally out of control and at least partially protected by powerful government figures.

The DEA reported that at least eighteen major drug gangs operated freely in and about Guadalajara, confirming this region as one of the world's most active drug centers. The inability of the relatively few DEA agents to impact the nearly hopeless situation finally discouraged Camarena. He requested a transfer and was only three weeks away from leaving the country with his family when he was abducted and murdered.

Witnesses reported that Camarena was last seen as he left his office, walking to his pickup in a nearby parking lot. Later it was learned that a number of men, including several Mexican police officers, forced him into their car at gunpoint. Two hours after Camarena's kidnapping, Captain Alfredo Zavala Avelar was also abducted. Avelar worked for the DEA as a pilot and had frequently assisted Camarena. When Camarena was reported missing by his wife, the DEA began an intense effort to locate him. Hampered by their inability to search or arrest without Mexican authorization, more than fifty American agents frantically searched for their fellow investigator.

On March 2, 1985, in an open field behind a small Mexican ranch, the bodies of the murdered agent and the pilot were finally located. Forensic evidence clearly indicated that they had been buried in another location and moved to that site. Autopsy results revealed that both men had been alive for many days following their abduction and had been tortured prior to being killed. Following these discoveries, U.S. officials became aware of a formidable effort to cover up the details of the murders. A conspiracy that had to involve officials of several Mexican governmental agencies attempted to protect drug dealers and government operatives directly involved in the crime.

In the more than four years that have passed since the brutal murder of KiKi Camarena, the investigation has produced only mixed results. In 1988 a jury in the federal district court of Los Angeles found three men, one a former Mexican police officer, guilty of complicity in Camarena's murder. However, few believe that all guilty parties were brought to justice. The Mexican government responded to the publicity and international pressure resulting from the murders by replacing some high-level police and judicial officials. Hundreds of police subordinates were also dismissed, with nearly 100 prosecuted for various criminal activities and official corruption. Nonetheless, the DEA has no intention of closing the murder investigation of KiKi Camarena. The agency continues to pursue new investigative leads, believing that many more guilty parties, including government officials, are still at large in Mexico.

The Mexican government continues to cooperate with our government, without fully committing to total drug eradication. Recently a mutual legal assistance treaty was signed between Mexico and the United States, yet the Mexican government has turned down requests by the United States for unrestricted access to Mexican airspace in the pursuit of suspected drug-carrying aircraft. A recent official U.S. State Department report summarized well the entire matter regarding the murder of KiKi Camarena. The International Narcotics Control Strategy Report dramatically understated the case when it reported that "the Mexican government's cooperation with the United States government investigation of the Camarena case has not been at the level of which Mexico is capable."

The narcotics situation in Mexico remains critical. And since Mexico shares large portions of our border, our drug problem is obviously linked to Mexico's. With Mexico's worsening economic situation, drug profits remain attractive to a people experiencing scarce jobs, poverty-level wages, and an uncertain political future. The future is not bright south of the border.

Sources: Elaine Shannon, *Desperados: Latin Drug Lords, U.S. Lawmen, and the War Americans Can't Win* (New York: Viking, 1988); "Death of a Narc," *Time,* 7 November 1988, 84–93; Michael P. Malone, "The Enrique Camarena Case," *FBI Law Enforcement Bulletin,* September 1989, 1–6.

5

Constitutional Limitations on Police Investigations

Jack Call
Radford University

In 1953 Earl Warren was appointed chief justice of the United States Supreme Court. Under his leadership the Court embarked on a period of liberal decision making, often referred to as the Due Process Revolution. In 1969 Chief Justice Warren retired and was replaced by Warren Burger, a decidedly more conservative leader of the Court. The Burger years have generally been viewed as a time during which the Court did not overturn the liberal decisions of the Warren Court but did limit their scope.[1]

Cases involving the rights of criminal defendants and suspects have figured prominently throughout both the Warren and Burger years. The Court decisions that have had the greatest actual or potential impact on police work fall into four general categories: seizures of persons, searches, confessions, and pretrial identifications. When the police violate any of the constitutional rules in these areas, the Court has applied the so-called exclusionary rule to prevent the use of any evidence obtained unconstitutionally. Before discussing these four areas in detail, it might be helpful to explore briefly the relationship of the Supreme Court to the Constitution.

The Constitution and the Supreme Court

The United States Constitution is the supreme law of the land.[2] This means that all other laws in our nation must be consistent with that document. In this context the word *law* includes state constitutions and any governmental action. Since police officers are employees of the government, their actions may not conflict with the Constitution. The Supreme Court's decision in *Marbury v. Madison*[3] in 1803 asserted the Court's power to declare a law or action of the government unconstitutional because it conflicts with the Constitution, even though the Constitution itself does not specifically give that power to the Court.

The original Constitution says virtually nothing of importance to the criminal justice system. However, the first ten amendments to that document—commonly referred to as the Bill of Rights—contain many provisions that directly affect the criminal justice system, such as the right to a public trial, the right to a jury trial, the right to counsel, and protection against double jeopardy, self-incrimination, and unreasonable searches and seizures. In 1833 the Supreme Court held in *Barron v. Baltimore*[4] that the restrictions of the Bill of Rights limited the actions of the federal government only and did not limit what state and local governments could do. However, after the Civil War the Fourteenth Amendment was adopted, which, among other things, prohibits the states (as well as counties and cities) from denying its citizens life, liberty, or property without "due process of law." In giving meaning to this rather vague and ambiguous phrase in the twentieth century, the Supreme Court has held that states must extend to their citizens most of the rights mentioned in the Bill of Rights, a process commonly referred to as selective incorporation.[5] In the 1960s the Court selectively incorporated for criminal defendants nearly all of the rights mentioned in the Bill of Rights.[6]

Over the years the Supreme Court has come to resemble a legislative body, creating hundreds of constitutional rules that law enforcement personnel must follow. That body of rules, which is constantly being refined and expanded, constitutes, in effect, a national code of procedure for criminal investigations.

Seizures of Persons

The Fourth Amendment prohibits unreasonable searches and seizures. Since an arrest is a seizure of the person arrested, the Fourth Amendment prohibits unreasonable arrests as well.

Stops and Frisks

The only major decision of the Warren Court in this area, *Terry v. Ohio* (1968),[7] gave the police a power they did not clearly possess previously. In *Terry* Officer McFadden observed three men engaging in suspicious behavior and concluded that they were planning a jewelry store robbery. When he approached them and inquired about what they were doing, one of the men mumbled something to one of the other two, causing McFadden to order all three to lean against a nearby wall. When he frisked them, he found an illegal weapon on Terry.

Long before the Warren Court era, the Supreme Court had established that a valid arrest required probable cause to think that the person arrested had committed or was about to commit a crime. So Terry argued that McFadden's search of him was improper because it was not pursuant to a valid arrest, for which there would have had to be probable cause.

The Warren Court rejected that argument. It held that McFadden had merely stopped Terry to make a brief investigation, which did not require probable cause but merely "reasonable suspicion" that criminal activity was afoot. The Court also held that such a stop could be accompanied by a frisk, that is, a pat-down of the outer clothing of the person stopped, if the officer had reasonable suspicion that the latter was armed and dangerous.

This constitutional permission for the police to stop and frisk, based on reasonable suspicion rather than probable cause, has provided the legal foundation for the aggressive practices of some police departments, which make extensive use of field interrogations (i.e., frequent stoppings of suspicious individuals). The Burger Court did little to restrain these practices. It even allowed a police officer to reach directly into the waistband of a suspect for a gun that the officer had been informed the suspect possessed (a search that goes beyond the limited pat-down permitted by *Terry*).[8] The Burger Court also permitted an officer to base his determination of reasonable suspicion on something other than personal observation and extended the stop-and-frisk doctrine to nondangerous offenses.[9]

The Burger Court did establish some limits on stops and frisks, however. The Court held that the police may not frisk people who are simply in a place that the police may search. In *Ybarra v. Illinois*[10] the police had a valid warrant to search a tavern but also frisked all the occupants of the tavern. The Court indicated that such frisks were unconstitutional unless the police had reasonable suspicion that each occupant searched was armed. In addition, the police may not require a person to go to the station house for fingerprinting unless they have probable cause to arrest that person.[11]

The Burger Court was not very supportive of police use of drug courier profiles as a basis for stopping suspicious persons. In the only case considered by the Burger Court where a stop was based solely on the fact that the person fit a drug courier profile, the Court found the stop unconstitutional.[12] However, in another similar case where the police had a little more to go on than just a drug courier profile, the Burger Court upheld the stop.[13]

Arrests

The Warren Court had little to say about situations in which the police arrest someone, and the Burger Court developed a somewhat mixed pattern in this area.[14] In probably its most important arrest case, the Burger Court upheld the power of the police to make arrests in felony cases without an arrest warrant, even if there is no reason to think that a delay to obtain a warrant would impede the arrest effort.[15] However, in another case the Court required that a person arrested without a warrant be brought promptly before a judicial officer for a determination as to whether the arrest was indeed supported by probable cause. The Burger Court also held that if the felony arrest is to be made at a home, an arrest warrant is constitutionally required, unless some pressing circumstance makes it likely that the delay to obtain the warrant would interfere with the ability of the police to make the arrest.[16] Furthermore, the Court held that a warrant for the arrest of one person does not justify entry into the home of another person to look for the former, without a warrant authorizing a search of the latter's home.[17]

In one other important arrest case the Burger Court limited the means that the police can use to effect an arrest. In *Tennessee v. Garner*[18] the Court struck down a

Tennessee statute that permitted the police to use any means necessary, including deadly force, to make an arrest of any criminal suspect, including one fleeing from the police. The Court held that the Fourth Amendment prohibition against unreasonable seizures requires that the police refrain from using deadly force to stop a fleeing suspect unless they reasonably believe that the suspect will otherwise escape and they have probable cause to believe that "the suspect poses a significant threat of death or serious physical injury to the officer or others."[19]

Searches

As indicated earlier, the Fourth Amendment prohibits unreasonable searches and seizures and requires that probable cause exist before an arrest or search warrant is issued. Although the amendment says nothing specific about when a warrant is required, the Supreme Court has generally interpreted the amendment as requiring a warrant before the police act.[20] The Court's preference for warrants has been based on the philosophy that it is better for a neutral, unbiased judicial officer to make a determination of probable cause than for the police to make this determination.

Of course, there are exceptions to the warrant requirement. One of the most important exceptions—the felony arrest—was discussed in the previous section. There are some exceptions to the warrant requirement in search situations as well, some of which are discussed here. However, in search situations, there is a very important preliminary question: What is a search? If the police are not conducting a search, the Fourth Amendment and the warrant requirement do not come into play at all.

Definition of a Search

The *American Heritage Dictionary* indicates that to search is "to make a thorough examination of or look over carefully in order to find something." However, the Supreme Court has never followed this definition. Because the language of the Fourth Amendment explicitly extends the right against unreasonable searches and seizures to "persons, houses, papers, and effects," many cases prior to the Due Process Revolution resolved the issue of whether a search had occurred on the basis of whether the police had trespassed into a physically protected area, such as a home. Electronic eavesdropping cases were especially troublesome.

By 1967 it was becoming increasingly apparent that modern technology had made obsolete this old trespass approach to the search question. In *Katz v. United States*[21] the police had attached an eavesdropping device to the outside of a public telephone booth without obtaining a search warrant. In holding that this action by the police constituted a search, the Warren Court indicated that the Fourth Amendment protects people, not places. Since the *Katz* decision the Court's determination of a search has centered on whether the person examined had a reasonable expectation of privacy that the police intruded upon.

Under the Burger Court "reasonable expectation of privacy" has been given a rather restricted meaning. Under the public exposure doctrine the Court developed the idea that individuals possess no reasonable expectation of privacy in places or things that they have exposed to the public. Thus, it is not a search when undercover agents wired for sound are invited by suspects into their homes, where the suspects make incriminating statements that are recorded.[22] Nor is it a search when the police require suspects to provide voice[23] or handwriting samples[24] or when they take paint scrapings from a car parked in a public parking area.[25]

Perhaps the most extreme set of public exposure cases are those involving the use of what one authority calls institutional agents (as opposed to undercover government agents).[26] In *Smith v. Maryland*[27] the Burger Court ruled that the police did not conduct a search when they obtained from the phone company a list of all phone numbers called from a suspect's telephone. Likewise, the Burger Court found no search when a prosecutor subpoenaed a suspect's bank records.[28] In deciding these cases, the Court relied somewhat on the idea that the suspects had accepted the risk that this information would be passed on to third parties by the institutions to whom the suspects had "exposed" this information.

Nonetheless, in two beeper cases the Burger Court indicated that there are limits to how far it will extend this line of reasoning.[29] The Court held in these cases that the police did not conduct searches when they placed electronic transmitters in packages of chemicals that they knew the suspects had bought. However, in the more recent of these two cases, the Court indicated that it was unconstitutional to use the beepers without a search warrant to obtain information "that could not have been obtained through visual surveillance."[30]

The open fields doctrine was also developed by the Burger Court to limit the applicability of the Fourth Amendment to police work. The open fields doctrine was first enunciated by the Supreme Court in 1924 and provided that the police are not searching when they look for or find something in a place outside the home or the fenced-in area around the home.[31] This means, for example, that the police can climb over a fence and walk through "the back forty," ignoring any no trespassing signs.[32] They can even observe things within the curtilage, the fenced-in area of a home, aerial surveillance without a warrant if they use aerial surveillance,[33] although physical intrusions into the curtilage require a search warrant.[34]

Search Warrant Exceptions

As indicated earlier, the Fourth Amendment has been generally viewed by the Supreme Court as requiring that a search warrant be obtained before a search takes place. Several of the exceptions to this warrant requirement merit our attention. One exception that affects a large number of cases concerns consent searches. The police need not have a warrant or probable cause if the person searched or a person having "common authority" over the place or thing to be searched voluntarily consents to the search.[35] Since a person generally has a constitutional right to require the police to search only with a warrant or probable cause, the person is waiving this right in consenting to a search.

Often, the Supreme Court requires that waivers of constitutional rights be made knowingly, that is, with knowledge of the right being waived. However, in *Schneckloth v. Bustamonte*[36] the Burger Court held that all that is required constitutionally is that the consent be voluntary. And voluntariness is decided on the basis of all the relevant circumstances, such as what age and mental condition the consenter is in and whether the consenter is under arrest at the time.

Another important exception to the search warrant requirement is searches made incident to an arrest. In *Chimel v. California*[37] the Warren Court held that the police do not need a search warrant to search someone they have arrested. The purpose of such a search is to protect the arresting officer and to prevent the destruction of evidence. Therefore, the search is limited to those areas within the immediate control of the arrestee.

Chimel left a lot of unanswered questions, one of which was whether the police could conduct a search incident to any arrest or only to an arrest in which it would be reasonable to think that the person arrested was armed or possessed evidence of a crime. The Burger Court addressed this important issue in two cases in 1973. In *United States v. Robinson*[38] the police had arrested Robinson for driving with a revoked driver's license. A search of Robinson pursuant to this arrest turned up a package of heroin in his coat pocket. The Court held the search to be constitutional because police officers should not have to make difficult judgments about whether a crime or the circumstances of an arrest justify a search. In *Gustafson v. Florida*[39] the defendant was searched incident to an arrest for not carrying his driver's license. The Court again upheld the search.

In these two cases the Burger Court seemed to be anxious to provide a clear rule that police could follow so that they would not have to make difficult judgments that courts might later second guess. The two cases together give the police rather broad authority to conduct searches incident to any custodial arrest. The Burger Court never had occasion to deal with a pretext arrest, in which the police follow a suspect around until they observe the suspect doing something for which he or she can be arrested (such as not coming to a full stop at a stop sign), which then justifies a search of the suspect.[40] However, the tenor of the *Gustafson* opinion suggests that the Burger Court would not have been inclined to inquire into the motives behind an officer's decision to arrest, as long as the arrest was supported by probable cause.

Chimel also created what some commentators have referred to as an armspan rule by limiting a search incident to an arrest to the area within the arrestee's immediate control. However, the Burger Court broadened the armspan rule for situations in which a defendant is arrested in a car. In *New York v. Belton*[41] the Court held that in such a case the police may constitutionally search the entire passenger compartment of the car, including any container in that compartment. Furthermore, the Court indicated that the passenger compartment can be searched even if the persons arrested have been removed from the car, as long as the search and the arrest occur at the same general time. Thus, a search is valid as long as the arrest is valid and as long as the search is limited to the area within the arrestee's control or to the passenger compartment of the arrestee's car.

The third important exception to the search warrant requirement is the so-called automobile exception. An automobile exception can be dated back as far as *Carroll v. United States* in 1925,[42] but its continued acceptance was somewhat doubtful by the time Warren Burger became chief justice. Nonetheless, in an early Burger Court decision the Court reaffirmed the automobile exception, espousing the *Carroll* philosophy that cars are so easily moved that the police may usually search them without a warrant *when* they have probable cause to think they will find contraband or evidence of a crime in the car.[43]

In addition, the Burger Court developed another basis for the automobile exception. In *United States v. Chadwick*[44] the Court indicated that warrants are not needed when probable cause exists to search cars because there is a diminished expectation of privacy in cars. The Court extended the automobile exception to a warrantless search of a mini–mobile home parked in a parking lot,[45] but did not uphold a warrantless search of a footlocker thought to contain drugs.[46] The Court pointed out that footlockers are not heavily regulated by the state, as cars are, and are more likely to contain objects that one does not want exposed to public view. In other words, footlockers carry a greater expectation of privacy.

Determination of Probable Cause

One other important area of law associated with searches—the determination of probable cause—has been substantially affected by the Supreme Court. Search warrants must be based on a finding of probable cause that contraband (i.e., objects that are themselves illegal, such as heroin or unregistered guns) or evidence of a crime will be found in the place searched. In addition, most warrantless searches must be based on a similar finding of probable cause. Often the facts used to establish probable cause come from firsthand knowledge possessed by the police, usually things they have observed directly. Sometimes, however, the facts are based on information provided by informants, who may themselves be criminals or other persons of questionable veracity.

To address the question of the reliability of information provided by informants, the Warren Court established a two-pronged test.[47] That test required hearsay information that formed the basis of a finding of probable cause to be sufficient to allow the deciding official to conclude reasonably (1) that the informant was credible (the veracity prong) and (2) that the informant's conclusions were based on reliable information (the basis-of-knowledge prong).

This so-called Aguilar test (named for one of the controlling cases in this area, *Aguilar v. Texas*) was quite controversial. In 1983 the Burger Court indicated that the test had often been applied by lower courts in a hypertechnical manner that had failed to uphold findings of probable cause when common sense would have suggested that probable cause did exist. Consequently, the Court abolished the Aguilar two-pronged test in favor of a totality of circumstances test.[48] In other words, the Court expects police officers and judicial officers issuing warrants to look at all the facts present in a case and determine whether the facts as a whole indicate that probable cause exists. The Court conceded that veracity and basis of knowledge were important considerations, but it contended that a weakness in one of these factors might be overcome by the strength of the other factor. The result of this decision seems to make it less likely that probable cause determinations will be overturned by the courts.

Confessions

One of the most controversial of all the Warren Court decisions during the Due Process Revolution was *Miranda v. Arizona*.[49] Even though the average person can rattle off at least some of the Miranda warnings, *Miranda* is a somewhat misunderstood case.

Prior to 1966 the Supreme Court had found confessions unconstitutional only if they were obtained involuntarily. (Throughout our discussion of confessions, the word *confession* refers to any incriminating statement made by a suspect, regardless of whether it amounts to a full admission of a crime.) The test for voluntariness was a totality of the circumstances test: one examined all the circumstances to determine whether a confession had been coerced from a suspect. By 1966 it was clear that the Supreme Court had become quite frustrated with the failure of the voluntariness test to bring an end to aggressive and inappropriate interrogation practices that the police utilized, at least on occasion.

Miranda represented a new approach to protecting criminal suspects from improper police interrogation. The underlying concept is that if the police fail to advise a suspect of certain rights before interrogating that suspect in custody, it will be conclusively presumed (i.e., there is nothing the prosecution can do to disprove the presumption) that any incriminating statements obtained during the interrogation are the result of improper compulsion on the part of the police. The familiar rights of which suspects must be informed prior to custodial interrogation are the right to remain silent, the right to consult an attorney before interrogation and to have the attorney present during interrogation, the right to have the state provide an attorney if the suspect cannot afford one, and the understanding that anything the suspect says can and will be used against him or her in a court of law. The part of *Miranda* that is so often misunderstood is that it applies only when custodial interrogation takes place.

A Definition of Custody

The *Miranda* decision suggested that a suspect in custody was one that had been "deprived of his freedom of action in any significant way."[50] The Burger Court's interpretation of this phrase requires that the suspect be detained by the police in a way that resembles arrest. Thus, the Burger Court found no custody involved when a suspected tax evader was questioned by IRS agents in a private home where the suspect occasionally stayed.[51] Nor did the Court find the questioning of a probationer by his probation officer in the latter's office custodial.[52] In two cases the Burger Court even found the interrogation at a police station was not custodial, stressing the fact that both suspects agreed to meet with the police at the station house and were told that they were not under arrest.[53]

Unfortunately, it is difficult to extract any practical guidelines from these cases that make it easy to determine when custody exists. The closest we can come at this point is that custody probably exists if a suspect is not free to go, but even this guideline is quite slippery. The key point is that the Burger Court was not very strict in interpreting custody.

A Definition of Interrogation

Obviously, if the police ask questions of a suspect, interrogation has occurred. But can actions short of explicit questioning constitute interrogation? Here the Burger Court was not so lenient. In *Rhode Island v. Innis* the Court held that "any words or actions on the part of the police (other than those normally attendant to arrest and custody) that the police should know are reasonably likely to elicit an incriminating response from the suspect" are the functional equivalent of express questioning and therefore constitute interrogation.[54]

However, the Court was more strict in its application of that definition. In *Innis* the defendant was arrested for killing a taxi driver with a shotgun. At the time of Innis's arrest, the shotgun had not been found. While driving Innis to the station house, two police officers talked to each other about their concern that the missing shotgun might come into the hands of the students at a nearby school for hand-icapped children. Upon hearing this, Innis directed the officers to the shotgun, which was then used as evidence against him at his trial.

Although it has always seemed to me (and to many of my students as well) that the officers hoped this conversation would elicit a response from Innis, a majority of the Burger Court characterized the conversation as "nothing more than a dialogue between the two officers to which no response from the [defendant] was invited."[55] Thus, the Burger Court may have conceded that behavior other than express questioning might constitute interrogation, but it was not very generous to defendants in its application of that rule.

Waiver of Miranda Rights

There are two Miranda rights that a suspect may waive: the right to remain silent and the right to consult an attorney. If a suspect initially asserts these rights, may he later waive them? The Burger Court answer to this question was mixed.

In *Michigan v. Mosley*[56] the police questioned Moseley about a series of robberies for which he had been arrested but then ceased their questioning when he indicated that he did not want to talk to the police about them. More than two hours later, another detective read Moseley his rights again and asked him questions about a murder unrelated to the robberies. In response to those questions, Moseley made some incriminating statements. The Burger Court held that Moseley's "right to cut off questioning" had been properly honored by the police, citing that (1) questioning had immediately ceased when Moseley had initially asserted his right, (2) a significant period of time passed between his assertion of that right and the next attempt to question him, (3) he was readvised of his rights before the second attempt to question him, and (4) the second interrogation concerned a different crime from that about which he was initially questioned.

The problem with *Mosley* is that it is not clear how important the last of these four factors was to the Court's decision. If it was not critical, then it appears that the police may later question a suspect even after he has asserted his right to remain silent, as long as they wait at least a couple of hours and readvise him of his rights before questioning begins again.

The Burger Court took a stricter approach when a suspect invoked the right to an attorney. In *Edwards v. Arizona* the Court held that once an accused has "expressed his desire to deal with the police only through counsel, [he] is not subject to further interrogation by the authorities until counsel has been made available to him, unless the accused himself initiates further communication, exchanges or conversation with the police."[57]

However, this may be another strict rule that the Court does not intend always to apply strictly. In *Oregon v. Bradshaw*[58] the accused denied having committed a homicide with which he had been charged and asked to see his lawyer. The police terminated the interrogation and took the accused back to his cell. On the way to his cell, the accused asked an officer, "[W]ell, what is going to happen to me now?" The officer reminded the accused that he did not have to talk, but a conversation followed during which the accused made incriminating statements. The Court's opinion conceded that the defendant's question was ambiguous but concluded that it reflected "a willingness and a desire for a generalized discussion about the investigation; it was not merely a necessary inquiry arising out of the incidents of the custodial relationship."[59] Consequently, the Court found that the accused had initiated further communication with the police so that it was proper for them to question him without his lawyer present.

On the other hand, in *Smith v. Illinois*[60] the accused at one point expressed a desire to consult with an attorney, then shortly afterward indicated, somewhat equivocally, that he would talk to the police without consulting an attorney first, and subsequently did in fact talk with them, giving them incriminating statements. The Court found that the accused had invoked his right to counsel and indicated that statements made by the accused after invocation of that right should not be used to cast doubt on whether he had in fact invoked his right.

Public Safety Exception

The Burger Court also created what may be an important exception to the requirement that Miranda warnings be given prior to custodial interrogation. In *New York v. Quarles*[61] four police officers entered a supermarket looking for a man who reportedly had entered the store carrying a gun. When one of the officers found the man, the officer pointed his weapon at the man, ordered him to stop, frisked him, and found an empty shoulder holster. Without giving the suspect the Miranda warnings, the officer asked him where the gun was, and the suspect pointed to some nearby boxes. A search of the boxes turned up a gun that was used as evidence at the suspect's trial. The Court held that it was proper for the officer to ask this question without giving the Miranda warnings because public safety was threatened as long as the gun was unaccounted for, and the need to protect public safety outweighed the importance of advising the suspect of his rights. Because this is such a recent case, the Court has not had occasion to expand on the scope of this exception, but it obviously has the potential to limit the reach of *Miranda* substantially.

The Revivification of Massiah

Several years prior to its decision in *Miranda,* the Warren Court held in *Massiah v. United States*[62] that the police could not deliberately elicit statements from an accused in the absence of a retained counsel if the accused had already been indicted. After *Miranda* it was not clear whether *Massiah* retained any vitality, but in 1977 the Burger Court made it clear that *Massiah* was still alive and well.

In *Brewer v. Williams*[63] Williams was suspected of having killed a ten-year-old girl. The crime occurred in Des Moines, Iowa, but Williams was arrested in Davenport, about 160 miles from Des Moines. An initial appearance for Williams was held in Davenport, and counsel was appointed for him there. Then Des Moines police detectives went to Davenport to pick up Williams and take him back to Des Moines. Williams's Davenport lawyer was denied permission to accompany Williams on the trip but told the detectives that they were not to question Williams on the way to Des Moines. Nevertheless, during the trip one of the detectives, who knew that Williams was a former mental patient and was deeply religious, began talking to Williams about the fact that the little girl's body had not been found and it would be a terrible shame if the family was deprived of a Christian burial for her. Even though the detective had told Williams just to listen and not say anything, Williams eventually took him to the girl's body.

This case could possibly have been decided on the basis of *Miranda,* but the Court instead reversed Williams's conviction on the basis of the police failure to obtain an explicit waiver of Williams's right to counsel. This development is important because *Massiah* could affect the admissibility of statements obtained by the police from a suspect in a noncustodial situation after the initiation of judicial proceedings against that suspect. For example, in the case cited earlier, the Court held that the interrogation of a suspected tax evader in a private home was not custodial, so Miranda warnings were unnecessary. But if the suspect in that case had already been formally charged with a crime, *Massiah* would seem to require the exclusion at trial of any incriminating statements obtained during that interrogation unless the IRS agents had obtained an explicit waiver of the suspect's right to counsel.

Pretrial Identifications

Pretrial identifications are typically made by witnesses at a lineup, through a display of photographs, or in a one-on-one confrontation between the witness and the suspect. Often these procedures are of critical importance to a suspect, whose arrest or conviction may hinge on whether a witness makes that identification. The danger, of course, is that the procedure may be conducted in such a way as to make it likely that a particular suspect will be identified, even if the witness's memory of the event is not strong.

Recognizing this danger, the Warren Court issued two important decisions in 1967. In *United States v. Wade*[64] the Court held that a lineup identification made after Wade's indictment was inadmissible at trial because Wade had not been represented by an attorney at the lineup, thereby violating his right to counsel. On the same day of the *Wade* decision, the Court held in *Stovall v. Denno*[65] that any identification procedure violates a suspect's right to due process of law if it is conducted in an unnecessarily suggestive manner that creates a substantial chance for a mistaken identification.

The Burger Court expanded on these Warren Court holdings. In *Kirby v. Illinois*[66] the Court held that a lineup may be conducted without a suspect's being represented by counsel if it takes place before the initiation of judicial criminal proceedings—that is, before a "formal charge, preliminary hearing, indictment, information [sworn charges filed by a prosecutor in lieu of a grand jury indictment], or arraignment."[67] Thus, *Kirby* may have only limited effect on *Wade* since it "appears to apply only to the short period of time between detention and the initial appearance in front of a judicial officer."[68] However, *Kirby* itself does not mention "initial appearance," and the term *arraignment* has two different meanings. Most often it refers to a formal appearance before a trial court to enter a plea, in which case *Wade* would not come into play until a prosecutor filed formal charges, well after the initial appearance. At this point the full impact of *Kirby* is still unclear.

Of more importance than *Kirby* is the Burger Court's decision in *United States v. Ash*,[69] in which the Court ruled that counsel is not required at an identification that involves only a photographic display, regardless of when the display occurs. Although a photo display seems just as fraught with the potential suggestiveness as a lineup, the Court distinguished between the two on the questionable basis that the defense counsel could adequately reconstruct the photo identification process by viewing the photos used and questioning the identifying witnesses, but counsel could not adequately reconstruct the lineup identification process.

The *Stovall* due process test for suggestiveness has three aspects: (1) Was the identification procedure suggestive? (2) If so, was it necessary to conduct the procedure as it was conducted? (3) If so, was there a good chance that the identification made was erroneous? The Burger Court made it clear that even if an identification procedure was unnecessarily suggestive, it would be admissible if the identification seemed reliable. In *Stovall* an undercover police officer purchased heroin from a seller and two days later was shown a single photo of the defendant, whom the undercover agent immediately identified as the seller. The Burger Court upheld the admission of this photo at the defendant's trial even though it was clearly unnecessarily suggestive because the following indicators of reliability accompanied the identification: "the witness was a trained police officer, had a sufficient opportunity to view the suspect, accurately described him, positively identified his photograph, and made the photographic identification only two days after the crime."[70]

The Exclusionary Rule

The rights of criminal suspects are of little good unless the police are motivated to observe those rights. The primary motivator utilized by the Supreme Court is the exclusionary rule, which provides that the prosecution may not use at trial any evidence obtained unconstitutionally to help convict the person whose rights were violated when the evidence was obtained. Although the Constitution says nothing about an exclusionary rule, the Supreme Court has found it a necessary implication of the Constitution. In 1961 the Warren Court issued one of its most controversial decisions in *Mapp v. Ohio,*[71] holding that the states must exclude evidence obtained in violation of the Fourth Amendment. Prior to *Mapp* only the federal courts had been required to exclude such evidence.[72] In addition, *Miranda* and *Wade* provide that improperly obtained confessions and pretrial identifications must also be excluded by the states. These decisions are of great importance because the vast majority of criminal cases are handled by state, rather than federal, courts.

Many critics argue that the exclusionary rule exacts too high a price from society, permitting many guilty defendants to go free. The Burger Court displayed little affection for the rule, but it did not eliminate it. Instead, it issued a number of decisions that significantly restricted the reach of the rule.

Situations in Which the Exclusionary Rule Does Not Apply

The Burger Court generally limited the application of the exclusionary rule to criminal trials. For example, it held that unconstitutionally obtained evidence could be used at grand jury proceedings,[73] civil trials,[74] and deportation hearings.[75]

The Burger Court even found a situation in which unconstitutionally obtained evidence could be used at trial. In *United States v. Harris*[76] the police had obtained a confession from Harris but had failed to administer Miranda warnings first. Thus, the prosecution could not introduce the confession as evidence that Harris had committed the crime. However, at trial Harris contradicted statements he had made in the confession, so the prosecution was allowed to use the confession for the limited purpose of proving that Harris's testimony was not worthy of belief. The Burger Court held that this use of the improperly obtained confession was permissible because the failure to give Miranda warnings did not give Harris a license to commit perjury. The Burger Court also held subsequently that a confession could be used for impeachment purposes even if it was obtained after the suspect asserted and was denied his right to consult with an attorney.[77] Likewise, it held that evidence obtained in violation of the Fourth Amendment could be used for impeachment purposes.[78]

Good Faith Exception

The Burger Court also found a good faith exception to the exclusionary rule. In *United States v. Leon*[79] the police had conducted a search within the scope of a search warrant it had obtained. The trial court judge later determined that the magistrate had not had probable cause to issue the warrant. The Court noted that the purpose of the exclusionary rule was to discourage the police from violating individual rights. And the Court failed to see how exclusion of the evidence under these circumstances would have this discouraging effect since it was the magistrate, not the police, who had erred. Consequently, the Court held that the evidence should have been admitted because the police had acted in good faith.

It is not clear whether *Leon* creates a full-blown good faith exception to the exclusionary rule. A full-blown good faith exception would allow the prosecution to make full use of any evidence obtained in violation of the Constitution as long as the officers obtaining the evidence believed they were not violating the Constitution and as long as reasonably well informed police officers would have thought the same thing. In *Leon* the police acted in good faith, and it was not their mistake that resulted in a violation of rights. However, one cannot yet say whether the good faith exception created in *Leon* would also apply to a case where the police acted in good faith, but their mistake resulted in a violation of rights.

Fruit of the Poisonous Tree Doctrine

An important aspect of the exclusionary rule is the fruit of the poisonous tree doctrine, which states that evidence is also inadmissible if it was obtained by the police as a result of other evidence that was obtained unconstitutionally. Thus, if the police coerce a confession from a suspect who tells them in the confession where the murder weapon can be found, both the confession (the poisonous tree) and the murder weapon (the fruit of the poisonous tree) are inadmissible. The Burger Court proved to be quite generous in finding exceptions to the fruit of the poisonous tree doctrine.

Independent Source Exception. Prior to the Burger Court years many lower courts had recognized an independent source exception to the fruit of the poisonous tree doctrine. Under this exception, fruit of the poisonous tree is admissible if the prosecution can show that it was obtained by a means independent of the illegal behavior. For example, in our hypothetical murder weapon situation, if an informant known to the police prior to the illegal confession gratuitously called the police and informed them of the murder weapon's location, the weapon would be admissible because it was obtained from a source independent of the illegal confession.

The independent source exception is often at issue in pretrial identification cases. If a pretrial identification is conducted without counsel present after the initiation of judicial proceedings against the defendant or in a manner so suggestive as to make the identification unreliable, *Wade* and *Stovall* make it clear that the pretrial identification is inadmissible at trial. But may the eyewitness still identify the suspect in court?

The Burger Court held in *Neil v. Biggers*[80] that the eyewitness may still identify the suspect in court if there is not a likelihood of misidentification stemming from the suggestive pretrial identification. In assessing that likelihood, the Court indicated that the following factors should be examined:

> The opportunity of the witness to view the criminal at the time of the crime, the witness' degree of attention, the accuracy of the witness' prior description of the criminal, the level of certainty demonstrated by the witness at the confrontation, and the length of time between the crime and the confrontation.[81]

Of course, the effect of *Biggers* is that the prosecution still has a very good chance of being permitted to have an eyewitness make an in-court identification of a defendant who was identified prior to trial in a suggestive identification procedure.

Not surprisingly, the Burger Court was also generous in permitting in-court identifications after pretrial identifications that were improper for reasons other than suggestiveness. In *United States v. Crews*[82] the police had improperly arrested Crews for a robbery and then photographed him at the police station. The robbery victim later identified Crews in an array of eight photos. The pretrial identification was inadmissible as fruit of the improper arrest; however, the Court upheld the in-court identification.

Some of the liberal justices believed that Crews's in-court identification was permissible because he was already a suspect in this crime before his illegal arrest. Thus, even if Crews had not been improperly arrested, the eyewitness would have had an opportunity at some point to identify Crews. But a majority of the justices went even further.

> Assume that a person is arrested for crime X and that answers to questions put to him without *Miranda* warnings implicate him in crime Y for which he is later tried. The victim of crime Y identifies him in the courtroom; the identification has an independent, untainted basis. I would not suppress such an identification on the grounds that the police had no reason to suspect the defendant of crime Y prior to their illegal questioning and that it is only because of the questioning that he is present in the courtroom for trial. I would reach the same result whether or not his arrest for crime X was without probable cause or reasonable suspicion.[83]

Thus, even if the police improperly arrest a suspect and improperly question him, whereupon he implicates himself in a crime for which he is not yet even a suspect, five justices of the Burger Court would still have permitted an in-court identification of the suspect in the second crime.

Purged Taint Exception. If the connection between the illegal behavior of the police and the fruit of that behavior is quite remote, in terms of either the length of time between the two or the length of the "chain" connecting the two, one might say that the taint of the illegal behavior had dissipated or been purged. One commentator stated it this way: "[T]he weaker the link between the initial unlawful conduct and the subsequent lawful discovery of evidence that results from the initial conduct, the less likely the poisonous tree doctrine will be invoked."[84]

This exception is quite nebulous and can be easily used to avoid the exclusionary rule. Although the Burger Court was somewhat generous to the prosecution in its application of the purged taint exception, it was not as generous as it could have been. For example, the Burger Court made it clear that the mere giving of Miranda warnings is not sufficient to purge a confession of the taint from an illegal arrest. Thus, in *Taylor v. Alabama*[85] the Court disallowed a confession after an illegal arrest even though the defendant was given Miranda warnings three times between the time of his arrest and his confession (a period of six hours) and even though the defendant had talked with two friends during that time.

However, the Burger Court was not always consistent. In *Rawlings v. Kentucky*[86] the Court allowed a confession that was given only forty-five minutes after the defendant was illegally arrested because the defendant was given Miranda warnings just before he gave his confession, the interrogation occurred in a house (rather than in the police station) in the presence of several friends, the confession was spontaneous rather than responsive to a direct question and was voluntary, and the police had apparently made the illegal arrest in good faith.

In a common variant of this situation, the police may improperly obtain a confession from a suspect (typically because of a failure to give proper Miranda warnings), then give the suspect proper Miranda warnings, and obtain another confession. In such situations the Burger Court focused on whether the initial confession was coerced. If it was, the subsequent confession was also inadmissible. If it was not, the Court found that proper Miranda warnings were sufficient to purge the second confession of the taint of the illegal first confession; therefore, the second confession was admissible.[87]

Another common situation in which the purged taint exception is often at issue is one in which the police become aware of a useful witness as a result of information that they obtain unlawfully. For example, in *United States v. Ceccolini*[88] a police officer was talking with an acquaintance who was working in Ceccolini's store. The officer noticed an envelope sitting on the cash register and illegally looked inside the envelope, discovering evidence of gambling activities. As a result, the employee was questioned and found to possess knowledge that incriminated Ceccolini. In holding that the testimony of the employee was not the fruit of the poisonous tree, the Burger Court emphasized that such witnesses are likely to be found by legal means eventually anyway and typically testify of their own free will some time after their initial discovery by the police.

The outcome of purged taint exception cases follows the application of totality of the circumstances tests, making it difficult to apply previous cases to present cases in a predictable fashion. Such cases are what lawyers call fact-specific cases, and the Burger Court's performance in this area was not consistent. Overall, however, the Burger Court seemed fairly generous to the prosecution in its willingness to find factors that dissipated the taint of previous evidence obtained illegally by the police.

Inevitable Discovery Exception. Prior to the Burger Court era, most lower courts had held that fruit of the poisonous tree was admissible if it would have been discovered inevitably by legal means, but the Supreme Court had not yet recognized an inevitable discovery exception. The Burger Court did so in 1984 in *Nix v. Williams.*[89] In that case the police improperly obtained from a defendant the location of a murder victim's body. The Court held that the information about the body was admissible because the police were already conducting a search for the body, which would have included the area where it was ultimately found.

This exception seems fair, since it can be argued that the prosecution should not be deprived of evidence that it would have had anyway, even if the police had not violated the defendant's rights. Nevertheless, the exception has troubling aspects. First, determining whether evidence would have been discovered anyway is a highly speculative venture. For this reason, two of the liberal justices on the Court were willing to accept the inevitable discovery exception only if the prosecution could prove inevitable discovery by clear and convincing evidence, rather than by the present standard of proof, which is preponderance of the evidence. Second, this exception deprives courts of the ability to penalize the police for bad faith behavior. For example, in *Nix* the police intentionally questioned the defendant after explicitly agreeing with his lawyer that they would not question him. In cases where the police have lost hope for a successful investigation, this exception may encourage the police to violate known rights to obtain evidence that they can later try to demonstrate they would have found anyway.

From Past to Future

In their excellent book on criminal procedure, Whitebread and Slobogin note four traits or positions that they believe characterized the Burger Court and its approach to criminal procedure:

1. The primary purpose of the criminal justice system is "to convict the guilty and let the innocent go free."[90]
2. The Burger Court exhibited a preference for totality of the circumstances analysis, which makes it difficult for lower court judges to find firm guidance in Supreme Court decisions.
3. Burger Court decisions reflect "greater faith in the integrity of the police and other officials who administer the criminal justice system"[91] than was demonstrated by the Warren Court.
4. Burger Court decisions reflect greater faith in the willingness of state court judges to protect federal constitutional rights than was demonstrated by the Warren Court.

What can be expected in the foreseeable future? There is no reason to expect the Rehnquist Court to deviate significantly from the trends established by the Burger Court. Chief Justice Rehnquist and Justices White, O'Connor, Scalia, and Kennedy seem to constitute a firm conservative majority on issues of criminal procedure. Although rumors of White's impending resignation have surfaced on occasion, all of these justices are relatively young as Supreme Court justices go and can be expected to serve on the Court for at least several more years.

The three oldest justices (Brennan, Marshall, and Blackmun) represent two consistently liberal votes (Brennan and Marshall) and one occasional liberal vote (Blackmun). Since these are the three most likely justices to leave the Court next, the Court could become even more conservative if a Republican president chooses their successors.

The trend toward the use of totality of the circumstances tests is also relevant in discussing the future of criminal procedure in the courts. When these tests are applied by federal lower court judges, about half of those judges are individuals who were appointed to their lifetime tenure positions by President Reagan. And Reagan was diligent in selecting conservative (and often young) nominees, who can be expected to shape the jurisprudence of the federal courts for years to come. When these tests are applied by state court judges, it is more difficult to generalize. However, many observers of American courts believe that state court judges, and particularly state lower court judges, tend to be more conservative than federal judges.[92]

Prognostication is always tricky business, and where the courts are concerned—especially the Supreme Court—it is particularly tricky business. Justices sometimes fail to behave as predicted. President Eisenhower, for example, was burned twice in this regard, with his appointments of Earl Warren and William Brennan. Justices sometimes change their philosophies while they are on the Court. Justice Blackmun is the most recent notable example of this phenomenon, and some believe that there are indications that Justice O'Connor may be undergoing a similar change. Nevertheless, given the current composition of the Supreme Court, the short-term prospects for change of that composition, and the current climate of public opinion concerning crime and the criminal justice system, it would be quite a surprise indeed if a Court even remotely resembling the Warren Court were to emerge in the foreseeable future.

Notes

[1] See, for example, Stephen A. Saltzburg, "The Ebb and Flow of Constitutional Criminal Procedure in the Warren and Burger Courts," *Georgetown Law Journal* 68 (1980): 151; Yale Kamisar, "The Warren Court (Was it Really so Defense-Minded?), the Burger Court (Is it Really so Prosecution-Oriented?), and Police Investigatory Practices," in *The Burger Court: The Counterrevolution That Wasn't,* ed. Vincent Blasi; Yale Kamisar, "The 'Police Practice' Phases of the Criminal Process and the Three Phases of the Burger Court," in *The Burger Years,* ed. Herman Schwarz (New York: Penguin Books, 1987).

[2] United States Constitution, Article VI, Section 2.

[3] Marbury v. Madison, 1 Cr. 137 (1803).

[4] Barron v. Baltimore, 7 Peters 243 (1833).

[5] See Henry J. Abraham, *The Judiciary: The Supreme Court in the Governmental Process,* 7th ed. (Boston: Allyn and Bacon, 1987), chap. 3, for a good discussion of selective incorporation.

[6] The right to indictment by grand jury is the only right of criminal defendants in the Bill of Rights that the Supreme Court has explicitly declined to apply to the states. *Hurtado v. California,* 110 U.S. 516 (1884).

[7] Terry v. Ohio, 392 U.S. 1 (1968).

[8] Adams v. Williams, 407 U.S. 143 (1972).

[9] Ibid.

[10] Ybarra v. Illinois, 444 U.S. 85 (1979).

[11] Hayes v. Florida, 470 U.S. 811 (1985).

[12] Reid v. Georgia, 448 U.S. 438 (1980).

[13] Florida v. Royer, 460 U.S. 491 (1983).

[14] The question of what constitutes an arrest is somewhat complicated, and space limitations preclude a more detailed discussion here.

[15] United States v. Watson, 423 U.S. 411 (1976).

[16] Payton v. New York, 445 U.S. 573 (1980).

[17] Steagald v. U.S., 451 U.S. 204 (1981).

[18] Tennessee v. Garner, 471 U.S. 1 (1985).

[19] Whitebread and Slobogin, *Criminal Procedure,* 102.

[20] Under the Burger Court there has been some tendency to engage in an analysis of whether the search was reasonable. See, for example, Whitebread and Slobogin, *Criminal Procedure,* section 4.03.

[21] Katz v. United States, 389 U.S. 347 (1967).

[22] On Lee v. United States, 343 U.S. 747 (1952) and United States v. White, 401 U.S. 745 (1971).

[23] United States v. Dionisio, 410 U.S. 1 (1973).

[24] United States v. Mara, 410 U.S. 1 (1973).

[25] Cardwell v. Lewis, 417 U.S. 583 (1974).

[26] Whitebread and Slobogin, *Criminal Procedure,* 112.

[27] Smith v. Maryland, 442 U.S. 735 (1979).

[28] United States v. Miller, 425 U.S. 435 (1976).

[29] United States v. Knotts, 460 U.S. 276 (1983); United States v. Karo, 468 U.S. 705 (1984).

[30] Quoted from United States v. Karo, 468 U.S. 705 (1984) in *Basic Criminal Procedure,* 6th ed., eds. Yale Kamisar, Wayne LaFave, and Jerold Israel (St. Paul: West, 1986), 252.

[31] Hester v. United States, 265 U.S. 57 (1924).

[32] Oliver v. United States, 466 U.S. 170 (1984).

[33] Dow Chemical Company v. United States, 106 S. Ct. 1819 (1986) and California v. Ciraolo, 106 S. Ct. 1809 (1986).

[34] United States v. Dunn, 107 S. Ct. 1913 (1987).

[35] Whitebread and Slobogin, *Criminal Procedure,* 242.

[36] Schneckloth v. Bustamonte, 412 U.S. 218 (1973).

[37] Chimel v. California, 395 U.S. 752 (1969).

[38] United States v. Robinson, 414 U.S. 218 (1973).

[39] Gustafson v. Florida, 414 U.S. 260 (1973).

[40] See, for example, the discussion in Kamisar, LaFave, and Israel, *Basic Criminal Procedure,* 393.

[41] New York v. Belton, 453 U.S. 454 (1981).

[42] Carroll v. United States, 267 U.S. 132 (1925).

[43] Chambers v. Maroney, 399 U.S. 42 (1970).

[44] United States v. Chadwick, 433 U.S. 1 (1977).

[45] California v. Carney, 105 S. Ct. 2066 (1985).

[46] United States v. Chadwick, 433 U.S. 1 (1977).

[47] Aguilar v. Texas, 378 U.S. 108 (1964) and Spinelli v. United States, 393 U.S. 310 (1969).

[48] Illinois v. Gates, 462 U.S. 213 (1983).

[49] Miranda v. Arizona, 384 U.S. 436 (1966).

[50] Ibid., 444.

[51] Beckwith v. United States, 425 U.S. 341 (1976).

[52] Minnesota v. Murphy, 466 U.S. 945 (1984).

[53] Oregon v. Mathiason, 429 U.S. 492 (1977) and California v. Beheler, 463 U.S. 1121 (1983).

[54] Rhode Island v. Innis, 446 U.S. 291 (1980).

[55] Ibid., 302.

[56] Michigan v. Mosley, 423 U.S. 96 (1975).

[57] Edwards v. Arizona, 451 U.S. 477 (1981), 484–85.

[58] Oregon v. Bradshaw, 462 U.S. 1039 (1983).

[59] Ibid., 1045–46.

[60] Smith v. Illinois, 105 S. Ct. 490 (1984).

[61] New York v. Quarles, 467 U.S. 649 (1984).

[62] Massiah v. United States, 377 U.S. 201 (1964).

[63] Brewer v. Williams, 430 U.S. 387 (1977).

[64] United States v. Wade, 388 U.S. 218 (1967).

[65] Stovall v. Denno, 388 U.S. 293 (1967).

[66] Kirby v. Illinois, 406 U.S. 682 (1972).

[67] Ibid., 689.

[68] Whitebread and Slobogin, *Criminal Procedure,* 418.

[69] United States v. Ash, 413 U.S. 300 (1973).

[70] Whitebread and Slobogin, *Criminal Procedure,* 421.

[71] Mapp v. Ohio, 367 U.S. 643 (1961).

[72] Some states had established an exclusionary rule of their own, but the Supreme Court had not required them to do so prior to Mapp.

[73] United States v. Calandra, 414 U.S. 338 (1974).

[74] United States v. Janis, 428 U.S. 433 (1976).

[75] Immigration and Naturalization Service v. Lopez-Mendoza, 468 U.S. 1032 (1984).

[76] United States v. Harris, 401 U.S. 222 (1971).

[77] Oregon v. Hass, 420 U.S. 714 (1975).

[78] United States v. Havens, 446 U.S. 620 (1980).

[79] United States v. Leon, 468 U.S. 897 (1984).

[80] Neil v. Biggers, 409 U.S. 188 (1972).

[81] Ibid., 199.

[82] United States v. Crews, 445 U.S. 463 (1980).

[83] Ibid., 478–79.

[84] Whitebread and Slobogin, *Criminal Procedure,* 38.

[85] Taylor v. Alabama, 457 U.S. 687 (1982).

[86] Rawlings v. Kentucky, 448 U.S. 98 (1980).

[87] Oregon v. Elstad, 470 U.S. 289 (1985).

[88] United States v. Ceccolini, 435 U.S. 268 (1978).

[89] Nix v. Williams, 467 U.S. 431 (1984).

[90] Whitebread and Slobogin, *Criminal Procedure,* 3.

[91] Ibid., 6.

[92] See, for example, Burt Neuborne, "The Myth of Parity," *Harvard Law Review* 90 (1977): 1105.

6

Miranda: Twenty Years of Clarification

George Watson, Jr.
Chadron State College

In 1936 the United States Supreme Court handed down the first significant confession case in *Brown v. Mississippi,*[1] and there has been extensive litigation on the admissibility of confessions ever since. For nearly thirty years after *Brown,* the Supreme Court followed a Fourteenth Amendment due process test that required all confessions to be made voluntarily. For such purposes voluntariness was determined by the totality of the circumstances surrounding the interrogation and the confession. In 1964, however, the test for admissibility of confessions changed when the Court ruled in *Massiah v. United States*[2] that the right to counsel was required at all critical stages in the proceedings. Also in 1966 the Supreme Court ruled in *Miranda v. Arizona*[3] that a confession obtained during a custodial interrogation is not admissible unless the defendant was first given his or her Miranda rights and then voluntarily and knowingly waived those rights. After *Miranda* the Fifth Amendment protection against self-incrimination became the cornerstone for evaluating the admissibility of confessions. This reading focuses on the development of confession law since *Miranda,* with emphasis on the major questions facing investigators.

When Is a Person in Custody?

The *Miranda* decision applies only to situations in which "a person has been taken into custody or otherwise deprived of his freedom of action in any significant way." Thus, statements made to an investigator before an individual is in custody are admissible. However, a person need not be under formal arrest to be in custody for the purposes of *Miranda.*[4]

A review of the cases in this area indicates that the Court focuses on a number of variables in defining *custody*—the purpose of the questioning, the location of the questioning, and the length of the detention. In *Oregon v. Mathiason*[5] the Supreme Court ruled that the questioning of a suspect at the station house did not in itself constitute custody. The police had initiated contact with Mathiason, a parolee, and had left a note at his apartment saying they would like to discuss something with him. Mathiason called in response to the note, and the officers questioned him at the state patrol office about two blocks from the defendant's home. One of the investigators advised Mathiason that the police believed he was involved in a burglary and then stated falsely that the defendant's fingerprints had been found at the scene, whereupon the defendant admitted that he had taken the property. The Supreme Court's ruling included this clarification:

> Any interview of one suspected of a crime by a police officer will have coercive aspects to it, simply by virtue of the fact that the police officer is part of a law enforcement system which may ultimately cause the suspect to be charged with a crime. But police officers are not required to administer Miranda warnings to everyone whom they question. Nor is the requirement of warnings to be imposed simply because the questioning takes place in the station house, or because the questioned person is one whom the police suspect.[6]

The custody issue has also arisen in situations outside the station house. In *Berkemer v. McCarty*[7] the Court ruled that questioning after a routine traffic stop did not constitute a custodial interrogation. According to the Court a typical traffic stop is public, temporary, and brief; therefore, warnings do not have to be given. However, if a traffic stop is atypical and if the defendant's freedom is curtailed to the "degree associated with formal arrest," the warnings must be given.

Case law suggests that reasonable investigative responses to these situations include (1) advising the person prior to any questioning that he or she is not under arrest; (2) asking the suspect to come to the station house for questioning; (3) taking every step to ensure that the suspect knows that the questioning is voluntary and that he or she is free to leave at any time; (4) making clear to the suspect the purpose of the interrogation and keeping the interview as short as possible; and (5) making the setting as noncoercive and unintimidating as possible.

What Is an Interrogation?

In a 1980 Supreme Court case, *Rhode Island v. Innis,*[8] the Court defined interrogation as any "express questioning or its functional equivalent," including "any words or actions on the part of police (other than those normally attendant to arrests and custody) that the police should know are reasonably likely to elicit an incriminating response from the suspect." Thus, the Court clearly stated that interrogation does not necessarily require questioning. Voluntary statements made to the police do not require prior warnings, but such warnings should be given before follow-up questions are asked if a person has made an incriminating statement. Threshold questioning is not a problem since, under *Mathiason,* the person is not in custody.

When Must Miranda Warnings Be Given?

In *Miranda* the Supreme Court intended that all suspects be informed of their rights when they are taken into custody. The simple rule is that warnings should be given to every suspect in custody even if no interrogation is presently contemplated.

However, the Court has fashioned two exceptions to the warning rule. First, the Court ruled in *New York v. Quarles*[9] that there are times when no warnings need to be given at all if the police can show that there was a public safety reason for not doing so. This is known as the public safety exception. Second, the Court has ruled that the warnings or "their fully effective equivalent" must be given, creating an exception for "de minimis," or minor, variations.[10] Despite these exceptions investigators should routinely give the Miranda rights to avoid violation.

What Constitutes a Valid Waiver?

If Miranda warnings have been given, subsequent statements made by the suspect are admissible if there has been a valid waiver of the right to remain silent and the right to have an attorney present during questioning. A valid waiver must be voluntarily and intelligently given and will be judged on the totality of the circumstances surrounding the questioning. The Supreme Court focuses on a number of relevant factors in making a waiver determination: the age, education, and intelligence of the suspect; the influence of alcohol, drugs, or medicine that might have impaired the suspect's thought processes; and the presence of any physical abuse, psychological pressure, or any other tactics aimed at breaking down the suspect.

What If a Suspect Fails to Assert His or Her Rights?

Miranda seems to imply that a valid waiver cannot be inferred from a suspect's silence. However, the Supreme Court has also ruled in *North Carolina v. Butler*[11] that an express waiver is not necessarily required. In the latter case the Court stated that silence is not enough by itself to constitute a valid waiver but should be considered in light of other factors such as age, education, intelligence, the absence of a coercive environment, and the absence of other tactics by investigators. The prudent investigative response to this issue is always to obtain an articulated waiver of the Fifth Amendment right to silence and the Sixth Amendment right to counsel, preferably in writing.

What If a Subject Is Unsure or Makes an Equivocal Request?

Uncertainty by a subject about waiving his or her rights does not constitute an assertion of the right to remain silent or to request counsel. Neither does it constitute a waiver of Miranda rights. As a result, interrogation does not need to stop, but the investigator must clarify what the subject wants to do. The investigator should be very careful in asking any clarifying questions and should not make statements that are aimed at influencing the subject.

Some of the same problems are encountered with a subject who makes equivocal assertions of the right to remain silent or to obtain counsel. For example, in *United States v. Webb*[12] the subject stated, "Yes, I want you to tell me what I am charged with, and then I'm going to call my lawyer." The Fifth Circuit, the highest court to hear the case, ruled that this was not an assertion of the right to counsel, the subsequent interrogation was permissible, and the confession was admissible. Whenever an assertion is unclear, the investigator should stop the interrogation and clarify the request. Again, it is important that the investigator make no statements that could be interpreted as an attempt to influence the subject during the clarification questioning.

What If a Suspect Partially Asserts His or Her Miranda Rights?

A common problem encountered by investigators occurs when a subject places restrictions on the questioning so that there is a partial assertion of Miranda rights. The subject may agree to talk about certain crimes or certain subjects but will not discuss others, or the subject may not want to discuss the matter until a later time. When limitations are asserted, the investigator should make very clear what the limitations are and should then respect those limitations, refraining from any statements or promises that could be interpreted as an attempt to influence the subject or go beyond the limitations. Any attempt to ask questions concerning items made off limits by the subject would certainly be in violation of *Miranda*.

What Happens When a Suspect Asserts His or Her Right to Remain Silent?

The *Miranda* opinion makes it clear that once a subject asserts the right to remain silent, the interrogation must cease. The Court stated that "without the right to cut off questioning, the setting of an in-custody interrogation operates to overcome free choice in producing a statement after the privilege has been invoked." However, a critical question remained: under what circumstances may an investigator resume interrogation after a subject has asserted the right to remain silent?

In *Michigan v. Mosely,*[13] decided by the Supreme Court in 1975, the Court addressed that question. The defendant had been advised of his Miranda rights and had declined to discuss the robberies; consequently, the investigator ceased the questioning. Two hours later, after giving Miranda warnings to the subject, a different investigator questioned the defendant about an unrelated murder. The subject made incriminating statements that were later used against him in a murder trial that resulted in his conviction. The Supreme Court decided that a resumption of questioning is permissible if the suspect's "right to cut off questioning was scrupulously honored."

The *Mosely* decision focused on three important factors: (1) the police immediately ceased the interrogation; (2) there was a significant passage of time before the resumption of questioning; and (3) the second interrogation focused on a crime that had not been the subject of earlier interrogation. The Supreme Court has not yet decided under what circumstances an investigator may resume questioning on the same charge that was the subject of the first interrogation.

What If a Subject Asserts His or Her Right to Counsel?

In *Miranda* the Supreme Court stated that "if an individual states that he wants an attorney, the interrogation must cease until an attorney is present." However, the Court decided in *Edwards v. Arizona*[14] that "a defendant having expressed his desire to deal with the police only through counsel, is not subject to further interrogation by the authorities until counsel has been made available to him, unless the accused himself initiates further communication, exchanges, or conversations with the police."[15] Thus, the Court created a general rule that prohibits police-initiated custodial interrogation after an assertion of the right to counsel but created an exception when the subject initiates the second interrogation. Investigators are not prohibited from initiating further contact with a subject to determine whether the subject has discussed the matter with an attorney. However, the limited questioning should cease at that point.

In the Absence of an Assertion of the Right to Counsel, Must Police Advise a Subject That an Attorney Has Attempted to Reach Him or Her?

In *Moran v. Burbine*[16] the Supreme Court ruled that police do not have an affirmative duty to disclose to a suspect an attorney's attempt to contact the suspect if the defendant has not asserted the right to counsel. Furthermore, police efforts to keep a defendant's attorney from contacting the subject do not necessarily violate the Fifth Amendment. In *Moran* the subject's sister had contacted an attorney, who contacted the police. The subject's attorney was assured that the subject would not be questioned until the following day. However, the police questioned the subject that same day, and Burbine confessed, having heard the Miranda warnings but having no knowledge that the attorney had called. It is important to point out that Justice Stevens, in his dissent in Footnote 41, listed seven state courts that require the police to disclose attempts by an attorney to reach a subject.

What If a Subject Asks for a Nonattorney?

Law enforcement officers often find themselves in situations where an in-custody subject wants to speak to a probation officer, a friend, a relative, or a member of the clergy. The Supreme Court has found that such requests do not constitute an assertion of the right to remain silent or a request for counsel; as a result, such requests do not require that custodial interrogation be stopped. In *Fare v. Michael*[17] the suspect, a sixteen-and-a-half-year-old male asked for his probation officer after being told his rights. The officers refused to contact the probation officer and continued to question the suspect, after reminding him that he could obtain an attorney. The Supreme Court, in a five-to-four decision, refused to recognize the request for a probation officer as an assertion of Miranda rights.

Several problems exist for an investigator. First, if the requested friend or relative happens to be an attorney, the courts may determine that it was a valid assertion of Miranda rights even if the investigator did not know that the friend or relative was an attorney. Certainly, a clarification that the friend or relative is not an attorney is important before continuing interrogation. Second, the Supreme Court in the *Fare* case makes it clear that a request by a juvenile for family or relatives may constitute a valid assertion of Miranda rights. The younger the juvenile and the more times the request is made, the greater likelihood the Court may recognize it as a valid assertion. Third, although the *Fare* case makes it clear that an interrogation does not have to cease, a request to speak with a nonattorney will be an important factor in the totality of the circumstances determining whether a person waived Miranda rights. In such a situation, the prudent response would be to stop the interrogation and allow the subject to meet with the nonattorney.

Does *Miranda* Apply to Misdemeanor Cases Involving Traffic Violations?

The *Miranda* decision is not limited to felonies or certain kinds of offenses. The Supreme Court ruled in *Berkemer v. McCarty*[18] that the warnings must be given before any custodial interrogation, with no exception for misdemeanors or traffic cases. Justice Marshall, writing for a unanimous court, pointed out that custody is the key, not the type of offense committed.

Notes

[1] Brown v. Mississippi, 297 U. S. 278, 56 S. CT. 461 (1936).

[2] Massiah v. United States, 377 U. S. 201, 84 S. CT. 1199 (1964).

[3] Miranda v. Arizona, 384 U. S. 436, 86 S. CT. 1602 (1966).

[4] Orozco v. Texas, 394 U. S. 324, 89 S. CT. 1095 (1969).

[5] Oregon v. Mathiason, 429 U. S. 492 (1977).

[6] Ibid.

[7] Berkemer v. McCarty, 468 U. S. 420, 104 S. CT. 3138 (1984).

[8] Rhode Island v. Innis, 446 U. S. 291 (1980).

[9] New York v. Quarles, 467 U. S. 649, 104 S. CT. 2626 (1984).

[10] California v. Prysock, 453 U. S. 355, 101 S. CT. 2806 (1981).

[11] North Carolina v. Butler, 441 U. S. 369, 99 S. CT. 1755 (1979).

[12] United States v. Webb, 633 F. 2d. 1140 (5th Civ. 1981).

[13] Michigan v. Mosely, 423 U. S. 96, S. CT. 321 (1975).

[14] Edwards v. Arizona, 451 U. S. 477, 101 S. CT. 1880 (1981).

[15] Ibid.

[16] Moran v. Burbine, 106 S. CT. 1135 (1986).

[17] Fare v. Michael C., 442 U. S. 707, 99 S. CT. 2560 (1979).

[18] Berkemer v. McCarty, 468 U. S. 420, 104 S. CT. 3138 (1984).

7
The Sexual Abuse of Children

James N. Gilbert
Kearney State College

A lthough the abuse of children can take many unfortunate forms, the sexual exploitation of a child is surely the most offensive. The first insights into child molesters and the frequency of child abuse became widely known with the publication of the Kinsey Report. That nationwide survey conducted during the 1950s was one of the first systematic attempts to survey sexual practices throughout the United States. However, the true depth and frequency of family violence and abuse was not clear until contemporary research highlighted the problem. Research first began to focus generally on family abuse, then more specifically on child abuse, and finally on sexual abuse of children. By the end of the 1970s an ever-growing number of researchers had documented a level of violence and abuse beyond what most people had imagined.

There are no accurate data available to determine the true number of child sexual abuse cases in the United States. Authorities know that the estimated 100,000 cases officially reported annually are but a fraction of the actual cases. Because of the unique nature of this crime there are numerous inherent obstacles to accurate reporting. First, the offense contains a sexual element, which always limits reporting because of societal embarrassment and suspicion. Second, the majority of perpetrators are well known to the victims, making the offenses psychologically more difficult to report. And third, the victims are children whose limited age and maturity levels make them less likely to report their own victimization to law enforcement authorities.

The Victims

The first Kinsey Report documented that 24 percent of the women interviewed reported a sexual encounter with an adult before they were thirteen years old. A similar survey conducted a generation later put that figure at 26 percent, and found that only 6 percent of the cases had been reported to the police.[1] More recent data concerning child sexual assault confirms a similar situation: one in four females is molested or raped by the time she reaches age twenty, and that a female is more at risk for sexual victimization by a family member than by any other potential suspect.[2] The statistical findings for male victims are more difficult for researchers to determine because male victims are more reluctant to admit their victimization. However, some researchers indicate that boys may be at equal risk for sexual victimization, whereas other limited data suggest that males may be even more likely victims than females since they are the preferred target of habitual child molesters (pedophiles).[3]

Pedophilia, sexual lust by adults for children, is a crime that is intensely age specific. That is, offenders limit their victim selection based entirely on the youthful appearance of the victim. In the vast majority of known cases, the child is abused in the home by a close relative, direct family member, friend, or neighbor. Alarmingly, the single largest group of suspects is parents. According to the secretary of Health and Human Services, 77 percent of child abusers are parents.[4] Children are also sexually abused by nonfamily adults who occupy a position of trust. Since many child molesters purposely seek out vocations, hobbies, or volunteer positions that place them in close contact with children, there are frequent reports of child sexual abuse in children's social organizations, religious youth groups, day-care centers, and other social settings where numerous children are brought into contact with authoritative adults.

Nonetheless, research has indicated that the statistical risk of a child's being sexually abused in a day-care center is lower than a child's risk of being abused at home. A study by the Family Research Laboratory of the University of New Hampshire estimated that 5.5 children are sexually abused for each 10,000 enrolled in day care compared with 8.9 per 10,000 children cared for in their own homes.[5] Day-care centers came under intense media focus as potential sites of sexual abuse following an infamous 1984 California case. That particular investigation involved seven teachers in a day-care center who were accused of 208 counts of molestation involving more than 100 children. All but two of the suspects were subsequently released because of a lack of evidence.

The Perpetrators

Adults who sexually abuse children are linked with many false stereotypes. In reality, sexual abusers of children come from all social and economic backgrounds and are equally represented as to race. Nonetheless, there are some common factors that surface in the majority of criminal investigations. The most prominent characteristic of child abusers is the pattern of their own past abuse; family violence and sexual abuse is a pattern of activity that reproduces itself. The majority of rapists were preyed upon sexually as children, just as most violent criminals have been raised in violent homes.[6] Sexually abused boys often become pedophiles and rapists, whereas sexually victimized girls are likelier to become battered wives.[7] A study in Minnesota found that fully 75 percent of adolescent female prostitutes had been victims of incest.[8] Thus, the majority of family abuse studies have demonstrated that child abuse progresses geometrically; that is, the abused have an increased probability of becoming abusers.

In addition, child molesters typically have an obsessive fixation on sex with children that is often difficult for others to comprehend. Molesters view sexual activity with children as such an intensely pleasurable activity that they may be considered sexually addicted. In fact, many offenders have other personal addictions that are separate from their pattern of child abuse—for example, drug addiction, alcoholism, gambling, or other destructive-obsessive behaviors.

Psychologically, molesters distort reality to rationalize their criminal behavior. Accordingly, many offenders admit during interrogation that they believe victims have actually enjoyed or encouraged their victimization, even when victims are as young as three or four years of age. Some offenders rationalize that sexual abuse is a positive way to teach children about sex.

Many child abuse suspects, like other types of sexually oriented criminals, also have difficulty forming adequate social relationships. However, it is not uncommon for abusers to be married. And even though many of the offenders may be considered sexual psychopaths (individuals unable to feel guilt concerning their criminal acts), they are rarely insane in a legal sense.

As indicated earlier, most sexual abuse against children is committed by persons who are known to the children. Although most children are taught to be cautious of strangers, they more easily fall victim to acquaintances, neighbors, or relatives. When youthful victims are strangers, abusers commonly use these "child lures," which were compiled by the National Coalition for Children's Justice.

☐ *Affection/love.* Child molesters commonly prey on children who are the most vulnerable, who may lack adequate love and affection in their home situations. Initially, molesters focus noncriminal attentions on these children and then use the relationship to persuade them to consent to criminal molestation or to keep secret a nonconsensual attack.

☐ *Assistance.* A common approach has been the assistance ploy, asking for directions to common landmarks, schools, and other locations or finding lost pets. Perpetrators are often quite creative and convincing in explaining their needs to children and obtaining their cooperation.

☐ *Authority.* Many children are taught to respect authority figures, and some suspects take advantage of this conditioning by acting or even dressing like common authority figures. Perpetrators also lure victims by telling them that some emergency has occurred with their parents.

☐ *Bribery.* Some molesters use desirable items that are sought by most children to lure victims into an abuse situation.

☐ *Ego/fame.* Other molesters pose as agents for modeling firms or acting organizations. Children are promised a modeling job or the chance to star in some type of media presentation if they cooperate in a sexually abusive act.

☐ *Games and fun.* This lure uses seemingly innocent play to lead to intimate bodily contact of an abusive nature. This method of operation is most commonly encountered when molesters are familiar to their victims.

☐ *Threats/fear.* Many abusers commonly employ violent threats to abduct or coerce victims, often with the use of a weapon. Although this method is generally used in an initial contact, it may also be used to silence a victim through intimidation after an attack.[9]

Investigative Issues

Investigation of the sexual abuse of children is a most difficult matter. Initial difficulty is encountered because of the lack of reporting associated with this type of crime. Unfortunately, research studies indicate that reporting this type of crime to the police is the exception, rather than the rule.[10] One thorough research study conducted in Massachusetts documented this lack of reporting. The study revealed that in 62 percent of all cases a report was not made to the authorities. The study also documented that in nearly 70 percent of the cases, the offender coerced the child to comply through either threats or actual aggression, with parents as likely as all other categories of suspects to be the aggressive perpetrators.[11] According to that same study, most individuals who did report the crimes to the police were either parents or primary caretakers of the victims. Very few cases were reported directly by the child victims. Not surprisingly, a greater number of cases seem to be reported when offenders are not relatives or family friends but are total strangers to the victims and their families.

Serious investigative difficulty also revolves around the age of the abuse victims. Children are immature in most aspects that are of importance to a successful criminal investigation. By definition, their cognitive and emotional development is limited. Many remain confused as to why the police have even been called and exhibit feelings of guilt and self-blame when confronted with the reality of their abuse. In addition, the psychological stress of this type of crime is intense; when the abuse becomes public, victims often regret having reported the crimes. And the need to repeat the details of the crimes to many enforcement and prosecution officials serves to keep the memory of the assaults alive, often at great psychological expense to the victims.

When investigations reach the judicial stage, an entirely different set of problems can face investigators and prosecution officials. The credibility of children's testimony will be directly attacked, as will their ability to accurately distinguish fact from fiction. Moreover, court officials frequently use language children do not comprehend. Consequently, when victims do not fully understand what information is being called for, it is not surprising that they have a difficult time testifying effectively, even though they may have given very complete statements to criminal investigators prior to court sessions.[12]

Another complicating factor results from the fact that children are generally the sole witnesses to their abuse. In addition, because offenses are frequently reported late, there is often a total lack of evidence. Thus, defense strategy will pit an adult's word against that of a child victim, and a confident adult may appear more truthful than a confused child.

When the child abuser is a parent, the investigator must be particularly aware that the child victim is in a difficult no-win situation. The child believes that by telling the truth and cooperating with the investigator, he or she will lose the love and support of one or both parents.[13] Since children are taught to obey and respect parents, abusive parents can control child victims by threatening to withdraw their love. Thus, the children feel constant parental and self-induced pressure to recant their original reports to the police. That pressure increases with time and reaches its most intense point when the victim faces the abuser in court.

Strategies to Improve Abuse Investigations and Prosecutions

Evidence indicates that a primary obstacle to successful prosecution of molesters is repeated interviewing of the young victims. To avoid this problem, an investigator should limit the number of interviews to the bare minimum and consider videotaping the first statement of the victim. Videotaping is often of great value because it captures a victim's most candid reaction to the crime and is highly effective in obtaining a guilty plea prior to trial. Additionally, police investigators and prosecutor's officials should consider combining their interviews of child victims to lessen the damaging effects of repeated interrogation.

In the last ten years the use of anatomically correct dolls has gained popularity in aiding child victims to reconstruct their victimization. Since the verbal abilities of young children are limited, a trained interviewer may elicit greater detail by asking victims to demonstrate their abuse through the dolls. Several research studies have documented that anatomically correct dolls do not lead to false reports but greatly enhance the accuracy of statements.[14] However, it is highly important that only trained individuals use the dolls to interview victims. If the defense could demonstrate that an untrained individual obtained the statement through the use of the doll, much of the evidence could be barred from being presented in court.

Additional measures to minimize difficulties can be implemented during the judicial phase of a case. Such measures as those identified in Table 7–1 should be instituted before the actual trial and should intensify during the trial.

Importance of Apprehension

Particularly disturbing to investigators is the alarming number of victims molested by a single perpetrator. One recent detailed study found that pedophiles are convicted of fewer than three acts per offender but are actually responsible for an

TABLE 7–1
Measures to minimize investigative and prosecution difficulties in abuse investigations.

Problem	Remedy
Investigative Phase	
Repeated interviews	Joint interviewing
	Videotaping of first statement
Difficulty of victim to verbalize what happened	Use of anatomically correct dolls
Fear of harm or loss of affection from parent or other family member who is perpetrator	Obtaining no-contact court order
	Removing victim or offender from home
High level of stress and embarrassment due to media reporting of offense	Media cooperation in suppressing identifying information
Judicial Phase	
Fear of courtroom	Alternative setting for victim's testimony
	Tour of courtroom
	Judge sitting at victim's table
Inhibiting effect of jury and/or courtroom spectators	Exclusion of spectators
	Videotaped deposition
	Closed-circuit TV
Inhibiting effect of defendant's presence	Closed-circuit TV
	Alternative seating arrangements
	Instruction to child to look elsewhere during testimony
Difficulty in describing events because of age	Expert witnesses to explain child's limitations in observation and perception
	Presence of victim advocate
	Use of artwork or dolls

Source: Deborah Whitcomb, "Prosecuting Child Sexual Abuse—New Approaches," *NIJ Reports,* May 1986, 6.

average of 281 molestations prior to arrest.[15] The study noted that the 153 offenders studied were responsible for 43,100 completed acts of sexual abuse against 22,981 child victims.

Also disturbing is the fact that incarceration rates are significantly lower for child molesters than for offenders who commit sex crimes against victims of all ages. A Justice Department study of four states found that only 13 percent of the persons arrested for sexual assault against children are sentenced to prison for more than one year. By comparison, 17 percent of persons charged with sexual assault against victims of all ages were sentenced to prison. As indicated in Table 7–2, there are also striking differences in the percentages of offenders convicted for sexual child abuse and those who actually go to prison. Even though 90 percent of all arrests for sexual

TABLE 7–2
A comparison of sex offenses against children and those against victims of all ages, showing the percentage of persons arrested who are subsequently prosecuted, convicted, or incarcerated.

	Prosecutions (%)	Convictions (%)	Incarcerations (%)
Sexual assault			
Child victims	90	65	13
All-aged victims	86	54	17
Other sex offenses			
Child victims	95	81	8
All-aged victims	95	65	10

Source: U.S. Department of Justice Study, Bureau of Justice Statistics, *Los Angeles Times,* 28 December 1984, p. 6.

assault of children result in prosecution and 65 percent of those arrested are subsequently convicted, only 13 percent are actually incarcerated in a state or federal penitentiary. Similarly, 81 percent of those arrested for other sex crimes against children are convicted, but only 8 percent go to prison.[16]

As this research indicates, sexual abuse of children does not often result in long-term confinement. That knowledge should motivate criminal investigators to be vigilant in their detection of such cases and to use only the most professional and effective methods of investigation to ensure successful prosecutions.

Notes

[1] Sheila Crowell and Ellen Kolba, "Men Who Molest/Children Who Survive" (New York: Filmmakers Library, Inc., 1985), 3.

[2] "Preventing Sexual Abuse of Children," *Parade Magazine,* 26 May 1985, 16; Robert J. Barry, "Incest: The Last Taboo," *FBI Law Enforcement Bulletin,* Jan. 1984, 2–9.

[3] Albert P. Cardarelli, "Child Sexual Abuse: Factors in Family Reports," *NIJ Reports,* May/June 1988, 9–12.

[4] "Preventing Sexual Abuse," 16.

[5] "Sex Abuse More Likely at Home, Study Says," *Roanoke Times,* 22 Mar. 1988, A–3.

[6] Ed Magnuson, "Child Abuse: The Ultimate Betrayal," *Time,* 5 Sept. 1983, 19–22.

[7] Ibid., 21.

[8] Crowell and Kolba, "Men Who Molest," 3.

[9] Untitled brochure, National Coalition for Children's Justice, Washington, DC, n.d.

[10] Cardarelli, "Child Sexual Abuse," 9–12.

[11] Ibid., 10.

[12] James R. Wise, "Differentiating Fact from Fantasy: The Reliability of Children's Memory," *Prosecutors Perspective,* Jan. 1988, 15–16.

[13] Barry, "Incest: The Last Taboo," 2–9.

[14] Michael D. Bradbury, "Anatomically Correct Dolls," *Prosecutors Perspective,* Jan. 1988, 1–2.

[15] Norm Maleng, "Self-Reported Sex Crimes of Nonincarcerated Paraphiliacs," *Prosecutors Perspective,* Jan. 1988, 18.

[16] Michael Wines, "Penalties Found Light in Crimes Against Minors," *Los Angeles Times,* 28 Dec. 1984, 6.

8

Child Abuse Investigation

Howard Tritt
Kent State University

The number of children living in a family environment that is detrimental to their physical and/or psychological well-being is rising at an alarming rate. The exposure of these rising numbers has awakened public awareness to the problem of abuse and has intensified court scrutiny of abuse incidences. As a result, the days of apathetic investigation of abuse accusations are over.

An investigator taking action in an abuse situation today must be prepared to produce independent evidence supporting the action taken, and that evidence must be free of the investigator's moral values and biases. In order to withstand court scrutiny, the evidence should address these basic questions:

1. Do the circumstances meet all legal requirements for physical, sexual, or emotional abuse? In particular, is the intent to abuse present and supported?
2. Are the circumstances severe enough to warrant the actions taken?
3. What other solutions were available, based on the circumstances present, and why were they ruled out?
4. Were the actions taken in cooperation with appropriate support agencies as identified by state statute, local ordinances, and departmental policy?

In acquiring the evidence necessary to answer these questions, investigators have encountered numerous problems. The first is definitional; the second is a determination of investigative responsibilities. Third, officers need to identify their roles in such investigations, and they must understand the investigative requirements of abuse cases. Last, they must be familiar with the support services available.

The definitional problem is not isolated to investigators. Few in the field can agree on what constitutes abuse, and many of its definitions are subjective and vague. The Federal Child Abuse Prevention and Treatment Act of 1974, as amended, provides an example of this problem. The act defines *abuse,* essentially, as the threatening of a child's health and safety by physical or mental injury, sexual abuse or exploitation, lack of medical care, neglect, or maltreatment by one responsible for the child's safety. Examination of *Black's Law Dictionary, Webster's New World Dictionary,* and several other dictionaries clarifies some of the key terms in this definition.

☐ *Threaten* is a communication or expression of an intent to cause harm to another.

☐ *Health* is the sound well-being of a person free from injury or sickness.

☐ *Safety* is a preventive approach to one's security.

☐ *Injury* is damage or harm to another.

☐ *Exploitation* is a daring or unethical use of a person.

☐ *Neglect* is a failure in or disregard for the providing of a required duty in a proper and accepted manner.

☐ *Maltreatment* is the rough, improper, or unskilled care of a person because of one's ignorance, neglect, or willfulness.

Putting these terms together would result in the following working definition of *abuse:*

> The communication or expression of rough, improper care or the unethical use of a child through the ignorance, neglect, or willfulness of one responsible for preventing such improper care or unethical use of the child, which results in harm or damage to the child's well-being as a person.

This definition may, at first glance, appear to provide some clarity. However, it is still very global. Many parental acts that would not ordinarily be considered abuse could easily be accused. Such accusation is happening with enough frequency that organizations are being formed in some areas by falsely accused parents to protect their rights and stop harassment by various governmental agencies.

Compounding the definitional issue is the subjectivity employed in determining the degree of improper care or unethical use of a child needed to prompt official action. For example, is the use of corporal punishment appropriate discipline or an abusive act? Is it a lack of moral judgment to allow family members to roam though the house in various states of undress or is it sexual exploitation? Is verbal correction or negative expression aimed at a child constructive or damaging? What an investigator may interpret as sufficient cause for action may not be seen as such by a prosecutor or court, or vice versa.

Still another problem associated with the definitional issue is the lack of investigative direction in these definitions. The first step in any investigation is a clear, concise definition of the problem to guide the investigator in the fact-finding process. Without this guidance the investigator is unsure of what facts are to be collected or what value to place on the evidence gathered. Some may contend that this is not a problem, as evidenced by the increase in the number of abuse prosecutions and convictions. However, this increase is not necessarily the result of increased quality of investigation, and an increase in prosecution and conviction without an improvement in quality is dangerous.

If investigators are able to develop a working definition of abuse, they must then determine what their responsibilities are in the investigation of abuse cases. Some would contend that the investigation of abuse is a public function. In many states, however, the statutes for reporting abuse require police, along with other professionals, to report all abuse to the local children's protective services agency for investigation. This investigative mandate is often given without the support of police power, placing the protective services investigator in a precarious position. Because of the current encompassing perspective of abuse, many acts that are criminal violations are being viewed as abuse. Thus, some agencies are trying to handle matters beyond their capabilities.

This problem of a dual system of investigative responsibility can be seen in the handling of many acts against children. Often, how an act is classified determines which agency has the primary responsibility for its investigation. If a child is beaten, is that assault or abuse? If a child is deliberately killed, is that murder or abuse? If a child is photographed nude, is that pornography or abuse? Criminal violations are the primary responsibility of the police, whereas abuse is the primary responsibility of children's protective services. To add to the confusion, our response often depends on the perpetrator: if one of these acts is committed by a parent, we tend to classify it as abuse, whereas that same act committed by a stranger is more apt to be classified criminally.

The question of classification and its effect on the subsequent investigation can be illustrated by a father-daughter incestuous situation. If the offense is classified as abuse, the age of the victim may be viewed as important for treatment but not so much for prosecution purposes. If the act is defined as rape, however, the age of the victim may be critical in prosecution. Many states specify stiffer penalties for rapes involving children below a certain age. In Ohio the rape of any child thirteen years of age or younger carries a possible life imprisonment.

Another element affected by classification and investigation is treatment. If the incestuous situation is considered abuse, efforts are made to keep the family together, if possible, and treat the culprit and the family. On the other hand, if the situation is viewed as rape, data are collected for prosecution, conviction, and often incarceration. Not surprisingly, whichever agency is assigned the responsibility of investigation leaves the other at a disadvantage; not many police officers are versed in the investigative needs of a protective services agency, and the reverse is also true.

According to much of the literature, the solution to this dilemma is to have a team approach in abuse cases. This sounds excellent on paper but has failed to materialize in practice. We are still experiencing jurisdictional arguments, loss of valuable evidence, fragmentation of skills, lack of cooperation and communication, and a duplication of effort. At times these behind-the-scenes differences have resulted in a failed prosecution and certainly a loss of respect for both agencies. Until this responsibility issue is resolved, progress in combatting the rising number of reported abuse cases will be slow.

Another problem for abuse investigators is to understand their role in these investigations. Abuse investigators function somewhat differently from those investigating other types of offenses; but abuse investigators are still investigators, and all of the basic principles of investigation apply. To be successful, they must utilize the basic investigative tools:

☐ observation

☐ perception

☐ patience

☐ logic

☐ complete knowledge and understanding of the subject under investigation

In addition, abuse investigators must serve as observers and data collectors for other professionals that will become involved through dispositional and treatment action. Abuse investigators should not take on the roles of other professionals but should become their eyes and ears, witnessing and recording the behaviors that are exhibited under the stress of the situation. Such information may provide additional insight for dispositional recommendations and treatment and may spell success in dealing with the culprit and/or the victim. Investigator failure to accept this additional role brings only more hard work, discord between agencies and personnel, duplication of efforts, and possible misdiagnosis.

The multidisciplinary requirements of abuse investigation present another problem to investigators. Perhaps no other area of investigation requires such a diverse background—a basic understanding and working knowledge of sociology, psychology, physiology/anatomy, and law. And these requirements are in addition to a full complement of investigative skills.

Many of the families encountered in abuse situations are multiple-problem families. They may be in an almost constant state of crisis from which the abusive act may have resulted or to which it may add more stress. In either case investigators must be skilled in crisis intervention techniques. Until a state of equilibrium is restored, little investigative activity can transpire.

Sociological and psychological knowledge is also needed to identify and interpret the many behavioral indicators present in most abuse cases. Although many investigators can cite a list of such indicators, only a few can analyze what messages these indicators convey or can apply them advantageously to their investigations. Many indicators with limited prosecutorial or treatment value may indirectly assist an investigation. For example, comments like "My child doesn't love me" or "My child doesn't eat for me" may indicate a possible role reversal on the part of the parent, and role reversal is a defense strategy often employed by abusive or neglecting parents who perceive their own lack of love or self-worth. Skilled investigators record such comments and forward them to professional counselors for clinical interpretation.

Behavior indicators may also assist investigators directly in several ways. They may reveal an abusive parent's need or an abused child's feelings, both of which should guide the selection of appropriate interviewing strategies. Such indicators may also signal an intent to commit or conceal the abusive act, as is often the case when hospital shopping occurs. And indicators may shed light on whether the act has happened before in the past or may happen again in the future unless some form of intervention is taken. The assistance of indicators is limited only by the ingenuity and resourcefulness of investigators.

In addition, abuse investigators need a basic working knowledge of physiology and anatomy, especially when it is necessary to match a child's injury to a parent's story of what happened. Without this knowledge investigators may miss parental comments of evidentiary value, they may not recognize a parental lie, or they may miss an opportunity to collect valuable physical evidence at the scene. Any case would be weakened or perhaps lost by such an oversight.

Legally, in addition to knowing both criminal and juvenile codes, search and seizure laws, and the procedures for taking custody of a child, investigators must be versed in a variety of legal issues that may arise in abuse cases. They must be acquainted with domestic relations and parental custody issues in cases involving separated or divorced parents. Investigators also need to be aware of the legal issues involved in reviewing medical and school records, both of which may contain valuable information. Another legal issue involved in abuse cases is the rights of parents and children in family matters, such as the right to discipline or the right to support. Lack of knowledge of such issues may result in the loss of a case on a technicality or may expose an investigator or an agency to a liability suit.

One final problem confronting abuse investigators is the need to be familiar with community support services. These may include a host of government, private, religious, and civic services; and investigators must know the services provided, their availability, and any costs associated with their use. Investigators should also be clear on the rules and procedures to follow when using specific services. A close working relationship with the staff members of the service agencies most frequently contacted may be beneficial to both the agencies and the investigators. One never knows when an emergency may arise.

As investigators cope with the problems of abuse investigation, they must learn to recognize and deal with their own feelings and emotions. They must look beyond the pain, hurt, and sorrow they see in abused children; they must remember that perpetrators are people, too, entitled to basic rights and human dignity. No matter how difficult, investigators must remain objective.

9
Informant Is a Dirty Word

Robert R. Reinertsen & Robert J. Bronson
Western Illinois University

The use of criminal informants in law enforcement operations is an area that has been largely neglected by commentators within the criminal justice system. Informants are generally unsavory types, engaged in marginal activities that involve betrayal of others. Nonetheless, despite their negative image, informants play such a large and important role in law enforcement efforts that they cannot be ignored.

Periodically the news media have focused attention on the role of the informant in the criminal justice system. This attention is inevitably generated by high-interest criminal cases that feature informants as major prosecution witnesses. The DeLorean cocaine trial and the Chicago Greylord investigation (which resulted in the prosecution of several sitting judges for accepting bribes) have raised several recurring issues concerning the use of informants as prosecutorial tools. First, there is the fundamental question of whether any moral and/or legal basis exists for the use of informants by law enforcement agencies. Then, if some legitimacy can be established, the question arises as to the proper role of informants. Finally, there is the dilemma of dealing with informants: on the one hand, informants are deemed indispensable sources of information and valuable prosecutorial tools; on the other hand, law enforcement agencies are loath to publicly embrace criminal informants and all their baggage.

Traditionally, the public image of the informant, or informer, has been a negative one, to say the least. The news and entertainment media have characterized informants as snitches, finks, stoolies, stool pigeons, and so on. And when informants are on public display as witnesses in criminal trials, they generally live up to their negative stereotypes. Timothy Hoffman, informant and key accuser in the DeLorean cocaine case, was described as "a hulking, 250 lb. convicted drug dealer and admitted perjurer whose latest job was as a professional informer, setting up his friends and acquaintances for Government stings. When the obese Hoffman appeared in the videotapes that were the chief evidence against DeLorean, he was almost always eating."[1] Even though informants help to undermine others who are involved in criminal activity and deserve punishment, the American psyche is geared to fair play, and the acts of betrayal fundamental to informant activities strike a discordant note.

Law enforcement officials are understandably defensive in their rare public statements concerning the role of police informants in their operations. Officials have endeavored to convince the public of the importance of informants in solving and prosecuting crimes, while at the same time minimizing law enforcement's intimate association with them. In a 1982 speech FBI Director William Webster attempted to put the best face possible on that association:

> . . . the handling and use of informants. . . . These are sensitive, sometimes intrusive investigative techniques. We use them because they are extremely effective and often indispensable and because we have confidence in the safeguards we have put in place so that they are used only when necessary and in a matter that minimizes their intrusiveness.[2]

In that same speech Judge Webster makes several candid statements about the importance of informants in police operations.

> Informants . . . they're dramatically effective investigative tools which have been responsible for some of our most important successes. . . . The informant is perhaps law enforcement's most important tool. . . . Informants are often effective because of their proximity to and participation in the criminal world, a fact which has earned them a generally unsavory reputation.[3]

Finally, Judge Webster describes the bottom line in dealing with informants: "The test for using an informant is not his lovability; it is his reliability."[4]

The FBI and other police agencies have attempted to cope with the unstable world of dealing with informants by creating elaborate bureaucratic mechanisms to control them and those law enforcement officers who deal directly with them. The FBI, for example, has formulated exhaustively detailed policies concerning the recruitment, control, and payment of criminal informants. Nonetheless, the need to maintain absolute confidentiality in working with informants precludes any meaningful oversight by the agency. In other words, in most cases the only source of control over an informant is his or her individual handler, or law enforcement contact person.

Protecting the confidentiality of informants' identities has been an unshakable article of faith for law enforcement agencies. This was dramatized in 1978 by then-Attorney General Griffin Bell, who risked a jail term on a contempt-of-court citation for failing to reveal the identities of informants. At the time Bell was quoted as saying that revealing informants' identities "would cause incalculable harm to the nation's ability to protect itself against enemies, foreign and domestic." He went on to say, "The continued flow of information from informants to authorities rests on the confidence of informants that their identities will not be revealed unless they consent."[5]

Thus, no matter how extensive or rigid agencies' policies are for dealing with informants, in most cases the agencies are unable to determine whether they are being implemented. Since individual officers deal one-on-one with their informants, maintaining the secrecy of their identities even within the agency, it is up to the officers to exercise their discretion in implementing agency policies. The agency must rely on their good faith and good judgment because there is simply no way to monitor the actual relationships. As an FBI agent, one of the authors saw other agents work "graveyard" informants, who didn't actually exist (their names came from tombstones in the cemetery). Information from other sources was attributed to the nonexistent informants in criminal investigative reports, and the agents maintained the required number of reliable C.I.s (criminal informants).

Cases are legion in which informants have embarrassed the law enforcement authorities for whom they were working by being arrested for their own related or unrelated criminal activities. Such a problem was brought dramatically to public attention in 1977 with the scandal involving the alias program run by the U.S. marshal service. The alias program was developed to address the problem of "used" informants: "Informers are to criminal justice what uranium is to a nuclear reactor— they make the system go, but they're an awful lot of trouble to dispose of after- ward."[6] The congressionally funded alias program provided new identities and secret lives for criminal informants who testified against organized crime figures. Beyond the accusations against some U.S. marshals for irresponsibility, mismanage- ment, and outright corruption in administering the program, a furor erupted over the return of relocated informant/witnesses to criminal activities. The marshals were "doing their job almost too well—that is, of providing ex-hoods with such effective cover stories and grouping so many of them in one place that many are able to return to their criminal trades with some impunity." What was worse, the marshals systematically covered up the criminal activities.[7]

When informants provide lead information that can be independently cor- roborated by other sources, there is little danger of their going public, thus embar- rassing law enforcement officials and endangering criminal prosecutions. However, the use of informants can pose real difficulties for law enforcement when they must surface in the formal criminal justice process. Informants surface in the investigative process when their information is used in affidavits to support search and arrest warrants. They surface in prosecutions when they appear before grand juries and in criminal trials as witnesses for the prosecution. In most cases, it is only necessary to reveal informant identities when they testify in criminal trials.

The Supreme Court stand on the police use of informants in the criminal justice process can be seen in the evolution of the law on probable cause, as it applies to the issuance of search warrants. That evolution moved from the *Aguilar- Spinelli* two-pronged test developed by the Court during the 1960s to the current standards articulated in *Illinois v. Gates,* which permit a magistrate issuing a search warrant to evaluate the probable cause for the warrant in light of the totality of the circumstances made known to the magistrate.[8]

Aguilar-Spinelli had been interpreted as requiring two questions (two prongs) to be satisfied independently of each other before a magistrate could issue a search warrant.

1. What is the "basis of knowledge" of the informant, that is, how did he come into possession of the information and does it amount to probable cause?

2. On what is the veracity of the informant based? This second element of the test could be provided by information establishing (a) the credibility of the informant or (b) the reliability of the information.[9]

Adoption of the totality of the circumstances test in *Gates* was a clear refutation of the more rigorous *Aguilar-Spinelli* test. The Burger Court believed that

> anonymous informants are crucial to certain types of police investigations. Since anonymous tips play a significant role in the fight against crime, their utilization is to be encouraged. Because the informant is anonymous, his veracity can be quite difficult to establish. Thus, any rule that rigidly precludes the use of anonymous informants is unreasonable.[10]

Thus, the widespread use of informants by police agencies seems to have the wholehearted endorsement of the U.S. Supreme Court.

Nonetheless, informants have not fared nearly as well as witnesses in open court, where the rigors of cross-examination and scrutiny by critical juries have rendered government informants relatively ineffective. Following a series of recent government defeats, highlighted by DeLorean's acquittal, prosecutors now concede that it is nearly impossible to win a case that relies exclusively on informant testimony. "Corroboration is the key," says Stephen Trott, chief of the Justice Department's criminal division. "Without corroboration, you're probably dead in the water."[11] But as the DeLorean case demonstrated, even with corroboration—and lots of it—juries sometimes refuse to convict when informant testimony is involved.

Notes

[1] Michael Serrill, "Are 'Bad Guys' Good Witnesses?" *Time,* 3 Sept. 1984, 77.

[2] William Webster, "The Informant and the Undercover Agent," *Vital Speeches,* 15 May 1982, 453.

[3] Ibid.

[4] Ibid., 454.

[5] "At Stake in the Fight over Government Informers," *U.S. News & World Report,* 17 Jul. 1978, 30.

[6] Richard Boeth, "Your Cover Is Showing," *Newsweek,* 28 Nov. 1977, 66.

[7] Ibid.

[8] Aguilar v. Texas, 378 U.S. 108, 1964; Spinelli v. United States, 393 U.S. 310 (1969); Illinois v. Gates, 462 U.S. 213 (1983).

[9] John McLaren, "A Lawyer's Guide to Search Warrants and the New Federalism," *Criminal Law Bulletin,* Jan./Feb. 1986, 8.

[10] Ibid.

[11] Serrill, "Bad Guys," 77.

10

Reflections on Undercover Street Experiences

James J. Ness & Ellyn K. Ness
Southern Illinois University

L ittle has been written but much ado has been made of the attitude changes experienced by the professor-turned-policeman. Albrilton presented a series of reflections on his experiences with the Macon, Georgia, police department, and the well-known Kirkham recounted his experiences with the Jacksonville, Florida, police.[1] Albrilton and Kirkham both describe the attitude changes they experienced when they became police officers, whereas others such as Van Mannan, Terry, and Stratton explore the attitudes of police officers.[2] This reading examines the policeman-turned-professor-turned-policeman.

There is an old adage among police officers that says, "Once a cop, always a cop," and I am no exception. I have been involved in policing for twenty-seven years and have worked in a variety of assignments in several different agencies. In 1977 I moved to southern Illinois to complete work on my master's degree and, upon completion, remained at the university as director of the Police Executive Study, which was funded by the Law Enforcement Assistance Administration (LEAA). After the grant money ran out, I took a position as chief of police in a rural Illinois town but in 1983 decided to seek the serenity and complacency of university life rather than the political and emotionally diverse life of a police chief.

I joined the faculty at Southern Illinois University—Carbondale but found myself drawn to friends who were active police officers and executives because university faculty seemed aloof and snobbish. I was invited to join the local chiefs' association and eventually became involved in doing some active part-time policing in a small rural town. In April 1984 at the monthly chiefs' meeting, I was approached by Dennis Bowman, director of the Southern Illinois Enforcement Group (SIEG) wondering whether I would be interested in doing some undercover intelligence and investigative work for a local police agency. The offer intrigued me because I had never done actual undercover work. I had been a plainclothes officer and detective, but undercover was different. It seemed like movie material.

So, I had a project for the summer. The purpose of the project was twofold: it was to satisfy the desire within me to be involved in a somewhat dangerous, clandestine police activity and also to provide firsthand knowledge about this kind of police activity that could be brought back to the classroom. Academicians write about the way police work should be done, about the police personality and police culture, and about the criminal justice system. However, many academicians have never experienced the real world of the streets. Some have experienced the peripheral aspects of police training and research, but few can actually relate to the streets and thus tend to lose their credibility in the classroom.

Just as Albrilton (1985) and Kirkham (1974) reported their results through attitude changes, we, too, must share our personal reactions.[3] The work presented here is not by any stretch of the imagination empirical data, nor is it a case study. It is a reflection on the personal experiences of my wife and me, and a look at the questions raised by certain police methods and the frustrations that undercover police officers experience on a daily basis. It is a reflection on the stress involved in undercover work, and the intent is to share our experiences so that others may benefit.

Geographical Background

Southern Illinois, which is the geographical area south of Interstate 64, is primarily rural. There are a few large cities—Carbondale being the largest, with the exception of the metropolitan St. Louis area. There are a variety of industries, with agriculture being the mainstay. SIU is the major educational and cultural force in the area. A vast majority of the population is rural and southern in its philosophy and culture.

The city for the undercover project was Cairo, Illinois, the county seat of Alexander County and the southernmost city in Illinois, with a population of approximately 6,000. Cairo marks the point where the Ohio and Mississippi rivers join; its rich history dates back to the Civil War. More recently, Cairo has become an economically depressed city with high unemployment, a dwindling population, reduced social and medical services, and racial problems. Cairo employs fourteen police officers and experiences at least three to four murders per year.

The Mission

Shortly after my initial conversation with Director Bowman regarding the Cairo project, we met with then-chief Earl "Bud" Shepherd of the Cairo Police Department to outline the project parameters. Chief Shepherd was concerned about narcotics traffic in Cairo; he had some idea of what was going on but wanted confirmation of activities and updated intelligence. Chief Shepherd suspected that some police officers were involved, so he wanted someone totally unknown to the regional law enforcement community.

The primary objective of the project was to obtain leads into criminal activity (narcotics and other), confirm the activity of identified persons, and gain intelligence of what was going on in Cairo. Basically this was a fishing expedition with no real target in mind. Although I never asked or discussed the situation, I strongly suspected that there were some political overtones to this inquiry because the chief had almost a carte blanche check from the mayor.

I wanted assurances that no one in Cairo would know who I was or what my mission was. In the end only the chief and two of his most trusted detectives knew my identity. Even the mayor was unaware of my identity until after the project was completed. Bowman, Shepherd, and I met again in Anna, Illinois, at which time I was officially approved for the project, the necessary monetary remunerations and insurance and logistical details were agreed to, and I was sworn in as an investigator of the Cairo Police Department.

Preparing the Cover

A good cover is essential to any undercover operation, and playing the role is one of the most interesting facets of undercover work. The undercover agent must be an actor, able to assume another identity. It is important that the bogus identity be close to the agent's own so that he or she can be comfortable with it. Agents draw on their own experiences and relate them to their covers.

A week after our Anna meeting, I went to the SIEG offices, where Bowman and I began to develop my cover and bogus identification. The Cairo area is primarily rural agricultural, but I did not know enough about agriculture to pass as a farmer. Besides, most farmers were known locals. However, I did know about horses since I raise quarter horses, so I decided that my cover would be that of an itinerant horse trainer from Murphysboro, Illinois, working for a firm from Indiana. Murphysboro was far enough from Cairo to keep curious people from going through the bother of checking up on me, but it was close enough to be considered local.

Once I had established a cover story, I had to establish an identity. The name I used was James Nolan. With the help of SIEG and two local police agencies, I was fitted with real IDs in the name of Nolan—a real traffic citation, a real driver's license, prescriptions, and so on. When my wife, Ellyn, joined me in the operation, she, too, developed a bogus identity. I was given a set of Indiana license plates registered to a dummy address and a gas credit card issued to a dummy corporation. For a vehicle I had a 1977 Chevrolet pickup truck with a camper top. For show, I put one of my old saddles with assorted tack and ropes in the camper, along with a sleeping bag and some old clothes.

I carried the bogus ID like normal identification and carried my real ID and police ID in my boot. I did not carry a firearm but did have one available in the glove compartment. I did not have to make many changes in personal appearance since I was already comfortable wearing jeans and boots. However, I did have to get used to wearing a good-ole-boy cap and not wearing my ring, watch, and jewelry.

Once the cover was set, Chief Shepherd was contacted, and arrangements were made to meet at a motel in Cairo. I felt very uncomfortable at first. What if I met somebody I knew? I was sometimes self-conscious of the ID in my boot and worried that people would know instinctively that I was a cop. They did not. I also feared being stopped by the police. What would I do? That didn't happen, but the questions and anxiety were always there. In my conversations with agents in SIEG and other police units, I learned that my concerns were not uncommon to individuals going undercover for the first time, although the degree of fear and anxiety differ with the individual.

Opening Night

On June 15, 1984, at 2:15 P.M. I checked into a motel in Cairo under the name of Nolan. At 3:30 P.M. Chief Shepherd and his two trusted detectives came to the motel room, as agreed. These three people were the only ones in Cairo who knew my real purpose for being there. I was given emergency phone numbers in case I got arrested or needed help and was also given information regarding the chief's targets of concern. There were five liquor establishments in town that had reputations as places where drugs were sold, but the police had no real evidence. My job was to confirm or refute the rumors.

When the chief and his men left, I proceeded to drive around Cairo to familiarize myself with the location of the five bars and get the lay of the land. I became very conscious of every police vehicle and made mental notes of where I could find help if needed. I located telephone booths and all-night gas stations. I became very suspicious of every car that was behind me. I usually take note of vehicles, but then I was jotting down license numbers and makes of vehicles. I felt as if everybody knew what I was doing, but I resolved that I would not be found out. It was time to become a serious actor and immerse myself in my role.

Early in the evening I entered the first bar, the Club. There were about fifteen to twenty people there. I ordered a beer and just observed for about an hour. Then I left that bar, went to dinner, and went on to the second bar, the House. From there I went to the third bar, the King. There was no unusual activity in any of these establishments, and I began to wonder whether it was all worth it. I wanted action—I was keyed to be a player, but nobody would play.

Later that night I returned to the Club since my information said that this was the hot spot and center of activity. By then, there was a large crowd, and I noticed several people who had been in the other bars earlier. Shortly after I arrived, a fight broke out between two female patrons. It was a mean, knock-down, hair-pulling, shirt-ripping fight, but no one did anything to stop it, not even the bartender. After about five minutes of encouragement from the male patrons, a couple of the men broke it up. I then realized that these were hard people that I would be dealing with—not very intellectual, but very physical.

The remainder of that first experience did not produce anything of consequence, but the paranoia was still there. On my return trip to Carbondale, I noticed a white male riding a yellow motorcycle, following me out of town. I had observed the individual in two of the establishments I had visited. I gave him ample opportunity to pass, but he stayed a distance behind. He finally turned off in Mounds, Illinois, and to this day I don't know whether his following me was intentional.

Partners

After my first experience I felt quite alone and reasoned that I needed a female partner to add credence to my being in Cairo. I approached my future wife, Ellyn, who was aware of what I was involved in and thought it would be interesting. She had a degree in criminal justice and was very adaptable to this kind of work. I contacted Chief Shepherd, who had no objections, and Ellyn became my undercover police partner.

Thereafter, I would check out the bars early, and later we would both return. We made solid contacts with many of the patrons and bartenders and had some unique experiences. Nobody ever suspected our male/female team.

On one of my individual forays, I made contact with a white male who was intoxicated and spoke freely of being able to deal some drugs. I set up a meeting with him to buy some valium, speed, and marijuana. However, I was worried because I had never handled a buy, and neither had Ellyn. I went to Bowman, who assigned an SIEG agent to assist. Bowman warned me that this particular agent was a little strange: he had shot a bank robbery suspect from a helicopter a few months earlier, liked guns, was a little wild, but was a good cop. I met him the day before the buy—Curtis Ehlers, a big man with long blond hair, a beard, and a diamond earring. We talked briefly, and I made arrangements to pick him up the next day.

On the way to Cairo I told Curt that Bowman had warned me about him. We discussed what we would do in the upcoming situation, and finally the conversation got around to guns. Curt then explained that he just liked to be prepared for any emergency, that his safety was paramount in these situations. With that he opened up a small flight bag he had brought along and produced an RPB Mac 11, a Beretta 9mm auto, an S&W .38 special revolver, several pairs of handcuffs, and a commando knife, not to mention the weapon on his person. I reminded him that we were only going to make a small drug buy, not start World War III. But Curt was a good undercover cop, and the three of us shared many memorable experiences in our Cairo adventure.

The three of us developed a relationship of trust and understanding that I had never experienced before. Without any words being spoken, we knew when to back away from a situation and when to proceed. We all knew our safety was involved and took steps to protect our well-being. At times Curt and I became almost chauvinistic in our protective attitude toward Ellyn, but we managed to overcome it because we knew from the start that she could handle herself in almost any situation.

Analysis of the Operation

As Marx points out, undercover situations tend to be fluid and unpredictable.[4] Such was the case in Cairo. For five months we were engaged in an operation that required us to be persons we were not. We had to associate with criminal types and, in essence, become the criminal type. This role change presented a great deal of stress since we were basically the straight-and-narrow types. We did have the advantage of not having to play our roles twenty-four hours a day; we could come back to our own world. However, this advantage presented another problem—we could not tell our friends what we were involved in. And the process of changing from one mind-set to another can be confusing and frustrating. At one point as we partied all night with an outlaw biker gang, we thought that Curt had gone over the line.

At times throughout the experience, we wondered who we really were and what we were doing. We were befriending people we could arrest someday and were finding that they weren't really that bad. They had families, dreams, and needs just like the rest of us, but sometimes they crossed over the line between right and wrong. In general, they were not killers, rapist, or big-time drug dealers; they were ordinary people trying to stay alive by doing what they knew best.

Undercover work is not the glamorized and sensationalized experience seen in TV series. In reality, the hours are long and at times very boring. One can only frequent so many bars in an evening with great enthusiasm. Sometimes undercover agents get caught up in the myth and crave the action and the excitement. In Cairo we were certainly always on the edge, worried that someone might find out who we were or that we might not be able to handle the situation, but the excitement was not of the TV type.

A significant challenge of undercover work is adapting to the environment in which the project is taking place. For example, we found that working the bars increased our tolerance for alcohol; if you don't drink in those places, you don't fit in. We never did drugs, nor did we have to face that decision very many times. When we did, we made excuses and bowed out, but such situations can affect credibility. All undercover agents struggle with this issue: should they participate in an illegal activity to secure their cover and make the case?

The paperwork associated with undercover assignments is demanding; it requires detailed information so that logical conclusions can be drawn. One of the hardest parts of undercover work is remembering the details of events; agents can't carry notebooks with them or keep running out to their cars to jot down information. In this area we worked well as a team. I could not remember names but was great on details; Ellyn remembered the names. In addition, all money spent must be accounted for. All food and drink, gas, motel, and any other expenses require receipts. It can be very difficult to keep personal money and department money separated.

Recommendations

As a result of our own experiences, our conclusions and recommendations for undercover projects are few and simple. First, one officer is not enough. A person working alone is isolated, and the tendency for corruption is much greater. However, the primary factor is the safety of the individuals involved in the operation. Second, undercover operations are not cost-effective. They require a great deal of time and money to begin and should not be attempted on a part-time basis or without adequate support. Third, agents should never go into a situation cold. There should be goals set for any operation and a basis of sound, reliable information. Secrecy is a must.

Another area of concern, for which we did not have an opportunity, is training. We were lucky that our operation was small scale and we were trained as police officers, but we had no background in covert operations. We also recommend that operations be closely monitored by superiors and that mechanisms be available to help agents deal with stress.

And finally, it's important to know when to end an operation. When it is not producing the anticipated results, it should be terminated. We ended our experience five months after we started because we saw that we were getting nowhere. We had found evidence of drug and other illegal activities but not to the extent first imagined. And we could not find any indications that police officers were involved in any of the illegal activities.

From an academic standpoint the experience was tremendous. From an administrative point of view it was a waste of money. From a police officer's vantage point it was frustrating because we couldn't get enough evidence to make solid cases. We recommend that further research be initiated in this highly specialized area of law enforcement to address some of these concerns.

Notes

[1] J.S. Albrilton, "Professor/Policeman: Reflections on a Practicum in Policing" (paper presented at the Academy of Criminal Justice Sciences, Las Vegas, NV, 1985); G. Kirkham, "A Professor's Street Lessons," *FBI Law Enforcement Bulletin,* Mar. 1974: 14–22.

[2] For a discussion of the attitudes of police officers, see J. Van Mannan, "Police Socialization: A Longitudinal Examination of Job Attitude in an Urban Police Department," *Administrative Science Quarterly* 20, no. 2 (1980): 207–28; W.C. Terry, III, *Policing Society: An Occupational View* (New York: Wiley, 1985); J.G. Stratton, *Police Passages* (Manhattan Beach, CA: Glennon Publishing, 1984).

[3] Albrilton "Professor/Policeman"; Kirkham, "Professor's Street Lessons."

[4] G.T. Marx, "Who Really Gets Stung? Some Issues Raised by New Police Undercover Work," *Crime and Delinquency* 28, no. 2 (1982): 176.

CASE STUDY
Donnie Brasco Infiltrates the Mob

James N. Gilbert
Kearney State College

As discussed in the previous reading, the role of the undercover operative is both essential and difficult. No case in recent memory is a more striking example of these two aspects than the successful infiltration of La Cosa Nostra (the American Mafia) by an agent of the FBI. Operating under the cover identity of Donnie Brasco, Agent Joseph D. Pistone worked his way into the Mafia and moved freely among organized crime families for an astonishing six years. When he began his deep cover in 1976, Pistone walked out of his office and didn't enter another FBI office until six years later. As a result of his extraordinary undercover work, more than one hundred federal criminal convictions were obtained, dealing a severe blow to Mafia operations throughout the United States. Pistone's work also resulted in a half-million dollar murder contract being placed on his life, necessitating his resignation from the FBI and a change of identity for him and his family.

Agent Pistone began his law enforcement career in Philadelphia as a criminal investigator with the Office of Naval Intelligence. Using that experience, he joined the FBI in 1969, assuming for many years the normal array of investigative duties required of all agents. Then in 1976 Agent Pistone and a new direction in FBI policy joined to produce the most sensational undercover operation in the annals of the FBI. Prior to the late 1970s, the FBI did not officially engage in undercover assignments utilizing its own agents. Although FBI supervision and surveillance of non-agent undercover informants was very common, then-Director J. Edgar Hoover was strongly opposed to using his own agents as undercover operatives. However, when the FBI assumed new leadership, the Bureau began to allow its own agents to work in long-term undercover investigations. The undercover concept was so new to the

FBI that no formal set of official guidelines existed for agents and their supervisors to use until 1980.

Posing as Don Brasco—jewel thief, burglar, and all-around career criminal— Agent Pistone carefully constructed his new identity. With identification papers and a new checking account in his false name, he rented an apartment close to the various social haunts of several New York Mafia families. At that point Pistone began to develop various rules and operational principles that guided his actions throughout the next six years.

☐ Keep your fabricated past simple and as close to the truth as possible. Construct a criminal past that enables you to work alone and without violence.

☐ Don't indicate that you have a great deal of money; that marks you as a cop or a person who can be conned out of his money.

☐ Never keep notes or anything that could expose your identity. You never know when you will be searched.

☐ Try to become accepted in your target group without drawing attention. You can push a little here and there but very gently. Use brief introductions, short conversations, appearances in one place or another, or hints that show you know your way around. You strive to leave a trail of credibility, but one built slowly; the quickest way to be identified as a law enforcement officer is to move too fast. You have to play by the rules of the street, to show that you have the time. Let your target check you out and come to you.

☐ You must continue to be your own person and keep your personality intact. Some undercover agents think they must drink heavily or take drugs to blend in or demonstrate their toughness, but that is a serious mistake. If you compromise your own standards and personality, smart criminals will see right through your facade. In addition, Agent Pistone realized as all undercover agents must, that at some point down the line he would have to testify in court about his activities. If he had taken drugs or engaged in any serious wrongdoing, his credibility would have been seriously questioned, and the effectiveness of his testimony would have been greatly diminished.

☐ Not every law enforcement officer has the capacity to work undercover. Virtually no new police officers or criminal investigators are hired with undercover work in mind. Instead, they are selected and trained to perform overt police duties. Undercover assignments require a strong, disciplined personality, capable of working alone without backup. You must be a true individualist.

☐ While you are pretending to be somebody else, you will encounter the same personality conflicts you would find anywhere. There will be people you will like and people you will not. You must override your natural inclinations for association and learn to cultivate whoever can help your investigation. You must learn to swallow your gripes and control your temper.

☐ Undercover agents must make difficult decisions on their own often right on the spot. You must accept the consequences of being wrong and making mistakes, because you will have nobody to hide behind on the street. You must be street-smart, disciplined to work, and willing to take the initiative.

After months of carefully gaining the confidence of various lower-level criminal suspects, Agent Pistone became a "connected guy" to two targeted Mafia families. A connected individual is a person trusted by Mafia members, a criminal who often works directly with mob members but who is not a "made guy" or a "wise guy." These latter designations are for actual Mafia members, individuals who are formally attached to a family organization and who must operate within its organizational constructs and social norms, following chain-of-command and profit-sharing rules.

From that point on, Pistone was remarkably successful in gaining the confidence of many high-ranking Mafia officers and gradually became a trusted friend. Success had its price, however, for he rarely saw his family for more than a few days during a period of several months. He was gradually brought into many criminal operations and conspiracies, observing firsthand how La Cosa Nostra operated, and he was able to piece together its often confusing levels of membership. Finally, because of his continued success Pistone's undercover operation was forced to stop. He was about to be inducted into the Mafia as a made guy and was expected to kill another Mafia member.

At the end of Agent Pistone's six-year journey into the heart of the Mafia, federal charges were brought against hundreds of criminals. A series of federal trials began in 1982 and are continuing to this day. As a direct result of Pistone's undercover work and associated criminal investigations, the American Mafia's leadership was completely broken by the FBI. No Mafia family was untouched, and virtually every boss of every Mafia family was sent to prison or died before sentencing.

In 1986 Agent Pistone resigned from the FBI after seventeen years of service, ten of which were devoted to undercover work and the resulting court trials. The attorney general of the United States presented him the Distinguished Service Award as the outstanding agent of the FBI. No law enforcement officer had ever penetrated so deep into the Mafia.

Since then Joseph Pistone has reportedly undergone plastic surgery. His current identity and whereabouts are closely guarded government secrets.

Sources: Joseph D. Pistone, *Donnie Brasco: My Undercover Life in the Mafia* (New York: New American Library, 1987); "Undercover in the Underworld," *Macleans,* 16 Aug. 1982, 33–34; "I Was a Mobster for the FBI," *Newsweek,* 16 Aug. 1982, 26.

11

Public Administration Theory and the Study of Criminal Investigation

David M. Jones
University of Wisconsin—Oshkosh

There are few who would deny that in recent years the discipline of criminal justice has matured into a distinct field of study. Unfortunately, however, some would argue that it is currently suffering from arrested development.[1] A major reason for this condition is the paucity of attempts to use theoretical perspectives to help interpret existing data and provide directions for further research. As Willis has argued, "Facts without theory, no matter how voluminous, lack meaning. Furthermore, a field of study cannot advance as a scientific discipline on facts alone."[2] Theory construction must become a central concern of students of criminal justice.

One way of enriching the theoretical foundations of the field is to borrow from more mature disciplines those ideas, theories, and frameworks that seem appropriate to the study of criminal justice. For instance, scholars have argued that economics and anthropology have much to offer our emerging discipline.[3] In addition, public administration theory, the focus of this reading, can provide useful insights into the field of criminal justice, especially the area of criminal investigation.

Although there are a number of approaches to administrative theory, the one that is considered here is the political economy framework developed by Gary L. Wamsley and Meyer N. Zald. For their purposes the term *political economy* is defined as "the interrelationship between a structure of rule (polity) and a system for producing and exchanging goods and services (economy)."[4] The first element in that relationship deals with matters of legitimacy and power distribution and their effect on such things as an agency's existence, its niche in the system, and its goals. The second is concerned with the arrangement of labor and the allocation of resources for the accomplishment of tasks given to an organization. Both an organization's polity and its economy can be further divided into internal and external aspects, giving a political economy framework four analytic components: external polity, external economy, internal polity, and internal economy. An analysis of each of these can help us understand why investigative agencies tend to operate in the manner that they do and may point out ways of improving the investigative process.

External Polity

According to the originators of the political economy framework, it is important to understand that any public organization is part of a policy subsystem, which is defined as "an arena of individuals, groups, and organizations, of 'relevant others' affected by and interested in a given policy."[5] Those relevant others will vary in their power over, interest in, and attitude toward a particular organization, but all will work to influence the way in which that organization conducts its affairs. Some of the relevant others that the Federal Bureau of Investigation must deal with include the president, the attorney general, United States attorneys, federal courts, and other agencies. Local investigative units must deal with city officials, prosecutors, judges, other components of the police department, and more. All of these groups and individuals seek to influence various aspects of the criminal investigation process.

The extent to which and the means by which these relevant others influence the organizations in question vary over time and among agencies. For instance, the FBI in pre-Hoover days was staffed by agents appointed on the basis of their political connections, who were then used to harass political opponents of the incumbent attorney general. Such actions took place because that was what important political "players" expected of the agency.[6] Similarly, at the local level the Memphis, Tennessee, police department was at one time an adjunct of the Crump machine, in which recruitment and advancement were based on political connections. In that department, laws were enforced to meet the dictates of the political boss.[7] Thus, in both cases the impact of relevant others on the agencies in question was pervasive.

Even though such intrusive measures are probably not common today, political players still successfully seek to influence the investigative priorities of many agencies. For example, in spite of the fact that J. Edgar Hoover had long opposed FBI involvement in civil rights and had steadfastly denied the existence of an organized crime syndicate, the bureau became active in both areas in the 1960s because of the proddings of Attorney General Robert Kennedy and his brother, President John F. Kennedy.[8] An attorney general's values form the basis for his or her prosecutorial discretion (i.e., which types of cases are emphasized), which, in turn, affects the prioritization of offenses by local FBI agents. Local district attorneys seem to have a similar impact on city detective bureaus.[9]

Other participants in the criminal justice system—for example, the judiciary— also have an impact on investigative procedures, priorities, and workloads. Rulings by the Supreme Court in cases like *Miranda v. Arizona* and *Escobedo v. Illinois* have affected interrogation procedures in many investigative units. Moreover, it has been argued that the tendency of federal judges to give lighter sentences to cocaine dealers than to heroin dealers has strengthened the predisposition of drug enforcement agents to concentrate their efforts on the latter rather than the former.[10]

Other organizational players may also affect such things as the workload of investigative agencies. For instance, Skolnick and Woodworth found that one detective bureau was handling an extremely high number of statutory rape cases not because the investigators were particularly interested in such cases or because the "victims" were particularly eager to bring such cases to the police, but because that city's welfare agency insisted that pregnant minors who desired to receive welfare report their plight to the police. In nearby communities where the welfare department did not have such a requirement, the statutory rape caseload was much lighter.[11]

Another set of important relevant others are an investigator's informants. In some types of cases—narcotics, for instance—a network of informers is essential for the successful conduct of the investigative job.[12] Consequently, for many types of investigators "the ability to develop an informant is a vital investigatory skill."[13] Although people become informants for a number of reasons, most do so in order to obtain leniency on a criminal charge. Consequently, investigators often use threats and incentives to "flip" a person accused of a crime. Then, in order to keep informants once they have been recruited, officers often give them various interpersonal rewards and may overlook certain infractions in order to keep their informants on the street. Thus, the criminal justice system is manipulated in various ways to deal with this important, though often despised, relevant other.[14]

Nonetheless, it would be a mistake to view investigative agencies as mere pawns that are buffeted every which way by political winds over which they have no control. Lawrence Sherman has argued that "police departments are *not* closed systems responding passively to environmental demands. Police departments, or actors within them, may try to shape the nature of their environment and its demands in significant ways."[15] Indeed, it is a central tenet of Wamsley and Zald's political economy approach that organizations do seek to manipulate relevant others in various ways (and with varying degrees of success) in an attempt to create a relatively benign or neutral environment in which they can function with some degree of autonomy.

In fact, many of the actions taken by investigative agencies can be understood primarily as attempts to manipulate their environment. For instance, during most of J. Edgar Hoover's tenure, the FBI and its director were so respected by powerful relevant others that no prudent politician would seriously consider publicly denouncing anything that Hoover said or did.[16] And that situation did not occur by chance; Mr. Hoover worked hard to build strong ties with powerful others. For instance, he cultivated very friendly relations with the chairman of the subcommittee that oversaw the FBI budget, even praising him publicly. Hoover also ran the FBI in ways that pleased the chairman and his colleagues and loaned the subcommittee agents for its own use. Moreover, Mr. Hoover actively cultivated public support so that any inclination toward harsh treatment of either Hoover or his bureau would be inhibited by knowledge of the public's great admiration for the agency.[17] In effect, then, the FBI was able to manipulate its environment by affecting those politicians who supervised the workings of the agency.

Similar actions have been taken by some police agencies on a local level. For instance, in the 1970s police involvement in Minneapolis politics was considered to be a long-standing tradition, with members of the force working to elect friendly officials. In the law-and-order 1960s a number of former police officers and detectives even served in city government, with one ultimately becoming mayor and apparently impacting police behavior. The police in Minneapolis felt that Mayor Stenvig (a former detective) was more predisposed than was his liberal predecessor to taking restraints off the police, and the officers acted accordingly.[18]

Another way in which leaders of organizations can develop a benign or neutral environment is through the use of certain management devices. For instance, it has been argued that the extensive reporting system that was operative in J. Edgar Hoover's FBI was not used primarily to induce efficiency in the investigative behavior of individual agents but was a means by which the director maintained strong control over his agency in order to enhance public confidence in it. In a similar fashion the administrative system of the Drug Enforcement Agency (DEA) has been largely shaped by political considerations.[19]

The same thing tends to happen at the local level. Patrick V. Murphy contends, for instance, that many of the rules in local police departments have been designed not so much to control officer behavior as to protect the departments—and members of their upper echelons—in the event of a scandal. Indeed, certain rules adopted in some departments seem to serve political needs at the expense of investigative capability. For example, many police departments move patrol officers to different beats at regular intervals, supposedly to inhibit the development of illegal relationships among officers and citizens and thus lessen the potential for scandal. However, such a rotation policy works against the development of close relations among citizens and police and thus inhibits effective contacts and leads that are so essential to the solution of many cases. Thus, it appears that there are times in the world of law enforcement when political needs dictate that form take precedence over function.[20]

Political concerns may also have an impact on the time spent by detectives on some cases. In a study of a detective division, Sanders found that officers would spend extra time on a seemingly hopeless case because a victim had complained that so little was being done about it. Political maintenance, or public relations, strategies also affected investigative priorities in that same agency's juvenile division. For example, runaways were given a high priority largely because the law enforcement agency responsible for the case would be harshly criticized if something were to happen to a runaway.[21]

In a similar vein one critic of the FBI has suggested that for much of its history the bureau's involvement in organized crime was premised on its publicity value. Another authority contends that the FBI expended considerable resources in the area of domestic security, in spite of tenuous legal grounds, at least partially because such action helped the bureau maintain good relations with certain powerful relevant others.[22]

Political maintenance needs not only affect which tasks an investigative agency will engage in, but also which ones it will avoid. Director Hoover kept the FBI out of such activities as press censorship and relocation of Japanese Americans during World War II in large part because such activities required collaboration with other governmental agencies and that collaboration would have compromised the FBI's greatly prized autonomy.[23]

At times political or public relations considerations also have an impact on how investigators pursue their tasks. For instance, Patrick Murphy, citing a RAND study of detective work, contends that such activities as fingerprint dusting, mug-shot showings, and witness questioning are often performed largely because victims and reporters expect these actions to occur, not because they meet an intrinsic investigative need. "There was, the study seemed to be suggesting, an element of public relations, if not of show-biz, in the performance of detectives."[24]

Still another way in which police departments and investigative agencies have sought to attain a favorable or nonthreatening environment has been by manipulating various statistics that some relevant others may consider to be authoritative indices of investigatory accomplishments. For example, an annual Washington rite for many years was Director Hoover's recitation of the FBI's record accomplishments, presented before the House Appropriations Subcommittee. Even though the subcommittee chairman and his colleagues were apparently well aware of the rather flimsy basis for some of these statistical accomplishments, some part of the public was probably duly impressed by them.[25]

Concern for case clearance rates and the manipulation of those figures are another part of the attempt to impress relevant others. Skolnick found in his study of a local police department that a large number of citizen complaints were not filed as offenses but were, instead, categorized as suspicious circumstances. This practice had an important impact on the department's clearance rate, which was based solely on actual "offenses." In the same city Skolnick found that many detectives would cajole offenders to admit to a number of crimes, using the promise of a reduced sentence. This practice, too, improved the clearance rate.[26]

Other statistics in other cities have also been allegedly manipulated for political reasons. For instance, Seidman and Couzens contend that when Jerry V. Wilson was installed as police chief in Washington, DC, he informed commanders that they had to reduce crime or they would be replaced by people who could. Shortly after his announcement there was a dramatic rise in the proportion of larcenies in which the value of the items lost was reported at less than fifty dollars. Thus, the numbers of larcenies classified as index crimes fell.

Such a concern for statistical accomplishments would be of no more than academic interest if it did not affect a unit's investigative priorities. Unfortunately, it appears to do just that. For instance, some detective units have refused to handle certain types of cases partly because they would be hard to solve. Since failure to make an arrest, or close the case, would adversely affect a unit's performance record, such cases have simply been avoided.[27] Similarly, the Drug Enforcement Agency officially encourages agents to concentrate on making big cases against major distributors, yet the perceived importance of numbers impelled agents to go after the small fry on the streets.[28]

Concern for statistics can adversely impact the investigative process in other ways, also. For example, if officers are told, or if they perceive, that their performance ratings are based on their individual arrest records, cooperation among detectives may be discouraged, even though such cooperation might increase the total arrests made by the division as a whole. In a related situation collaboration among DEA field officers was dampened by the widespread perception that certain preferments were likely to go to those individuals who made the arrests of large drug distributors.[29]

In sum, then, a good bit of what is done by investigative agencies seems to be an attempt to create a relatively benign environment. Cases are pursued (or not pursued) and statistics are manipulated to influence those relevant others who are in positions to affect the well-being of an investigative organization. Thus, much of what investigative agencies do is affected by their external political environment.

External Economy

Another factor that is of some importance to investigative organizations is the external economy. Concepts important to this analytical component include industry structure, supply and demand considerations, technological innovation, and an agency's raw materials.

Because of this nation's tradition of decentralization in government, a multitude of law enforcement agencies exist. The consequences of this industry structure, however, are open to debate. To some this situation means that many agencies are woefully inadequate for the tasks set before them, but others contend that this is a healthy situation that enhances citizen respect for law enforcement. At least one commentator has pointed to the unhealthy competition that has occurred because of law enforcement fragmentation, but another has emphasized the cooperation that is found among different agencies. Thus, though many have noted the fragmented industry structure that characterizes law enforcement in the United States, there is disagreement about its consequences.[30]

Supply and demand considerations also affect investigative agencies. For one thing it is important for such organizations to be able to attract capable personnel, which has not always been an easy task. For example, Niederhoffer has noted that it was quite simple for many departments to recruit well-educated people during the Great Depression but not in subsequent years. Criminal investigation, like many other governmental services, is a labor-intensive industry. This fact, when tied to the higher wages demanded by all workers in recent years, has contributed to an urban fiscal crisis. Because of that crisis, retrenchment has been called for in many urban bureaucracies, leaving fewer investigators to deal with the work at hand.

The economy can affect investigative workloads in a number of other ways, too. For instance, one of the consequences of America's prosperity after World War II was a significant demographic trend known as the baby boom. That boom meant that, starting in the 1960s, a larger number of teenagers and young adults came onto the scene. And since that age range seems to be more crime-prone than others, the crime rate began to skyrocket.

As a result, the workload of investigative agencies drastically increased.[31] Thus, the external economy has an important effect on investigative agencies, but such organizations have little, if any, control over that external economy.

A third element of the external economy that has had profound effects on the criminal investigation process is technological innovation, which has had two important implications. One of these concerns how crimes are investigated and solved. For example, developments in the science of criminalistics have meant that some offenses that would have baffled investigators in earlier times are now being solved. The other implication is more ominous, however. Simply put, innovations in technology have brought new types of crimes. Computer-related crimes, for example, were unknown half a century ago but are now relatively widespread.

One final critical phenomenon connected with the external economy is, according to Wamsley and Zald, the fact that public organizations must obtain raw materials from the environment and process them into products offered to consumers. Investigative organizations can be seen as taking a raw material—a crime— and processing it into a product—an arrest—that can be offered to prosecutorial consumers. It is important to note that there are different types of crimes and, correspondingly, different ways to solve crimes. In other words, the type of crime that is committed determines the task of the investigative agency, and the nature of the task greatly affects the way in which the investigative organization operates.[32]

Different agencies often concentrate on different types of crimes. For example, the FBI has traditionally dealt with predatory crimes, those that produce victims who are willing to complain to authorities. Such crimes include embezzlement and auto theft. Given the nature of this type of crime and its victim, the agent's task becomes one of reacting to complaints by following leads, interviewing witnesses, checking with informants, and so on. In contrast, the DEA investigator must deal primarily with consensual crimes. In these cases the "victim" is highly unlikely to complain to authorities. Consequently, the investigator needs a different type of strategy to deal with such a crime. Generally speaking, DEA agents try to apprehend offenders through the process of instigations; that is, they often go underground and pose as drug customers in order to make a bust.[33] In a similar fashion, the job of the local vice squad officer, who deals with consensual crimes such as prostitution, is different from that of the burglary squad officer, who investigates predatory crimes.

Internal Polity

This component of organization deals with "the structure of authority and power and the dominant values, goals, and ethos institutionalized in that structure."[34] In terms of the structure of authority and power in investigative organizations, at the national level, at least, variation exists among agencies. For instance, the Federal Bureau of Investigation has traditionally been a highly centralized organization. At least in the past the assignment of agents to different offices was centrally determined, special agents in charge of local agencies were rotated with some frequency, and an agent desiring advancement in the bureau's hierarchy found it imperative to take on assignments that would lead toward a "headquarter's point of view." In contrast, the Drug Enforcement Agency is a highly decentralized organization. Regional directors remain in one place for long periods of time, central policy directives are not rigidly adhered to, and critical investigative decisions are arrived at locally.

The relative amount of centralization in an agency becomes important when changes in investigatory priorities are called for. For instance, when Hoover's successor decided that changes were necessary (e.g., when it was decided to move more forcefully against white-collar crime), he was able to effect those changes, even in the face of some local opposition. Managers in the DEA have not been so successful in their attempts to change local priorities.[35]

Related to the distribution of power within an organization is the allocation of prestige, that is, the relative importance attached to the work of the various divisions of an investigative agency. For instance, Sanders notes that in the department that he studied, a hierarchy of prestige existed. In that agency the juvenile division had the lowest status, whereas major crimes had the highest. Moreover, prestige levels appeared to be related to division workload. Thus, the major crimes division was faced with a relatively small volume of cases and consequently was not under the same pressure to inactivate important cases that other units experienced.[36]

Differentials in prestige may also have an impact on morale and efficiency in investigative organizations. For example, when the Philadelphia office of the FBI became more involved in white-collar crime, the work done by other units was seen as less important. Consequently, the belief developed that there was an A team and a B team in that field office. Those squads not involved with white-collar crime were given higher workloads, so high, in fact, that they were unable to deal effectively with pending matters. In order to come to grips with the problem, one particular squad simply refused to consider certain cases. Morale problems also developed because some agency members concluded that even if they did develop good cases, they would often lose them to more prestigious groups in the unit. As a result, the willingness to do nonpriority work subsided in many agents.[37]

A second important component of internal polity revolves around the values and ethos that are institutionalized within an agency. Of some importance here is the lack of lateral entry into most police departments in the United States. What this means is that most of the officers in a local detective bureau have spent a certain amount of time as patrol officers. Consequently, they have been subjected to those pressures that go to develop the working personality of a police officer.[38] A great deal has been written about this phenomenon, suggesting that officers tend to develop certain characteristic attitudes. These include such traits as suspicion, cynicism, authoritarianism, and a feeling of social isolation. Although the exact impact of these personality traits is unclear, such attitudes might inhibit effective interaction with relevant others.[39]

Another element in the ethos of one organization has had a demonstrable impact on its investigative activities. According to Wilson, street agents of the DEA work in a milieu that rewards heroin busts. That emphasis tends to discourage the practice of leaving informants in place for a substantial period of time to apprehend more important distributors. "As one experienced supervisor put it: 'Narcotics agents are a certain kind of animal—door-kicking heroin agents. Other agents think that there is something wrong with a guy who will pass up tonight's buy.' "[40] This dominant attitude has also contributed to poor relations between agents and intelligence gathering units in the DEA. The former regard the latter as mere paper-shufflers who contribute little to the real tasks at hand.[41]

Not all agencies, of course, have the same ethos. For instance, at least three styles of police work have been identified: the watchman, legalistic, and service styles.[42] And the style adopted does appear to have a policy impact. For example, in a city that has a highly professionalized force with a legalistic style, delinquents and minority groups are dealt with in a very different manner from that found in another city with a less professionalized force in which the watchman style predominates.[43]

Internal Economy

This component of an organization deals with how effectively and efficiently it performs its basic technical functions.[44] As applied to investigative organizations, internal economy relates to certain tactical decisions concerning how the investigative function operates. For instance, some agencies could operate somewhat more efficiently if detectives worked singly rather than in pairs in performing certain routine duties. Some authorities have also contended that detectives in some departments overspecialize in their handling of cases, perhaps hindering their ability to apprehend certain types of offenders.[45] Other technical considerations—such as appropriate forms for documentation of investigative work, the appropriate type of personnel to process a crime scene, and the proper means of managing the flow of cases—also fall into the category of internal economy. This component of an organization is significant because it impacts the efficiency and effectiveness of the organization.

Thus, the political economy framework of Wamsley and Zald provides a useful basis for understanding the functioning of investigative organizations. With such concepts as external polity, external economy, internal polity, and internal economy we may be better able to fathom some of the actions taken by investigatory agencies. Moreover, once we understand why certain things happen the way they do, we may be in a better position to deal with those elements that are dysfunctional. In short, organizational theory may have both theoretical and practical benefits for the criminal investigation process.

Notes

[1] C.L. Willis, "Criminal Justice Theory: A Case of Trained Incapacity," *Journal of Criminal Justice* 11 (1983): 447–58.

[2] Ibid., 448.

[3] T. Orsagh, "Is There a Place for Economics in Criminology and Criminal Justice?" *Journal of Criminal Justice* 11 (1983): 391–402; R.R.E. Kania, "Joining Anthropology and Law Enforcement," *Journal of Criminal Justice* 11 (1983): 495–504.

[4] C. Perrow, *Complex Organizations: A Critical Essay* (Glenview, IL: Scott, Foresman, 1978); G.L. Wamsley and M.N. Zald, *The Political Economy of Public Organizations: A Critique and Approach to the Study of Public Administration* (Lexington, MA: Heath, 1973); idem, 64.

[5] Wamsley and Zald, *Political Economy,* 26.

[6] J.Q. Wilson, *The Investigators* (New York: Basic Books, 1978), 177.

[7] A.E. Bent, *The Politics of Law Enforcement* (Lexington, MA: Heath, 1974).

[8] V. Navasky, *Kennedy Justice* (New York: Atheneum, 1971); Wilson, *The Investigators,* 190.

[9] J.Q. Wilson, "The Changing FBI: The Road to Abscam," *The Public Interest* 59 (1980): 3–14; P.V. Murphy and T. Plate, *Commissioner: A View from the Top of Law Enforcement* (New York: Simon and Schuster, 1977).

[10] Wilson, *The Investigator,* 121–22.

[11] J.H. Skolnick and J.R. Woodworth, "Bureaucracy, Information, and Social Control: A Study of a Morals Detail," in *The Police: Six Sociological Essays,* ed. D.J. Bordua (New York: Wiley, 1967), 99–136.

[12] J.H. Skolnick, *Justice Without Trial: Law Enforcement in a Democratic Society* (New York: Wiley, 1975).

[13] Wilson, *The Investigators,* 35.

[14] Skolnick, *Justice Without Trial,* 130–36.

[15] L.W. Sherman, "Police Corruption Control: Environmental Context Versus Organizational Policy," in *Police and Society,* ed. D.H. Bayley (Beverly Hills: Sage Publications, 1977), 113.

[16] Navasky, *Kennedy Justice,* 30–31.

[17] Ibid., 34–35.

[18] E. Eidenberg and J. Rigert, "The Police and Politics," *The Police in Urban Society,* ed. H. Hahn (Beverly Hills: Sage Publications, 1970), 291–306.

[19] Wilson, *The Investigators,* 192.

[20] Among those arguing that police departments adopt certain rules to serve political maintenance needs are Murphy and Plate, *Commissioner,* 198–99; Wilson, *The Investigators,* 199; C.E. Silberman, *Criminal Violence, Criminal Justice* (New York: Vintage Books, 1980).

[21] W.B. Sanders, *Detective Work: A Study of Criminal Investigations* (New York: Macmillan, 1977).

[22] Murphy and Plate, *Commissioner,* 86; Wilson, *The Investigators,* 176–79.

[23] Wilson, *The Investigators,* 169–71.

[24] Murphy and Plate, *Commissioner,* 186–87.

[25] Wilson, *The Investigators.*

[26] Skolnick, *Justice Without Trial.*

[27] D. Seidman and M. Couzens, "Getting the Crime Rate Down: Political Pressure and Crime Reporting," *Law and Society Review* 8 (1972): 457–94; A. Bequai, *White-Collar Crime: A 20th Century Crisis* (Lexington, MA: Heath, 1978).

[28] Wilson, *The Investigators,* 129–33.

[29] P.V. Bloch and D.R. Weidman, *Managing Criminal Investigations* (Washington, DC: U.S. Government Printing Office, 1975); Wilson, *The Investigators,* 118–19.

[30] Pros and cons of this nation's tradition of decentralization in government are addressed in Murphy and Plate, *Commissioner,* 70–76; E. Ostrom and G.P. Whitaker, "Does Local Community Control of Police Make a Difference? Some Preliminary Findings," *American Journal of Political Science* 17 (1973): 48–76; B.D. Rogers and C.M. Lipsey, "Metropolitan Reform and Citizen Evaluation of Police Performance in Nashville-Davidson County, Tennessee," *Publius* 4 (1974): 19–34; J.R. Nash, *Citizen Hoover* (Chicago: Nelson-Hall, 1972); J.C. McDavid, "Interjurisdictional Cooperation Among Police Departments in the St. Louis Metropolitan Area," *Publius* 4 (1974): 35–48.

[31] See A. Niederhoffer, *Behind the Shield: The Police in Urban Society* (New York: Doubleday, 1967); Y.H. Cho, *Public Policy and Urban Crime* (Cambridge, MA: Ballinger, 1974); J.Q. Wilson, *Thinking About Crime* (New York: Basic Books, 1975) for a discussion of how supply and demand considerations affect investigative agencies.

[32] Wamsley and Zald, *Political Economy*; Wilson, *The Investigators,* 8.

[33] Wilson, *The Investigators,* 39–56.

[34] Wamsley and Zald, *Political Economy,* 57.

[35] Wilson, *The Investigators.*

[36] Sanders, *Detective Work.*

[37] Wilson, *The Investigators.*

[38] Skolnick, *Justice Without Trial,* 42.

[39] Niederhoffer, *Behind the Shield*; Skolnick, *Justice Without Trial,* 42–70.

[40] Wilson, *The Investigators,* 75.

[41] Ibid., 155–57.

[42] J.Q. Wilson, *Varieties of Police Behavior* (Cambridge: Harvard University Press, 1968).

[43] J.Q. Wilson, "The Police and the Delinquent in Two Cities," in *City Politics and Public Policy,* ed. J.Q. Wilson (New York: Wiley, 1968), 178–205.

[44] Wamsley and Zald, *Political Economy,* 77.

[45] Bloch and Weidman, *Managing Criminal Investigations.*

12
Managing for Investigative Productivity

James R. Farris
California State University, Fullerton

The myth of Sherlock Holmes carefully sifting through a morass of evidence and cleverly ferreting out valuable information from a variety of colorful characters serves as a model of investigative techniques. In recent times the television character Lieutenant Columbo, with what appears to be a bungling approach, skillfully and methodically identifies the perpetrator of each carefully orchestrated murder. Both serve as models to be emulated. However, most crimes are not solved in the style of Holmes or Columbo. Nonetheless, we continue to shoot ourselves in the foot by doggedly clinging to these myths. Investigators must be more productive and work more efficiently to achieve the statistics that will prove their worth as detectives.

Let's be realistic and tell it the way it is. Let's stop crunching numbers to prove the productivity and worth of detectives when the basic model is flawed. Premier detectives or investigative agencies are able to control case inputs. Likewise, any investigative agency can be made to look productive—or nonproductive—based on subjectively selected inputs and outcomes for measurement.

The use of statistical methods and formulas to judge the productivity of investigative achievement is meaningless until appropriate investigative tactics, strategies, and goals can be determined. This chapter examines what the statistics have revealed about the investigative function and the difficulty in attempting to quantify investigative activity into meaningful information for formulating managerial policy and control. The chapter also suggests appropriate goals, strategies, tactics, and the use of investigative specialists.

Productivity and Measurement

Productivity, essentially, is the return received from a given unit of input. The term is basically synonymous with efficiency since the greater the output is relative to each unit of input or resources, the more efficient or productive the organization is. Effectiveness, on the other hand, is a measure of the extent to which an organization has accomplished its goals.[1] Cawley describes investigative productivity as the number of investigative outcomes or activities per person-hour or person-days.[2]

With rising costs and declining tax revenues, managers and policy makers at all levels of government have increased the pressure on law enforcement to produce more with less. In this respect law enforcement executives are constantly pressured to justify their activities and resources. Basically, the reason for developing measures of productivity for the investigative function is to justify current investigative personnel authorizations or to prove the need for additional authorizations.[3]

Probably the most common method of measuring productivity in investigations is comparing clearance rates with reported crimes. However, this method is fraught with many difficulties. For example, crimes cleared are not necessarily reflective of the crimes originally reported. In other words, if reported crimes are not cleared until subsequent months, an inaccurate relationship between crimes reported and crimes cleared may be portrayed in that month's statistics. Also, agencies vary in how they claim cases to be cleared, and clearance rates do not reflect investigative productivity and quality.[4]

Block and Weidman suggest that the productivity formula should be the number of criminals arrested and prosecuted by the investigative unit divided by the number of crimes reported. Additionally, they recommend that performance observation, ratings of investigative personnel, and review of investigative reports be incorporated into the measurement process.[5]

Cawley and colleagues identify three component parts of an effective monitoring system to judge productivity. The first of these is investigative outcomes, including the number of arrests, case suspensions, case continuances, case clearances, cases prosecuted, and cases resulting in convictions. The second component is investigative activities, which include investigative leads such as interviews, interrogations, crime scene searches, surveillance, and so on. Third, investigative productivity determines the number of investigative outcomes or activities per person-hour or person-day. In this respect, the number of personnel assigned to investigations and the overall personnel costs can determine the cost of each case and thus ultimate productivity, or the relationship of inputs to outputs.[6]

One eighteen-month study of the Birmingham, Alabama, Police Department, as a follow-up to the Rand study on criminal investigation, used economic analysis to evaluate the productivity of investigations. That formula essentially attempted to quantify benefits (monetary or personal) for the victims plus the joint benefit to the community and law enforcement minus the total joint costs divided by the total input resources, to arrive at a measure of productivity. The formula linked greater investigative productivity to a restructuring of the detective division, initiation of a case-screening system for selective input into the investigations unit, and emphasis on managing the investigative continuum from initiation to prosecution.[7]

There are numerous other methods for measuring productivity. Some are as simple as measuring the numbers of cases assigned, closed, and pending for each investigator at the end of each month. Others are as complex as the computer-based analysis system attempted by the investigations unit of the California Department of Motor Vehicles during the 1970s. That system attempted to measure the specific time expended on each lead by each individual investigator throughout the state for each case category. From the data a mean average for time expended was then compiled for each case type. If an individual investigator's time per case exceeded the state average, then pressure was placed on that investigator to be more productive. Like most other measures of productivity, this approach tended to measure quantity of work, but not quality.

The folly of attempting to judge the productivity of current investigative practices with any empirically based formula is best summed up by Cawley:

> All the data collected will be valueless unless they can be used within the context of what is expected, what is considered good performance, and what constitutes satisfactory investigative outcomes. Those standards are based on what is important to the administration of the department, such as high rates of clearance per total case load. The department administrator should decide what is important, based on local needs and local concerns, and should base judgments on those matters determined to be important.[8]

Investigative Approaches and Priorities

Traditional approaches to criminal investigation by specialized persons (i.e., detectives/investigators) have been shown generally to be unproductive. For example, the Rand study found that detectives in Kansas City, Missouri (one of the sampled cities), spent 55 percent of their time actually conducting investigations. Of that time approximately 40 percent was directed toward cases that were never solved; 48 percent was expended on cases that were already cleared; and only 12 percent was spent on crimes that they did, in fact, solve. In terms of specialized investigative techniques, such as crime scene searches and collection of physical evidence, for one of the most frequently reported serious crimes, burglary, only 1 percent of such cases were solved based solely on physical evidence. Furthermore, according to this study, most detectives actually investigate less than one case per day and close 9.2 cases per month in crimes against persons and 16.9 cases in crimes against property. Basically, the study recommends either that detective personnel strength be reduced and resources assigned elsewhere or that the investigative function be reexamined, strategies and utilization changed, and management professionalized for greater cost-effectiveness of investigative resources.[9]

With 8 to 22 percent of police personnel assigned to investigations, the question is how these individuals can be productively utilized.[10] Recommendations for reform include prioritizing investigative resources to emphasize investigative activities that lead to productive outcomes, properly utilizing talents, educating and training each investigator, and applying systems theory to the management of ongoing investigations. Further, Dintino suggests that a substantial shift from the traditional reactive types of investigation to proactive types would lead to more productive results. He contends that investigators would then be able to address other forms of crime (e.g., organized/economic crime) that are not productively investigated in reactive modes.[11]

A systems approach to investigations would suggest that goals be defined. Cawley suggests two good investigative goals: (1) the collection of facts leading to the identification, apprehension, and arrest of an offender and (2) the organization of those facts to present the evidence of guilt in such a way that successful prosecution can occur. With appropriate goals the issue then becomes one of gate keeping, or controlling inputs into the investigative subsystem.[12]

Appropriate case inputs are those that can be productively worked and that require specialized treatment. Some crimes currently pursued by police investigative units, such as residential burglary or other property crimes, should be reexamined to determine the most effective means of prevention and control. The Rand study found that residential burglaries are most often cleared by routine patrol activities, but in the past the national average of cleared burglary cases has never exceeded 20 percent.[13] Numerous studies have indicated that burglary is best prevented by such programs as neighborhood watch, property identification, home security plans, environmental design, and so on, rather than by reactive burglary investigation.

Fundamental to a systems approach is the recognition that resources and processes must be prioritized, that is, focused first on the most critical cases. For example, in case management the first priority might be persons in custody who have committed a crime; second, cases with known suspects and substantial evidence; and third, cases with substantial evidence but no known suspects.

However, prioritization must not be limited to this type of case management, or we may fail to focus on crimes that are the most deleterious to society. Certain types of organized/political/business crimes are extremely detrimental to the foundations of a free government and economy, yet the cry from law enforcement is that we do not have the time or resources to investigate these crimes. Perhaps we need to reevaluate our investigative emphases. This author suggests that investigative activity be limited to (1) crimes against persons (homicide, rape, robbery, and aggravated assault, prioritized in that order); (2) organized/political/business crimes; and (3) all other crimes that require specialized investigative methodologies or tactics. Crimes that do not fall into these categories should be handled by patrol officers.

Development of Investigative Skills

Education, training, and development of investigative personnel and the adaptation of new technologies provide the best opportunity to improve investigative productivity, once approaches and priorities have been determined. From an educational standpoint investigators must have a thorough and competent knowledge of all aspects of criminal law, especially as it relates to procedures and evidence. In addition, they must have the ability to communicate and write effectively in order to document all forms of investigative activity for court presentation. Investigators must also have a substantial exposure to the forensic sciences, an understanding of their applications and limitations in criminal investigations, and an appreciation of the laws of probability.

Competence in these subject areas requires more extensive education and training than is normally received in a police academy. Furthermore, a few years of experience on the job is sufficient to master only a few of the skills involved. Nonetheless, police officers are often promoted to the rank of detective with only the basic police academy training and three to four years of experience in patrol. Few departments offer any advanced training or expect additional education for their detectives, even though the required investigative skills are complex.

- ☐ interviewing and interrogation
- ☐ evidence recognition and collection
- ☐ informant selection, recruitment, control, and management
- ☐ planning, control, and management of undercover investigations, including sting operations
- ☐ techniques and effective utilization of physical surveillance
- ☐ intelligence collection analyses
- ☐ participation in special operations, such as protection of dignitaries and threatened informants, victims, and witnesses

With new technologies and burgeoning criminal activities—especially computer-generated crimes and complex economic and political crimes—it is apparent that investigators must gain expertise in computers, business finances, cash/product flow analysis, bankruptcy laws and procedures, and so on. Detective units are here to stay. The challenge is to nurture and develop their expertise.

Management Issues

Criminal investigations, although sharing commonalities, are uniquely different on a case by case basis. Hence, qualitative issues become paramount in judging positive outcomes, and management must focus on producing a quality product. An emphasis on monthly reports, statistics, and productivity formulas may reveal nonproductive outcomes but rarely provides remedies for improvement. Those remedies rest on a thorough knowledge of investigative theories and practice, a positive organizational environment, a thorough case review of reports, qualitative assessments of ongoing cases, and evaluation of personnel. Thus, objective qualitative analysis of investigative products requires substantial exposure to and experience in criminal investigation.

The organizational climate surrounding criminal investigation must foster open discussion, creativity, and mutual respect among participants. Most investigators have tremendous latitude and are rarely instructed by an overseer during the working day. Consequently, investigators must be persons who have demonstrated the maturity, responsibility, and judgment required to work effectively and productively without close supervision. Investigative supervisors, in turn, must rely on the talents of their people, engage in healthy dialogue about ongoing cases, and set acceptable standards of productivity. A supervisor should be a coach, motivator, or facilitator, not a boss or monitor of investigative statistics.

An integral component of a systems approach is adequate feedback and control. Management must constantly examine and reexamine investigative goals to ensure that they are appropriate and that they contribute in a positive way to the overall goals of the law enforcement agency. In this process, alternative courses of action should always be considered; perhaps certain types of crimes could be better addressed by prevention programs or legislative changes than by investigative activities. When appropriate goals are confirmed, strategies must be developed to achieve them, as well as a means to provide accurate and timely feedback regarding goal accomplishment. With this information investigative activity can be refined for greater productivity. Few of us can be Sherlock Holmes, but we can all be productive.

Notes

[1] Harry W. More, Jr., ed., *Effective Police Administration,* 2d ed. (St. Paul: West, 1979); James A. Anderson, "On Measuring Productivity Improvement," *Journal of Political Science and Administration* 12, no. 4 (1984): 373–78; Advisory Commission on Productivity in Law Enforcement, *Opportunities for Improving Productivity in Police Services* (Washington, DC: The National Commission on Productivity, 1973).

[2] Donald F. Cawley et al. *Managing Criminal Investigations Manual* (Washington, DC: University Research Corporation, 1976).

[3] Anderson, "On Measuring Productivity;" John Dintino and Clinton L. Pagano, "The Investigative Function: Reassessing the Quality of Management," *The Police Chief* 51, no. 6 (1984): 55–58; Cawley et al., *Managing Criminal Investigations Manual.*

[4] For the Rand Study, see Peter W. Greenwood, Jan M. Chaiken, and Joan Petersilia, *The Criminal Investigation Process* (Santa Monica: The Rand Corporation, 1975).

[5] Peter B. Bloch and Donald R. Weidman, *Managing Criminal Investigations* (Washington, DC: National Institute of Law Enforcement and Criminal Justice, 1975).

[6] Cawley et al., *Managing Criminal Investigations Manual,* 147.

[7] Vergil L. Williams and Raymond O. Sumrall, "Productivity Measures in the Criminal Investigation Function," *The Journal of Criminal Justice* 10 (1982): 11–122.

[8] Cawley et al., *Managing Criminal Investigations Manual,* 155.

[9] Greenwood, Chaiken, and Petersilia, *Criminal Investigation Process.*

[10] Bloch, *Managing Criminal Investigations.*

[11] Anderson, "On Measuring Productivity"; More, *Effective Police Administration*; Richard A. Myren and Carol Henderson Garcia, *Investigation for Determination of Fact* (Pacific Grove, CA: Brooks/Cole Publishing, 1989); Dintino, "The Investigative Function."

[12] Cawley et al., *Managing Criminal Investigations Manual,* 1.

[13] Greenwood, Chaiken, and Petersilia, *Criminal Investigation Process.*

13

Criminal Investigation and the Classical Application of Ethics

Peter Longo
Kearney State College

Ethics has been debated throughout the history of humankind and has recently been the focus of increased attention. Nationally, public officials who fail to follow exacting standards of ethics are being challenged by the media and the public. At the same time criminal justice forces are trying to handle increased crime and yet maintain ethics in enforcing the law. One would think that all of this debate and attention would have resulted in firm conclusions, but such is not the case. In fact, many questions remain. Is ethics a legal code? Is it proper upbringing? What is ethics? The student of criminal justice will spend a great amount of study time learning legal guidelines and mandates and countless hours mastering the art of criminal investigation. Yet it will not be enough to do what is legal and efficient. Criminal justice personnel will be called on in their discretionary decision making to do what is right.

It is this latter task, doing what is right, that serves as the focus of this reading. Some have called for a humanistic approach to the ethics debate (Gilbert, 1988), even though humanities tend to slow down our fast-paced world.[1] We are a society that enjoys fast food, fast cars, fast laughs; administrators are fixed on minute-manager theories and quick-fix solutions. Unfortunately, however, a quick-fix is usually short-lived. The lessons from the humanities, on the other hand, are deliberate and are aimed at endurance.

In response to this humanistic call, we will take several steps back into history, to revisit the well-known Greek and classical philosopher, Aristotle. Aristotle's message of ethical behavior is priceless and of particular worth to criminal justice students. In all probability Aristotle did not know much about the particulars of criminal investigation, but he did understand a great deal about ethics and human nature. Additionally, his messages are clear and understandable and directly applicable to criminal justice matters, since criminal justice is, essentially, a study of human nature gone astray.

Potential Ethical Dilemmas

Let's imagine that you are a new police officer, called to investigate the disappearance and possible abduction of a twelve-year-old girl. Your investigative leads take you to a suspect within your jurisdiction, who fits the description on all points and has a previous record of kidnapping and child molestation. You apprehend the suspect, but your instincts tell you that the missing child is dead.

The suspect hears the Miranda warnings and chooses to remain silent. As you drive him to the location of the crime, the silence becomes uncomfortable. It is Christmas Eve, the snow is falling at a steady rate, and your thoughts wander from your own young daughter to the victim. Something must be done, but what?

This scenario was derived from a 1984 Supreme Court case, *Nix v. Williams,* better known in legal circles as the Christian burial case.[2] In the Nix case the officer gave an emotional speech about a proper Christian burial for the victim, and the suspect responded by confessing to the homicide and telling the location of the body. The Supreme Court eventually ruled against the suspect's claim that the confession was unconstitutionally obtained from him. However, the exclusionary rule, which prevents the use of illegally obtained evidence in court proceedings, continues to present legal as well as ethical dilemmas. In the words of one New York judge, "The criminal is to go free because the constable has blundered."[3] The exclusionary rule has been modified through the years, but there are now many more legal gray areas that are often determined on a case by case basis.

Although the exclusionary rule is perhaps the most obvious ethical challenge to an investigator, it is by no means the only one. Investigators are called upon to obtain evidence in various forms and once again must not only know the legally required bounds and procedures, but must also act as ethical citizens. Police are highly unsupervised and experience great pressure to operate under an ends-justifies-the-means philosophy. In addition, there is always the temptation to do what peers are doing, even if it is wrong and/or illegal.

Aristotle's Ethical Framework for Criminal Investigation

Aristotle devotes less than two dozen lines to criminal law, yet those lines are quoted in thousands of volumes. In addition, Aristotle offers universal messages that have particular importance for criminal investigators.

As discussed previously, the exclusionary rule poses serious ethical dilemmas for criminal investigators. At times they may applaud the rule, at other times curse it. Aristotle clearly indicates that the law must be preserved and that it ultimately will lead us to a good life. That good life is based on ethical behavior, and Aristotle is harsh on lawbreakers.

> The fact is that the greatest crimes are caused by excess and not by necessity. Men do not become tyrants in order that they may not suffer cold; and hence great is the honour bestowed not on him who kills a thief, but on him who kills a tyrant.[4]

This passage has several important messages for criminal investigators. Generally, it urges moderate behavior. Moderation directly confronts overzealous behavior, which has the potential to harm citizens. According to Aristotle the greatest crimes stem from excess, not necessity. And excess, which is clearly a selfish act, breaks the spirit of the investigative community. Criminal investigators undoubtedly experience positive feelings when cases are broken, but the betrayal of one's ethics to solve a criminal investigation is inexcusable.

Aristotle's Understanding of *Good*

Good is probably easier to define in the technical field of criminal investigation than it is in the philosophical field of ethics. Good investigative methods include proper identification of a suspect, location and arrest of the suspect, protection of the chain of evidence, and so on. However, deriving a clear meaning of *good* in the abstract is a challenge. Aristotle gives *good* some universal meaning in his *Nicomachean Ethics,* which was originally intended for the statesman, or public servant. Criminal investigators can certainly be looked upon as public servants in the best sense of the phrase.

Aristotle states that "every art and every inquiry and similarly every action and choice is thought to aim at some good."[5] Thus, according to Aristotle's framework, criminal justice practitioners must aim each day to do what is good. Copleston, a scholar of Aristotle's work, adds to this notion, claiming that public servants should act "to make man, in a universal sense, happy."[6] Criminal investigators, then, are ethically bound to act on behalf of the citizens they serve—even when that task is made unpleasant by an unfriendly judge, a difficult police chief, an obnoxious drunk, or some other less-than-desirable character. Aristotle urges equity, not necessarily equality. Thus, each situation and each individual must be evaluated, and then investigators must do what is good—a formidable charge.

Fortunately, the teachings of Aristotle do not demand immediate perfection. Aristotle believed that life is an ongoing adventure in which each activity offers a learning aspect. Centuries ago he realized the frailty of humankind, even though he did not excuse it. Instead he queries, "Shall we not, like archers who have a mark to aim at, be more likely to hit upon what we should?"[7] If criminal investigators continually aim at what is good, they will accomplish much.

Truth: An Individual Responsibility

American government has grown accustomed to hiding behind the group. According to David Truman, a political scientist, democracy is served by having lawmakers listen to groups, which are a mere reflection of individual behavior.[8] Even though this might be true, such a scheme keeps individuals from accepting responsibility and encourages the non-Aristotelian excuse "Everyone else was doing it." Political figures in Washington, DC, have used this rationale, as have vast numbers of arrestees the world over.

The abdication of individual responsibility has had tragic consequences in both private and public sectors. The Valdez oil spill of 1989 showed how difficult it was to find an individual in the Exxon Corporation responsible. Individuals can hide in the bureaucratic maze of a corporate structure, blame the structure, and pay no ethical debt to society. The same loss of individual responsibility is at the heart of many police and/or correctional scandals. For example, the New York scandal that involved hundreds of police and was portrayed in the book and movie *Serpico* illustrates this point.[9] Large numbers of criminal investigators engaged in unlawful activities and then explained that so many others were doing it. The system, if it didn't tolerate, at least disguised such behavior. Aristotle's work swiftly condemns the group or pluralistic excuse:

> We had perhaps better consider the universal good and discuss thoroughly what is meant by it, although such an inquiry is made an uphill one by the fact that the Forms have been introduced by friends of our own. Yet it would perhaps be thought to be better, indeed to be our duty, for the sake of maintaining the truth even to destroy what touches us closely, especially as we are philosophers; for, while both are dear, piety requires us to honour truth above our friends.[10]

This message is of critical importance: ethical duty lies with the individual, even if that duty damages friendship. Criminal investigators will encounter a police subculture, which may be fine unless it prevents ethical behavior. Perhaps a detective friend will plant drug evidence on a drug dealer to effect the arrest of an evil individual who has continually evaded legal arrest. Ultimately, each individual must decide whether "to honor truth."

Obtaining Excellence in Individual Ethics

The quest for ethical behavior is ongoing. Aristotle observes that ethical excellence involves both intellectual and moral aspects:

> Intellectual excellence in the main owes both its birth and its growth to teaching (for which reason it requires experience and time), while moral excellence comes about as a result of habit, whence also its name is one that is formed by a slight variation from the word for *habit*. From this it is also plain that none of the moral excellences arises in us by nature; for nothing that exists by nature can form a habit contrary to its nature.[11]

In other words, experience and intellectual study can lead us to ethics, but it's not easy to be ethical. The ethical challenge is particularly difficult in the high-pressured world of criminal justice, where not only personal pressures, but also victims, the media, supervisors, and many others exert powerful influences. However, investigators can learn from their experiences and from study. Knowing all the legal mandates and achieving a sound moral base will result in ethical behavior.

Aristotle demands ethical behavior but knows that it is a never-ending challenge.

Anyone can get angry . . . that is easy . . . or give or spend money; but to do this to the right person, to the right extent, at the right time, with the right aim, and in the right way, that is not for everyone, nor is it easy; that is why goodness is both rare, honorable, and noble.[12]

The criminal justice journey may be difficult, but it will also be honorable if investigators follow the path of ethical behavior, striving always for goodness.

Twentieth Century Examples

The relevance of Aristotle to criminal investigators is seen in examples of potential real-life situations. In each of the situations described here, imagine that you are a conscientious investigator—and look to Aristotle for guidance.

Imagine that you are asked to testify in a court of law about a known drug dealer. You know the harmful results of the suspect's actions, and you also know that you do not have sufficient evidence to support the particular charge. The bailiff calls you to take the stand. What do you do? Aristotle's advice is simple: tell the truth. The real challenge is to convict the drug dealer through truthful means; if you lie, the process of justice is a sham. Ah, but everyone lies. Aristotle says that this is no excuse. You are a public servant and must serve *all* the public.

Suppose that you have been called to an area known for its high crack-cocaine use. You visit an apartment where a single mother has overdosed on crack and has killed her two young children. Something must be done, you think as you hit the streets searching for crack dealers. Is it OK to be excessive in your search, just this once? Aristotle answers no; necessity does not justify excess. You have spent a great deal of time and energy learning how to investigate in a legal manner. Arrest the crack dealer, but do it right.

Imagine that you have been investigating a child pornography operation. You could save two weeks of intense work by lying to obtain a search warrant. That approach would make a great number of people happy, and your job as a public servant is to make people happy. What do you do? Aristotle suggests that you execute the search warrant legally, for a situation that tempts an investigator to lie for the good of a single case does not ultimately serve the entire community well. In an Aristotelian manner Justice Brandeis said in his dissent in *Olmstead v. United States:* "Our government is the potent, omnipresent teacher. For good or for ill, it teaches the whole people by its example. If the government becomes a lawbreaker, it breeds contempt for law; it invites every man to become a law unto himself; it invites anarchy."[13] Do not be deceived into making one person happy or one police chief happy at the expense of making the community happy.

You have been asked to investigate a complaint of domestic violence. You work your way through a neighborhood of crime . . . crack dealers, drug pushing, prostitution. You are surrounded by human misery. You make your way to the door of the complainant. You knock, and a battered wife lets you in. The suspect has fled. You pursue the suspect and ultimately apprehend him. Is there anything wrong with letting the suspect feel a little of your anger and disgust? Once again, Aristotle cautions against excessive force. Responding in a manner consistent with a criminal lowers you to the level of the criminal. Instead, Aristotle says that public servants must treat humans as humans, even though not all humans act like humans. Criminal investigators will be frequently called upon to set the example. Aristotle's call is for ethical conduct.

Continuation of the Journey

Hopefully, the connection between classical ethics and criminal justice fieldwork has been made, but it must continue to be made. Ethical behavior requires ongoing practice and theory. Again, the words of Aristotle:

> But most people . . . take refuge in theory and think they are being philosophers and will become good in this way, behaving somewhat like patients who listen attentively to their doctors, but do none of the things they are ordered to do. And the latter will not be made well in body by such a course of treatment; the former will not be made well in soul by such a course in philosophy.[14]

It does an investigator no good to obtain a criminal justice education stressing legal investigative guidelines and then go out and violate the spirit of the law. The classical framework of Aristotle can serve both as a springboard for future discussions of investigative theories and as a practical guide to good actions, which will lead us ultimately to a good society.

Notes

[1] James Gilbert, "Investigative Ethics," in *Critical Issues in Criminal Investigation,* 2d ed., ed. M. Palmiotto (Cincinnati: Anderson, 1988).

[2] Nix v. Williams, 467 U.S. 431 (1984).

[3] People v. Defore, 150 N.E. 585 (1926), 587.

[4] Aristotle, *Politics,* in *The Complete Works of Aristotle,* ed. Jonathan Barnes (Princeton: Princeton University Press, 1984), 1267(a): 13–16.

[5] Aristotle, *Nicomachean Ethics* 1094(a): 1–2.

[6] Frederick Copleston, *A History of Philosophy* (Garden City, NY: Image Books, 1962).

[7] Aristotle, *Nicomachean Ethics* 1094(a): 24–25.

[8] David Truman, *The Governmental Process* (New York: Knopf, 1951).

[9] Peter Maas, *Serpico* (New York: Viking, 1973).

[10] Aristotle, *Nicomachean Ethics* 1096(a): 12–16.

[11] Ibid., 1103(a): 14–21.

[12] Ibid., 1190(a): 20–30.

[13] Olmstead v. United States, 277 U.S. 438 (1928), 485.

[14] Aristotle, *Nicomachean Ethics* 11056(b): 12–18.

CASE STUDY
The 77th Precinct: Casualties of Greed

James N. Gilbert
Kearney State College

During 1987 a police scandal rocked the city of New York, a city that was no stranger to official misconduct within its criminal justice system. However, that investigation was to have long-lasting negative consequences, not only for those officers directly involved, but also for the image of the New York City Police Department. What occurred in the 77th precinct was without precedent: an entire precinct station—some 220 police officers and 20 supervisors—was forced to transfer because of the level of corruption discovered there. Eventually, thirteen patrol officers were indicted for well over one hundred serious felony charges, which included taking bribes from drug dealers, stealing money and narcotics, taking money from dead bodies, and using drugs. Twenty-five other officers were disciplined on less serious charges. In an attempt to understand how such widespread misconduct could occur, one can gain much insight from an examination of the two principal officers involved in exposing the scandal.

The 77th precinct is located within Brooklyn's Bedford-Stuyvesant neighborhood, a once-stable middle-class bedroom and professional area that has deteriorated into one of the worst slums in the nation. To this patrol district two rookie officers were assigned—Henry Winter and Tony Magno. The two men soon became partners in the traditional sense as well as partners in crime. Both came from law-abiding middle-class backgrounds and, like most officers who work high-crime inner-city neighborhoods, lived far from their work environment. Winter and Magno were initially respected as hard-working, aggressive officers. However, they were ill prepared for the radically different world of Bedford-Stuyvesant. Annually, more than eighty criminal homicides are reported there, as are four hundred shootings and more than two thousand robberies. Narcotics trafficking is so common that it can be witnessed virtually anywhere within the boundaries of the 77th precinct. Not surprisingly, officers assigned to the 77th quickly developed a siege mentality, well illustrated by their nickname for the precinct—the Alamo. Widely perceived as a dumping ground for problem officers, the 77th was considered by most to be a downward career move.

The 77th had been the target of the police department's Internal Affairs Division for some time. The precinct had a reputation within the department for corruption, but specific proof had not been obtained. Numerous precinct commanders and other supervisors had notified their superiors about alleged corruption, particularly among officers of the early morning shift. But evidence did not become available until Winter and Magno found themselves facing long terms of imprisonment.

The beginning of the end came when a drug dealer, to avoid imprisonment himself, agreed to cooperate with the New York State special prosecutor for corruption. The dealer reported widespread corruption, involving money and drug payoffs to local police, and agreed to be recorded and filmed while paying off Winter and Magno to protect his narcotics operation. Thus, the pair were caught accepting a bribe, were shown the extensive evidence of their guilt, and were offered a deal. If they cooperated with the prosecutor by gathering evidence on other corrupt officers, they would not be prosecuted and would be granted immunity for all past crimes. The two partners became the first in the history of the department to gather incriminating evidence against an entire precinct.

Wearing small recording devices while on duty and recording all phone calls off duty, the pair quickly began to document an incredible network of police illegality. It was a police organization totally out of control, a precinct that had seemingly lost all concept of morality and ethical behavior among its officers. Officers were documented stealing anything of value: money, drugs, cigarettes, beer, and much more. Of particular concern to the internal affairs investigators was a group of thirteen officers who were systematically robbing drug dealers of their money and wares. It soon became clear that the level of corruption was so pervasive that those involved believed they were totally above the law and would never be caught. One officer was so blatantly confident that for five hundred dollars she agreed to provide protection for a shipment of cocaine while it passed through Brooklyn. The operation was really a sting in which undercover police officers posed as drug dealers.

When the prosecutor's office finally decided that enough evidence had been gathered, a special grand jury began hearing the evidence, and indictments quickly followed. By late 1987 most of the indicted officers had either pled guilty in agreement for lesser sentences or had been found guilty in jury trials. Many of the officers were sentenced to long prison terms, but officers Winter and Magno escaped prosecution in exchange for their extensive courtroom testimony. Even though the majority of officers assigned to the 77th precinct were not indicted or brought up on departmental charges, the precinct was deemed unsalvageable and all personnel were transferred.

The shameful story of the 77th precinct is unique only in its magnitude. Even though there is no doubt that the majority of law enforcement officers are ethical and highly professional practitioners, dishonest police officers continue to be convicted throughout the nation. Why would career officers do such things, knowingly placing their careers on the line, often for trivial rewards? The answers are, of course, complex. However, the constant element in many of the stories of corrupt police officers is that they appear totally unprepared to deal with the intensity of their work environments. Many are not initially dishonest, but dishonest peers and a gradual loss of faith in the system wear down their ethical resistance.

Officer Winter's case graphically illustrates this unfortunate process. Winter gradually lost faith in the ability of the system to deal effectively with his many quality arrests. He then began to take the law into his own hands, burning drug money in front of dealers or driving dealers many miles out of Brooklyn and forcing them to walk back without shoes or clothing. Additionally, Winter observed so many dishonest acts among other officers that he believed such behavior was the standard rather than the exception for police conduct. And underlying all of this was the constant stress of policing a population that lived in appalling poverty in a place where rampant violence and disregard for human life seemed commonplace.

Certainly such explanations do not exonerate corrupt behavior. Nonetheless, there has been a notable lack of academy and in-service training to prepare officers for the stress and temptation of modern policing. Officers should be realistically prepared for the difficulties that may await them, and they should be ethically trained to avoid an end-justifies-the-means mentality. In addition, an organizational attitude must be established in which officers no longer tolerate corruption but cooperate in attempts to investigate the illegal acts of their peers. In the 77th precinct resistance to the corruption investigation was so strong that officers refused to ride ever again in the patrol unit used by Winter and Magno, terming it the Ratmobile.

The successful battle against corruption in the 77th precinct did not, of course, end police corruption in New York City or in any other city. The bottom line may well be found in convincing police officers that the criminal justice system works. As one of the convicted officers of the 77th stated in attempting to explain his corruption, "I did it for the glory; it was all done as a way of getting back at the people you couldn't hurt. No one becomes a cop to steal."

Source: Mike McAlary, *Buddy Boys: When Good Cops Turn Bad* (New York: Putnam, 1987).

14
White Collar Crime

James Lovelace
Federal Bureau of Investigation

White collar crime (WCC) is a broad area of criminal activity that involves the taking of property by guile, deceit, violation of confidence, or abuse of official position. Although WCC is not characterized by violence, it is nevertheless a serious problem costing Americans more than $200 billion per year. Within the WCC area, the FBI differentiates among different subareas—specifically, financial crimes, fraud against the government, and public corruption.

Financial Crimes

Crimes Involving Financial Institutions

For the most part financial crimes involve criminal activity at banking and financial institutions. In about 25 percent of the banks that fail, significant criminal activity comes to light. And banks that fail are only part of the serious bank fraud and embezzlement problem. Losses in the million dollar range are not at all unusual in individual cases.

The FBI has jurisdiction over criminal activity at almost all banking and financial institutions because almost all of them are insured federally and the FBI has jurisdiction to investigate any federal violation. That same activity may also be a violation of state law, in which case state law enforcement authorities can also investigate it, and it can be prosecuted in either state or federal court. Sometimes bigger cases are investigated jointly by the FBI and state authorities.

Insider Activity. Most of the criminal actions seen at failed banks and much of that at solvent banks results from insider activity. Often it is in the form of outright embezzlement, just switching the money from one column to another and thereby into the embezzler's pocket.

There are also a lot of straw-man loan schemes, or accommodation loans. For example, let's say that a bank officer wants a loan to be made to a person or business. The borrower may already be at the legal lending limit or may be ineligible for the loan for some other reason, but the bank officer wants the borrower to get the loan anyway. What the bank officer may be tempted to do is to have another person come in and sign the loan papers so that the loan appears to be going to this other person. In many cases the bank officer and the real borrower may even forge the other name to the loan documents without telling the person about the loan, or they may list the loan in the name of a fictitious person. If the real borrower can't pay the money back and the loan goes into default, the bank loses the money. If the bank fails, the FDIC ultimately loses the money.

Outside Schemes. The main types of financial crimes that don't involve insiders are false statements, check kiting, and check forgery. False statements concern the financial statements submitted to obtain a loan, including the listing of collateral to secure the loan. All too often a bank finds no collateral when it goes to collect on it. A farmer or a rancher may have claimed a thousand head of cattle or three or four hundred acres in corn when, in fact, he had just a few hundred cattle or half that amount of land under cultivation. At other times the collateral may not be in the borrower's name free and clear; it may have been shared with others or encumbered by a mortgage. In many false statement cases people have gotten loans from two or three different banks and haven't listed all of the loans on their financial statements.

Check kiting is a scheme to manipulate an account so that the account balance appears much higher than it actually is. This deceit is usually accomplished by floating bogus deposits between several different accounts. When the check kite finally crashes, whoever happens to be holding the most checks at that time bears the brunt of the losses, which can amount to more than one or two million dollars.

Check forgeries in which the FBI takes an interest are those involving professional criminals who make their living from this activity. Although this crime can be as simple as forging a name on a check that has been lost or stolen, it often involves much more. There are many organized gangs that blow into a town, armed with dozens of fake IDs in several different names, and open up accounts at half a dozen different banks. They deposit bad checks from the previous town and, in just a few days, can spread several thousand dollars' worth of checks around town. They then move on before the checks start bouncing.

Sometimes a split-deposit scheme is utilized. In one variation a group comes into town and steals checks from mailboxes, thus gaining access to the established checking accounts of real people and to checks drawn on various companies and commercial entities. Sometimes these groups use stolen checks; at other times they use their own check printers. In either case they go to a branch of the victim's bank, usually a drive-in, and deposit forged checks worth four or five hundred dollars, taking one or two hundred dollars back in cash. By the time these checks bounce and the bank figures out what has happened, the forgers are long gone. Although the amounts in individual transactions are not large, by working several different accounts at several different branches, a group can realize a six-figure profit in one town very quickly. A variation of this scheme involves passing checks to local merchants and then returning the property for cash before the check bounces.

Other Financial Crimes

A good number of financial crimes do not involve banking institutions directly. One such scheme is the advance-fee swindle, in which a con artist masquerades as a money broker or loan arranger in order to collect underserved fees. These swindlers offer their victims loans for which the victims otherwise would not qualify. Sometimes the fakers claim to be able to arrange super-low rates; sometimes they promise that the loan will repay itself through reinvestment of part of the borrowed funds at an extremely high rate of return. Of course, to qualify, the borrower has to pay a fee up front—an advance fee. A one million dollar self-liquidating loan might require fifty thousand dollars up front. The rest of the story is obvious.

Other financial crimes include bankruptcy fraud; fraudulent investment claims, such as oil and gas leases; credit card fraud; and consumer fraud, that is, the selling of worthless merchandise, often by mail or via toll-free telephone calls.

Fraud Against the Government

Procurement Fraud

In areas where fraud against the government is a big problem, the major emphasis of the FBI is on procurement fraud. The tremendous expenditures of the Department of Defense (DOD) are made largely through contracts with private companies. Unfortunately, all too many of these firms are fattening their pockets by cheating the Department of Defense. As part of the government's overall effort to reduce expenditures, the FBI has been trying to crack down hard on DOD fraud, which is currently the agency's number one national WCC priority.

Home Loan Fraud

Another type of fraud against the government is FHA and VA home loan fraud. In these cases, once again, the FBI pursues those people who make a business of this type of fraud. Usually these white collar criminals have connections within the lending industry or the home real estate industry.

In a typical scheme a dishonest businessman might find a house to buy for $50,000 that needs some repairs to increase its value. The businessman buys it and then finds a straw buyer to pose as someone who is going to buy the home from the businessman, using an FHA or VA loan to finance the purchase. The straw buyer fills out the loan documents and puts the loan in his own name, appearing in all respects to be the purchaser of the home. However, the businessman pays all of the closing fees, puts up the down payment, and then pays the straw buyer a fee for the use of his name.

The businessman makes his profit by fraudulently inflating the value of the home. He doesn't make any repairs to the house yet sells it to the straw buyer for $75,000. Of the $25,000 profit he uses $5,000 or $6,000 to cover the closing costs and the down payment. Another part he uses to pay the straw buyer, which leaves the businessman with at least $15,000 for his efforts. If he completes the scheme ten times, he makes a quick $200,000.

The federal government's loss in such situations comes from the fact that the mortgages for these homes are FHA and VA insured. Thus, in our example the FHA or the VA would have received the $5,000 down payment and would have guaranteed a mortgage of $70,000. If the bank forecloses and goes to the FHA for the $70,000, the FHA or VA will attempt to sell the house. However, it's only worth $50,000 because the improvements were never made. Consequently, the government agency loses $20,000 plus the administrative costs of handling foreclosed loans. Because organized home loan fraud results in huge losses, the FBI pursues these cases aggressively.

Medicare/Medicaid Fraud

Another type of fraud against the government involves Medicare/Medicaid fraud. Here again, the FBI is most interested in the organized violators who abuse the system to rake in huge profits. These white collar criminals include unscrupulous doctors, pharmacists, and operators of health care centers for the elderly who bill the government for services that aren't rendered or for drugs or tests that aren't given. Sometimes a lower quality, cheaper drug or test is given, but the government is billed for the more expensive version. As a result, not only is the government defrauded, but the poor and elderly receive inferior treatment.

Public Corruption

The final type of white collar crime is public corruption. Investigations in this area involve federal officials, of course, but the vast majority of corruption cases focus on state and local officials. All of these investigations are conducted pursuant to a law known as the Hobbs Act, which states that a public official who obtains money or property under color, or authority, of official right has committed extortion.

A good example of such extortion is payoffs to get property rezoned. Property that is zoned for single-family residential use is worth much less than it would be if the zoning were changed to commercial or multifamily use. Thus, if a zoning change is needed to increase the value of a property by, perhaps, one million dollars, then it may be prudent to kick back ten thousand dollars to the public official who determines whether that rezoning request is granted. In such a case the public official who takes a payoff in return for official help is obtaining money under color of official right.

Public corruption is not limited to the big cities. In the early 1980s the FBI successfully investigated most of the county commissioners in the state of Oklahoma, who had been illegally obtaining payoffs to ensure that all county business went to certain construction companies and vendors. Even more recently a similar long-running investigation in the state of Mississippi resulted in the successful prosecution of many county commissioners in that state also, for accepting payments in return for exerting their influence over the awarding of county contracts.

Legal Basis for Prosecution

The FBI does not use a great many different laws to prosecute people guilty of white collar crime. Most of the criminal activity directed at financial institutions is prosecuted under one or more of five federal statutes. One of these simply forbids anyone from knowingly executing or attempting to execute a scheme or artifice to defraud a federally chartered or insured financial institution.

The other statutes are more specific. One prohibits the theft, embezzlement, or misapplication of the funds of a federally insured financial institution by a bank officer or employee. Another makes it a criminal violation for a bank officer or employee to make a false entry on the books of a federally insured financial institution. Sometimes this particular statute is used to prosecute employees or officers who have falsified bank records in order to cover up other criminal activities. A third statute makes it illegal to give a false statement to a federally insured financial institution in order to obtain a loan from that institution.

One final law, which the FBI utilizes in the prosecution of forged check cases, forbids the transportation through interstate or foreign commerce of any falsely made, forged, altered, or counterfeited security. For purposes of this law, checks and other negotiable instruments are considered securities, as are stocks, bonds, and numerous other types of commercial paper. Under this law a suspect need not be the one who physically transports a security across state lines; it is sufficient that the person causes the security to be transported. Thus, any time a person writes a bad check in one state and it is drawn on a bank in another state, that person is deemed to have caused the check to travel interstate.

Advance-fee swindles, as well as other common types of fraud perpetrated by con artists, are prosecuted under either the fraud-by-wire or the mail fraud statute. The wire fraud statute makes it a criminal violation for a person to cause the interstate transmittal of a wire, radio, or television communication that furthers a scheme to defraud or obtain money or property by false pretenses. The mail fraud statute makes it illegal to cause such a communication to go through the mail. Thus, if a con artist, in the course of defrauding someone, makes an interstate telephone call or sends the victim a letter—or even if the victim, as a result of the fraud, calls across state lines or writes the con artist or some other party—then the con artist is guilty of mail fraud or fraud by wire.

Another statute that is sometimes used in fraud cases makes it a criminal violation for a person to transport across state lines property worth more than five thousand dollars that has been stolen or procured by fraud. That same statute also makes it a violation to cause another person to travel interstate to further a fraud being perpetrated against that person. Consequently, if a con artist urges a victim to travel from New York City to Newark, New Jersey, to inspect some real estate or to sign some loan documents, for example, then that con artist can be prosecuted in federal court.

The laws that cover fraud against the government also identify both general and specific criminal violations. Some target specific acts committed against specific federal agencies. Others prohibit any fraud or theft committed against the United States or any of its agencies. In addition, the FBI uses the various statutes already discussed if the United States is a victim of wire fraud, mail fraud, and so on.

In the area of public corruption, the primary legal basis is the Hobbs Act, which was mentioned earlier. When federal officials are involved, a statute is also available prohibiting the bribery of those officials. Local officials can be charged under that statute, too, if their illegal activity occurred with programs financed by the federal government.

Investigation and Prosecution

Evidence must prove beyond a reasonable doubt that the suspect did, in fact, commit the acts specified by the applicable statute.

Financial Crimes

With most financial crimes against banks, cases are put together historically by analyzing bank records and tracing paper trails. In most such cases it is fairly clear that the bank has been defrauded, and available information usually casts suspicion on particular subjects. It is necessary then to go back over the bank's records to piece together exactly how the fraud was accomplished and to prove—with a paper trail supplemented by interviews and analysis of records—that the suspect did, in fact, commit the fraud.

In fraudulent check cases it is generally known at the beginning of a case exactly how a fraud was committed but not who committed it. Therefore, investigative techniques are needed that are more typical of general criminal investigations, such as robberies or burglaries. One of the first things to do is collect the physical evidence and submit it to a laboratory for fingerprint and handwriting analysis. The laboratory compares the fraudulent checks with other specimens in the national fraudulent check file in order to associate them with cases in other states with which the perpetrators may have been involved.

Many other avenues can also be explored. If the banks or stores where the checks were passed have surveillance cameras, those surveillance photos are sent to other law enforcement agencies to see whether any of the perpetrators are known to other investigators. In addition, driver's licenses and other pieces of identification used by the perpetrators can be traced. Sometimes a motel where the perpetrators stayed can be identified, and telephone calls made from that location can be traced.

Any leads that might help uncover the true names of the check passers are followed. If names can be ascertained, then fingerprints and handwriting from the checks and other evidence can be compared with prints and exemplars of the suspects to help prove responsibility for the bad checks.

Fraud. In fraud cases the con artist is known, and the victim's statement details what the subject is alleged to have said and done. However, in order to obtain a conviction on fraud charges, it must be proved that (1) the con artist did, in fact, make those statements and take those action that caused the victim to give the perpetrator money or property, (2) the victim was led to believe a gross misrepresentation, and (3) the con artist knew full well that the representation was not true. Unfortunately, none of these elements are easy to prove.

First of all, it is difficult to rely purely on the recollection of the victim, particularly when just one or two victims are involved. In most cases the perpetrator will deny saying what the victim alleges. One way to overcome this problem is to identify additional victims early on and enlist their assistance in getting the con artist to repeat the representations under conditions that allow the conversation to be recorded. Sometimes, an FBI agent can pose as a potential victim and talk to the perpetrator directly. This approach permits a fuller exploration of all the mis-representations.

To refute the representations, experts are contacted regarding the product being sold, and references and other customers are checked. The con artist's own background is also investigated in detail, particularly claims made about education and business history. If the perpetrator's own words can be recorded over a period of time, contradictions may be found in different conversations about the same topic. These contradictions, along with evidence that the con artist withheld infor-mation from the victim(s), can help show that the con artist knew the repre-sentations were false.

Fraud Against the Government and Public Corruption

The criminal activity that takes place when fraud against the government and public corruption occur is not as readily apparent as most financial crimes. In fact, fraud against the government and public corruption often occur without awareness on the part of either victims or law enforcement. Therefore, a great deal of the FBI's effort with these two types of white collar crime goes into detecting the fact that a crime has occurred.

Proactive Investigation. Rather than sitting back and waiting for criminal activity to be reported, the FBI engages in proactive investigation to uncover fraud against the government and public corruption that would not otherwise come to light. One component of that investigation is a close examination of the records of programs known to be prone to fraud. Trends or patterns may not clearly establish criminal activity, but they may call for further investigation. For example, a computer printout of all home mortgages that have gone into foreclosure in a particular area over a two- or three-year period should be examined for evidence that any particular real estate company or mortgage company has been involved in an abnormally high number of the foreclosures. It is also important to note whether the same person has been a seller or a purchaser of several different homes that were ultimately involved in foreclosure and to determine how many payments were made on the loan prior to default. Loans that go into default without any payments whatsoever being made on them are particularly good indicators of fraud. Similar surveys should be made of the records of the Department of Health and Human Services, especially regarding Medicare and Medicaid expenditures.

Development and proper use of confidential sources of information is also very important in uncovering and investigating fraud against the government and public corruption. Such sources of information may be personal or business acquaintances of the subject or even a bag man, the intermediary used by a corrupt politician to collect payoff money. A bag man is used to prevent the victim from being able to testify from personal knowledge that the perpetrator did, in fact, receive the payoff. Fortunately for the FBI, bag men often dabble in criminal activity and may trade their cooperation with law enforcement for consideration in their own cases.

Once information is acquired, it is necessary to establish that the principals to the crime did knowingly engage in the illegal activity. One approach is through traditional investigative techniques and the tracing of paper trails. Very often, however, the case against such subjects must be built around their own words and actions. In that situation a tape recorder might be used with the consent of the cooperating informant. If necessary and sufficient evidence exists for a court order, a wire tap or microphone surveillance might also be attempted to obtain conversations between various persons actually involved in the crime.

Undercover Operations. The investigative technique that is probably the most difficult to execute properly is the undercover operation. It can be very effective and is sometimes the only method available in certain fraud and corruption cases. The Abscam investigation of the late 1970s may well be the best known example of an FBI undercover operation. In Abscam, FBI agents passed themselves off as representatives of extremely rich businessmen from the Middle East, who wished to do business in this country. The undercover agents let it be known that the rich businessmen were willing to make payoffs to politicians in return for official favors.

The Abscam operation was, of course, very successful. Time and again bag men introduced the undercover agents to corrupt politicians willing to sell their offices for cash. The agents met the corrupt politicians in a townhouse in Washington, DC, on a yacht in Florida, and at hotels in Philadelphia and other cities. During their meetings the politicians told the undercover agents what they could do for the rich businessmen and stipulated what they would have to be paid for their help. Each of those who were ultimately convicted of criminal charges had accepted thousands of dollars in payoffs while FBI tape recorders and video cameras recorded their words and actions.

Even though the Abscam operation was more elaborate than most FBI undercover operations, the general objective is always the same—that is, to win the confidence of persons identified as engaging in illegal activity and convince them that the undercover agents are either already engaged in the same type of criminal activity or wish to become involved in such activity. The undercover agents then talk to the subjects regarding the illegal activity and pretend to break the law along with the subjects—while recorders and cameras capture the subjects' words and actions for use in court. The FBI has used this technique successfully in numerous investigations of various types of white collar crime.

The struggle against white collar crime cannot be won by the FBI alone. Nor can it be won by federal, state, and local law enforcement alone. It requires the cooperation of the public sector, private industry, and an informed and concerned populace. Law enforcement can only lead the way.

15

Ten Common Fallacies Relating to Investigations of Unattended Deaths

Robert R. Reinertsen
Western Illinois University

Unattended deaths are those that require at least some degree of inquiry by a governmental agency. These investigations, no matter how cursory, are necessary to resolve questions arising when no reliable witness can report the precise circumstances surrounding someone's death. After autopsies are performed by forensic pathologists, coroners or medical examiners attribute the majority of unattended deaths to natural causes. But the circumstances surrounding some unattended deaths suggest unnatural causes. If attendant circumstances raise questions of a possible homicide, suicide, or accident, further investigation is required.

Anyone investigating an unattended death must put initial effort into determining two things: the manner of death and the cause of death. The manner of death concerns the way in which the death occurred: by natural causes, accident, suicide, homicide, or undetermined factors. The cause of death, on the other hand, relates to the means used to produce the resulting death. For example, Jones may shout, "Goodbye, cruel world," jump off the Golden Gate Bridge, and die after hitting the water. Here the manner of death is suicide, and an autopsy may identify the cause of death as drowning, heart attack, or even a skull fracture.

Despite the apparent simplicity of this example, death investigation is extremely complex and is fraught with the potential for many terrible mistakes. Large urban police departments, such as that in New York City, maintain highly specialized homicide units staffed by well-trained, experienced professionals.[1] On the other hand, many medium-sized and most small-sized police departments are ill-equipped to handle investigations of unattended deaths. An inexperienced or untrained investigator in any setting is apt to rely on one of several common fallacies, which may result in homicides going undetected and murderers going free. A fallacy is "an idea or opinion founded on mistaken logic or perception; a false notion."[2] This investigator has identified ten such mistaken notions commonly associated with unattended death investigations.

Fallacy #1

Top-notch death investigators are made with hard work,
training, and experience; they are not born.

This fallacy makes the following assumptions:

1. The Puritan ethic of hard work, perseverance, and moral rectitude is the key to success in any worthwhile endeavor.

2. Complex homicide investigations constitute something less than an art form.

3. Uniformed patrol work prepares an individual for investigative work.

4. Human behavior is relatively predictable.

These assumptions, when coupled with average abilities, add up to mediocre investigation.

My view, admittedly and unashamedly, is elitist. It maintains that the really good investigators are born with the high intelligence, native intuition, aptitude for logical thinking, and necessary intangibles to become a truly top-notch investigator. The foremost, and absolutely essential, intangible is the innate and peculiar ability of great investigators to focus every particle of knowledge and past experience on the case at hand. This quality is analogous to the unexplained capacity of great baseball hitters to consistently hit a hard-pitched ball, one of the most difficult feats in sports. Anyone can become a reasonably good hitter with hard work, but the great ones are naturals. So it is with top-notch investigators.

How does an individual with the requisite abilities translate them into the accoutrements of a great homicide detective? The following must be acquired:

☐ A formal education with emphasis on forensic science, medical pathology, logic, abnormal psychology, and criminal law and evidence. (The ideally educated homicide investigator would have an undergraduate degree in philosophy and criminal justice, a law degree, and a medical degree in forensic pathology.)

☐ Interest in problem solving (from picture puzzles to critiques of logical syllogisms), popular crime literature, and motion pictures and selected television programs relating to crime.

☐ A strong sense of moral values.

Fallacy #2

Virtually all homicides are solved.

First, what is meant by "solved"? In police parlance a crime is solved, or cleared, "when at least one person is arrested, charged with the commission of the offense, and turned over to the court for prosecution."[3] According to the latest available FBI Uniform Crime Report (UCR) estimates, there were 20,613 reported murders and nonnegligent manslaughters in the United States in 1986. The clearance, or solution, rate was 70 percent. This means that fully 30 percent, or 6,184, of the known homicides went unsolved. If several thousand unreported and "hidden" homicides are figured in, the actual solution rate may fall below 60 percent.

Unreported and hidden homicides stem from several sources:

1. *Serial murders.* Serial murderers are homicidal psychopaths acting out violent sexual fantasies. Typically, a number of victims are killed over a period of time. There do not appear to be any discernible relationships between serial murderers and their victims, and there are no apparent motives for the killings. Often, victims of serial murderers are runaways, prostitutes, and other rootless unfortunates who are neither missed nor searched for. An unknown number of serial murder victims are buried in unknown graves across the United States; a conservative estimate of unreported serial murders is 500 to 800 yearly.

2. *Mercy killings.* Another source of unreported homicides is euthanasia, or mercy killing. Most such killings performed by medical personnel go undetected. Many others, committed by spouses and other close family members, are either undetected or officially ignored. Here again, no data exist on the number involved, but it could be as high as several thousand annually.

3. *Infanticides.* For reasons not fully explained, the criminal justice system of the United States collectively avoids treating infanticide—the murder of children—as real homicide. It appears, many times, that our criminal justice agencies have given parents (the vast majority of perpetrators) license to kill their children. Law enforcement agencies often accept whatever explanation homicidal parents give for their infants' deaths and let it go at that. Some hospitals, for example, routinely classify infant beating deaths as SIDS, even though a baby may be covered with bruises. I estimate two to three thousand infanticides each year.

4. *Mistakes in investigations.* This category includes all other unreported homicides—for example, homicides erroneously characterized as suicides, accidental deaths, or undetermined; cases where an apparent murder is not prosecuted because the victim's remains cannot be found; and homicides that are too complicated for some local departments to solve and merely remain open.

Fallacy #3

At the scene of every homicide a specific search pattern should be chosen and implemented.

A crime scene can be defined as the specific physical setting of a crime and its general environs. The purpose in searching a crime scene is to locate physical evidence. Criminal investigation texts typically prescribe several patterns for searching crime scenes: spiral, zone, grid, strip, and pie, or wheel. The frequent charge to would-be investigators is to first carefully choose one of the patterns and then proceed with the search, always adhering to the pattern of choice.

In my view, placing the emphasis on choosing the right search pattern detracts from the primary objective of a search, which is to locate physical evidence. Each and every crime scene—especially those involving homicides—is completely unique. Thus, rather than engaging in a futile exercise to choose a search pattern, the homicide crime scene investigator should focus attention on locating physical evidence in the most expeditious manner possible. In conducting a thorough crime scene search, an investigator should seek to provide answers to these three questions:

1. What has been removed from the crime scene?
2. What has been added to the crime scene?
3. What has been altered or contaminated at the crime scene?

Fallacy #4

Estimating the time of death is relatively easy and certain.

Representations by the popular media—mystery stories and novels, motion pictures, and television productions—help perpetuate this myth. Actions taken by investigators in compliance with this fallacy have resulted in some grievous errors. Put simply, estimating the time of death is one of the most imprecise areas of death investigation. According to one medical examiner, the only way to accurately estimate the time of death in a homicide case is to have the victim shot by a bullet that passes through his watch on the way to his heart.

Nonetheless, most textbooks dealing with criminal investigation devote at least a portion of a chapter to estimating time of death. The techniques listed here are typically presented as accurate means of estimating time of death:

☐ *Loss of body heat.* The texts state that the average loss of body heat after death in an environment of 70°F is 1.5 degrees per hour. Thus, obtaining the body temperature, either rectally or by cutting an incision in the abdomen and placing the thermometer in the liver, should lead to the precise time of death. However, this method has proved to be wildly inaccurate. Variables such as body type and general health of the victim cause this calculation to vary greatly.

☐ *Rigor mortis.* Rigor mortis is a stiffening of the body muscles caused by the gradual buildup of lactic acid in the muscle tissue. Supposedly the onset of rigor mortis comes within four hours of death, is fully formed within 24 hours, and is totally reversed within 48 hours. But factors such as atmospheric and surface temperature, humidity, and body fat percentage skew the estimates. This investigator has observed rigor mortis in victims known to have been dead for three days or more.

☐ *Post mortem lividity.* At death, blood stops circulating and settles in those portions of the body closest to the ground. Subsequent blood stains would be purple in color. All that can really be determined from lividity stains is whether a person has been moved after being dead approximately an hour or more.

☐ *Putrefaction.* A host of variables—including air temperature, moisture, general health, presence of insects, and individual body chemistry—make it impossible to give any realistic estimate relating to the rate of bodily decomposition.

Fallacy #5:

Homicides can easily be made to look like suicides.

In truth, victims rarely cooperate in their own murders, and making a homicide appear to be a convincing suicide would require the complete cooperation of the victim. Certainly, victim cooperation does occur in some mercy killings and in some sadomasochistic encounters that result in homicides. But by and large, these instances are rare. Devising a homicide to look like a suicide is actually the second most difficult trick in perpetrating homicides. (The most difficult task is rigging a suicide to look like a homicide.[4])

I believe that any reasonably competent investigator should be able to detect a homicide. However, investigators must adhere to the first principle of homicide investigation: assume that any unattended death is a homicide and investigate it accordingly. In other words, all possibilities of homicide should be eliminated before moving on.

Investigators should look for certain things in questionable homicide/suicide death scenes. In violent deaths these elements should be checked:

☐ precise location of weapon

☐ configuration of blood spatters

☐ trace elements of possible perpetrator on victim (check victim's fingernails)

☐ signs of struggle

☐ suicide note (found only 49 percent of the time)

☐ family problems

☐ recent behavior of deceased

In nonviolent deaths all of the preceding elements should be checked, plus these:

☐ precise cause of death

☐ medical history (look for terminal illness)

☐ drug use

Fallacy #6

There is little, if any, difference between a coroner and a medical examiner.

There are a number of differences between the systems of coroners and medical examiners and between their orientations. Coroners' offices are political bureaucracies with political orientations, whereas medical examiners' offices are medical bureaucracies with technical predispositions. Thus, the overriding difference is politics. The coroner system had its roots in medieval England and seems to be perpetuated in states that are less progressive politically. The medical examiner system, on the other hand, has appeared in states and large cities concerned with depoliticizing and professionalizing the medical aspects of death investigation.

Events following the death of Mary Jo Kopechne at Chappaquiddick in July 1969 illustrate how a coroner's office can be used politically. When Teddy Kennedy drove off the bridge at Chappaquiddick with Mary Jo Kopechne in the car, Kennedy swam free, but Kopechne did not and either drowned or suffocated. After leaving the scene of the accident, Kennedy waited several hours before reporting it. If Mary Jo died of suffocation, it would mean that she had remained alive in the submerged car for a period of time ranging from twenty minutes to three hours, or as long as the air pocket held out. Death by drowning would have taken only a few minutes. Consequently, it may have been very important to the Kennedy family that an autopsy not be done because of the risk of discovering that the death had been caused by suffocation. By choosing not to do an autopsy on Mary Jo, the coroner helped avoid the possibility of a ruined political career, not to mention serious criminal charges against Teddy Kennedy.

Here are some of the differences between the two systems:

☐ Coroners are elected; medical examiners are appointed.

☐ Medical examiners are required to be licensed physicians; coroners may be laypersons.

☐ Coroners are primarily politicians, with political agendas, whereas medical examiners are physicians, whose primary focus is on autopsies.

☐ Coroners tend to be better administrators than medical examiners are.

☐ Medical examiners are required to perform autopsies for all unattended deaths, but coroners can exercise varying degrees of discretion in determining whether an autopsy will be performed.

□ Coroners generally have more power to stimulate or impede the investigation of unattended deaths; medical examiners are limited to autopsies.

Fallacy #7

It is very difficult to elicit information from those who are close to suspects.

Prisons would be virtually empty if criminals and those associated with them could keep their collective mouths shut regarding their knowledge of illegal activities. People in criminal trouble—and their families, friends, and associates—are likely to talk about illegal activities for these reasons:

□ the basic human inability to keep a secret

□ feelings of guilt and the need for expiation

□ the need to brag and thus prop up fragile egos

□ the effect of alcohol in loosening tongues

□ the innate arrogance and carelessness of many criminals

□ the fact that familiarity breeds resentment among people

□ greed

If the assumption is correct that criminals and those close to them are eager to talk, what might keep them from doing it? The only deterrent seems to be fear of being identified as the source of the information. No one wants to be labeled a snitch. Investigators, then, must be able to convince potential informants that they will not be found out.

Fallacy #8

A corpse must be physically located in order to convict a person of murder or some other form of criminal homicide.

Although widely accepted, this belief is nonsense. If it were true, murderers would simply dispose of their victims' remains and then have no fear of prosecution.

According to the law, if it appears that a homicide has taken place but no corpse has been found, courts may rely on circumstantial evidence to determine that a homicide has taken place and that a particular individual committed the homicide. Thus, hiding or disposing of a victim's remains will do the murderer no good if circumstantial evidence leads to the inescapable conclusion that an individual was murdered and that the person in question committed the murder.

Fallacy #9

Homicide cases are most often solved by miraculous sleuthing.

The myth of the dedicated, doggedly determined, innovative homicide detective pervades the popular culture. In reality, very few homicides are solved by anything resembling detective work. Most solutions result from information from witnesses at the scene, confessions from perpetrators at or near the scene, and information from those closely associated with perpetrators. In fact, most of the solved homicides result from uniformed officers being advised of the identity of the perpetrator *at the crime scene*. And most crimes that are solved are solved within three hours of their occurrence; very few homicides are solved after that time. Thus, if there is no one at the scene to identify the perpetrator by name, then there is little likelihood that the homicide will be solved. So why bother to maintain homicide investigation units? The truth is that they are not cost-effective in all cases, and most police departments would be better advised to disband their homicide units in favor of putting more uniformed officers on the street.

Fallacy #10

Serial murderers have no motives.

Several factors explain why serial murderers in the United States are so difficult to apprehend:

- *Unlimited freedom.* U.S. citizens have obvious constitutional protections and have no restrictions on travel.

- *Complete mobility.* Relatively cheap gasoline, a good road system, and generally favorable economic and political conditions allow for vast numbers of people, including serial murderers, to range far and wide. In addition, the social mobility in U.S. society makes it quite easy for individuals to blend into virtually any setting.

- *Fragmented law enforcement.* Unlike most other Western countries, the United States does not have a centralized police force. There are well over 50,000 federal, state, and local police agencies in the country, each with a separate command structure and jurisdictional area. In addition, there is little cooperation in the form of information exchange or coordinated operations.

- *An open society.* It has been said that Americans are too open and trusting. This characteristic may be especially true as one moves west and south and away from large metropolitan areas.

- *Availability of potential victims.* There are many thousands of unaccounted-for persons traveling about in our society. These are people who remove themselves to unfamiliar surroundings, where they are not known or cared for. Teenage runaways, fugitives, bums, the homeless, prostitutes (both male and female), and adventurers of various descriptions fit this category. Collectively they constitute a pool of potential victims for serial murderers.

Nonetheless, lack of apparent motive is cited as the most important reason that serial murderers are so difficult to catch. In nonserial murders perpetrators and victims have some sort of connection—they are spouses, lovers, friends or enemies, relatives, or acquaintances. These connections provide various motives for murder. But since serial murders are most often an encounter of strangers, no motives seem to emerge.

Despite appearances, there *is* a discernible motive common to all serial murders. Serial murderers are psychopathic killers whose motive is to act out their violent sexual fantasies, either hetero- or homosexual. Thus, their obsession is their motive, but knowing that does not make it any easier to solve serial murders.

The ten fallacies discussed here are not the only ones that can complicate investigations of unattended deaths. However, dispelling these myths would constitute a significant step forward in this area of criminal investigation.

Notes

[1] See Carston Stroud, *Close Pursuit: A Week in the Life of an NYPD Homicide Cop* (New York: Bantam, 1987) for an account of NYPD homicide detectives in action.

[2] *The American Heritage Dictionary,* New College Edition, s.v. "fallacy."

[3] Federal Bureau of Investigation, *Crime in the United States* (Washington, DC: FBI, Crime Records Division, 1986), 154.

[4] A. Conan Doyle, "The Problem of Thor Bridge," in *The Complete Sherlock Holmes* (Garden City, NY: Doubleday, 1960), 1054.

16

The Investigative Challenge of Serial Murder

Steven A. Egger
Sangamon State University

Murder has traditionally been a crime for which police show a high clearance rate. However, part of the well-kept secret of this success is that a criminal homicide is a relatively easy crime to investigate and solve. Once the victim is identified, the investigator simply begins to reduce the number of associates, friends, and relatives who have a high probability of having committed the crime. Most murders are committed by a person(s) in one of these categories.

Furthermore, about 66 percent of murderers are in custody within twenty-four hours. If murders are not solved within forty-eight hours, the chance of solving the case and apprehending the killer drops markedly.[1] A study of Memphis murders from 1974 to 1978 found that all those involving relatives were solved within twenty-four hours; 84 percent were solved in a day if the persons were known to each other but were not relatives. For strangers the success rate dropped to 69 percent.[2]

A review of Uniform Crime Reports for the last twenty years reveals that murder and nonnegligent manslaughter have increased numerically by 300 percent, and the rate per 100,000 population has doubled during this period. However, the most dramatic change is that police clearance rates for murder have dropped from

An expanded revision of this chapter will be published in *Serial Murder: An Elusive Phenomenon,* by Steven A. Egger, forthcoming in 1990 by Praeger Publishers.

93 percent in 1962 to 70 percent in 1987. Currently, more than one-quarter of all murders are not solved by law enforcement. This drop is generally attributed to the dramatic increase in homicides among strangers. Wilbanks found an increase in such murders in Dade County, Florida, between 1917 and 1988;[3] and on the national level murders with unknown motives increased by 270 percent during a recent seven-year period. During that same period, murder increased approximately 12 percent. Thus, it appears that police effectiveness in apprehending murderers has been substantially reduced in part because of the dramatic rise in seemingly motiveless murders and those among strangers. Serial murders comprise most of the unsolved category.

Robert Keppel states that catching multiple murderers "is very, very difficult. Police departments aren't organized to catch serial killers. They're organized to catch burglars and robbers and to intervene in family fights." Pierce Brooks, an FBI consultant, states that serial murderers "are very mobile, they don't leave a great body of physical evidence, and they kill strangers." Levin and Fox add, "Some time may pass before law enforcement investigators realize that a series of seemingly unrelated homicides is actually the work of a single individual—by that time, he may be long gone." There is a greater suspicion today that many unexplained homicides are committed by serial murderers crossing city, county, and state lines. Terrence Green, former head of the police homicide division in Oakland, California, maintains, "Every police department in the United States has dealt with a serial murder, perhaps without realizing it."[4]

Technically, an unsolved murder is never closed. However, other murders occur, and resources must be allocated on a cost-effective basis. Greater solvability and currency of the event are given higher priority. Nonetheless, when unsolved murders are identified as part of a serial sequence, the police must respond.

The various ways in which law enforcement has responded to serial murder can be grouped into several categories: holding conferences with involved or potentially involved agencies; acting as a clearinghouse of information on serial crimes; forming a task force for the coordination of multiple-jurisdiction investigations; using an outside investigative consultant team; and using psychological profiling. All of these responses are, of course, after the fact and reactive in nature. A less reactive response, although certainly not preventive, is the development of a centralized point of analysis from which to identify patterns of serial murders as they emerge and to communicate such patterns to the appropriate agencies for necessary and combined action. In addition, there are other responses to serial murder that are used less frequently: specially developed computer software programs, geoforensic pattern analysis, and payment to an identified serial killer for necessary criminal evidence.

Before analyzing these various responses by law enforcement to serial murder, we must emphasize our major conclusion: very little of scholarly substance and empirical knowledge has been developed around the phenomenon of serial murder. And without an empirically validated knowledge base, law enforcement's response to serial murder is frequently unsuccessful and, even when successful, is more a product of chance than of planning.

Conferences

Law enforcement conferences are almost a tradition in police work. They are normally convened on an annual basis by professional associations to provide for socializing, sharing new techniques and technology, and updating various areas of specialization. Recently conferences have been convened to address specific problems facing multiple jurisdictions, and only very recently have such conferences attempted to deal with serial murder. Conferences dealing with serial murder have been of two types: those dealing with numerous unsolved murders and those responding to the ramifications of the identification and confessions of a serial murderer.

One such conference dealing with numerous unsolved murders was convened at the Texas Department of Public Safety Training Center in Austin, Texas, in October 1980. The discovery of an unidentified homicide victim found along Interstate 35 near Waco, Texas, and numerous other unsolved homicides occurring along this highway in a three-year period were the catalyst for the conference. Representatives from thirty-two cities, counties, and political jurisdictions in Texas attended this conference, and nineteen new leads to unsolved area crimes were developed as a result of the information shared among law enforcement officers. Other such conferences have been held in response to the Green River killings in the Seattle, Washington, area (1983); the Michigan murders in the Ann Arbor-Ypsilanti, Michigan, area (1968); and the Hillside Strangler case in the Los Angeles, California, area (1979).

Two examples of conferences convened in response to an identified serial murderer were those organized by the Monroe, Louisiana, Police Department in October 1983 and January 1984. In the wake of the arrest and subsequent confessions of serial murderer Henry Lee Lucas in Texas, more than 150 investigators from twenty-four different states met during those two conferences, compared notes on unsolved murders in their areas, and were briefed by the Texas rangers regarding Lucas's known travels and modus operandi. Similar conferences were held in 1984 in Wisconsin and Georgia, centering primarily on Henry Lee Lucas and unsolved murders in those states. Another example was the conference in December 1984, organized by Florida agencies after the arrest of Robert Joe Long, who was charged with eight counts of sexual battery, nine counts of kidnapping, one count of aggravated assault, seven counts of murder, and one count of first degree murder in the Tampa, Florida, area. Information was shared regarding Long and unsolved murders and rapes in Florida and Georgia that could be attributed to him.[5]

Information Clearinghouse

A response similar to the conference approach is the information clearinghouse. Again, such a response may occur because of the apprehension of a serial murderer or the existence of a number of unsolved murders involving multiple law enforcement jurisdictions. An example of the former on a national scale was the Lucas Homicide Task Force in the state of Texas. Authorized by the governor of Texas in

November 1983, the task force operated until April 1985, communicating with law enforcement agencies requesting information on Lucas, compiling and distributing information on Lucas to requesting agencies, coordinating interviews of Lucas that were conducted by law enforcement investigators from numerous states, conducting preliminary interviews of Lucas for other agencies that sent investigative information by mail, and providing for Lucas's security. During the task force's existence approximately 600 different law enforcement agencies interviewed Lucas; total interviews involved more than 1,000 different people from forty states and Canada. In addition, the task force cleared a total of 210 homicide cases, of which 189 were directly attributed to Lucas.[6]

Another example of an information clearinghouse can be found in Tennessee. In 1985, responding to eight unsolved homicides of unidentified females since October 1983, the Tennessee Bureau of Investigation began serving as an information clearinghouse for law enforcement agencies from five different states (Pennsylvania, Kentucky, Tennessee, Mississippi, and Arkansas) and the Federal Bureau of Investigation. The clearinghouse provided information to all jurisdictions and was the catalyst for a network among them.[7]

Task Forces

The formation of a task force is one of the most traditional methods of responding to a multiple-jurisdictional crime investigation. In the early summer of 1969 a task force comprised of five separate law enforcement agencies was established in Ann Arbor, Michigan, in response to six unsolved homicides of young females that had occurred in that county in the previous 2 1/2 years. When a seventh young female homicide victim was found, the governor of Michigan ordered the Michigan State Police, one of the five agencies, "to concentrate and coordinate the efforts of all state and local agencies."[8] John Norman Collins was arrested two days later for the murder of the seventh victim and was subsequently convicted.

Levin and Fox state that a task force is the usual law enforcement response to difficult investigations but that it "has never proven to be overly successful." The task force in the Hillside Strangler case, according to Levin and Fox, was too large and decentralized. They contend that the killings would never have been solved if Bianchi had not killed on his own in Washington: "Until his arrest in Washington . . . the Los Angeles Task Force had been stumped for a year and had been labeled a total failure."[9]

In July 1980 a task force formed to look into the problem of missing and murdered children in the Atlanta, Georgia, area. The original task force consisted of five police officers but grew a great deal larger and eventually resulted in the arrest and conviction of Wayne Williams for murdering two of twenty-eight homicide victims and suspected responsibility for the deaths of many of the other victims. Chet Dettlinger, former assistant to Atlanta's chief of police, is extremely critical of the Atlanta task force, particularly for their failure to include some homicide victims among those related to task force efforts and for their inadequate analysis of the geographic distribution of the homicides. Levin and Fox are also critical of the

Atlanta task force for its late formation and its failure to consider the geographic evidence in a broader context.[10]

In addition, Levin and Fox are critical of the Boston Strangler task force, which they say was poorly focused and used techniques ranging from traditional forensics to the use of psychics. "The capture of Albert DeSalvo actually resulted from his arrest by the Cambridge Police for a breaking and entering and an assault, rather than for one of the stranglings."[11]

Darrach and Norris contrast the Atlanta task force with the Green River task force set up to investigate the killings of more than thirty young women in the general vicinity of the Green River in the Seattle, Washington, area.

> Everything that went wrong in the Atlanta investigation has been going right in Seattle. The Green River Task Force, set up to investigate the killings, now includes 30 talented detectives and is clearly one of the best organized, least politicized and most effective units in the country. Protected by a strong sheriff, the group has shrewdly controlled the release of information to prevent hysteria and keep the killer guessing.[12]

However, as of November 1988 no arrests had been made by the Green River Task Force.

Past experience with multijurisdictional task forces has revealed the crucial need for a well-managed and coordinated response. To meet this need, specific guidelines were developed in the form of a manual—*Multi-Agency Investigation Team Manual* (MAIT). This manual resulted from the documentation and synthesis of a two-week conference of experienced serial murder investigators held in August 1986.[13] Even though the MAIT manual has been criticized for its traditional approach to organization and management and its cookbook approach to the problem, there are some particular points worthy of highlighting.

> The serial murderer often selects his victim from an urban area but disposes of the body in the privacy of a rural area, crossing jurisdictions in the process. Law enforcement agencies are generally accustomed to operating as self-contained units and often do not have the organizational structure, personnel or inclination for coordinating with other agencies. Historically, the Achilles' heel of most prolonged serial murder investigations has not been that of the investigative function per se, but the viability of the law enforcement agencies involved to
>
> ☐ manage the massive amounts of information received and generated
> ☐ effectively communicate internally or externally with other involved agencies.
>
> With most serial murder investigations, the amount of information and the rate of accumulation far exceeds human capabilities for management. Case coordination, review and analysis provides an opportunity to examine all investigative activities so that leads are not overlooked or links between them missed.[14]

Investigative Consultants

In October 1980 the police chief of Stamford, Connecticut, offered to loan Atlanta one of his skilled investigators with experience in a similar case to assist in the missing and murdered children investigation. As a result of the discussions that followed, the Police Executive Research Forum agreed to underwrite a cooperative effort to provide a team of qualified and experienced investigators to assist in the Atlanta case.[15] A group of five investigators was subsequently selected from police departments all across the country, with Pierce Brooks of Eugene, Oregon, selected as the team leader.

In November 1980 this team traveled to Atlanta and served as investigative consultants for two weeks.

> The responsibility of this investigative consultant team was . . . to come to Atlanta as consultants to the task force investigators and share with them any insights they might have by virtue of their experience in working complex cases in their respective jurisdictions. To that end, they were expected to review the case files and interact with the investigators responsible for the investigation involving the missing and murdered children.[16]

Even though the use of this team did not directly result in a successful resolution to the Atlanta homicides,

> The November 1980 venture of the Investigative Consultant Team (ICT) in Atlanta is believed to be the first time police investigators, all from separate departments, were invited to participate as consultants in a major criminal investigation in a city other than their own.[17]

This participation of officers from other agencies was seen by many as a bold and creative step taken by the Atlanta Police Department.

Psychological Profiling

Another response to serial murder has been the use of psychological profiling in an attempt to provide investigators with more information on a yet-unidentified serial murderer. Hazelwood and Douglas define a psychological profile as one "based on characteristic patterns or factors of uniqueness that distinguish certain individuals from the general population."[18] Reiser states,

> The arcane art of psychological profiling of suspects in bizarre and multiple murder cases is actually a variant of psycho-diagnostic assessment and psycho-biography. It involves an amalgam of case evidence, statistical probabilities based on similar cases, available suspect and victim psychodynamics, knowledge of unconscious processes, and interpretation of detectable symbolic communications. The factual materials and speculative possibilities are combined using an inferential-deductive process.[19]

The actual origins of criminal profiling are obscure. However, it is known that during World War II, the Office of Strategic Services (OSS) employed a psychiatrist, William Langer, to profile Adolf Hitler. The material assembled by Langer included a psychological description of Hitler's personality, a diagnosis of his condition, and a predictive statement suggesting how Hitler would react to defeat. Such cases as the Boston Strangler and the Mad Bomber of New York City were also profiled in a similar manner by Dr. James A. Brussels.[20]

The Federal Bureau of Investigation became involved in psychological profiling in 1970, when Agent Howard Teten began developing profiles. Teten was teaching an applied criminology course at the FBI Academy at that time, and students from various police departments brought their criminal cases to him.[21] The FBI began formally developing psychological profiles shortly thereafter, believing "that in most crime scenes, the killer leaves his signature there. If you're sensitized to what these things are, you can construct a profile of the killer."[22]

Kessler, Burgess, Douglas, and Depue describe psychological profiling as "the process of identifying the gross psychological characteristics of an individual based upon an analysis of the crimes he or she committed and providing a general description of the person, utilizing those traits" (p. 3). Kessler et al. state that the process normally involves five steps:

1. a comprehensive study of the nature of the criminal act and the types of persons who have committed this offense

2. a thorough inspection of the specific crime scene involved in the case

3. an in-depth examination of the background and activities of the victim(s) and any known suspects

4. a formulation of the probable motivating factors of all parties involved

5. the development of a description of the perpetrator based on the overt characteristics associated with his or her probable psychological makeup.[23]

According to FBI Agent Robert K. Kessler,

All people have personality traits that can be more or less identified. But an abnormal person becomes ritualized even more so and there's a pattern in his behavior. Often times, the behavior and the personality are reflected in the crime scene of that individual. . . by studying the crime scene from the psychological standpoint, rather than from the technical, evidence-gathering standpoint, you could recreate the personality of the individual who committed the crime. If the crime scene is abnormal, it would indicate their personality is abnormal.[24]

Roy Hazelwood, another member of the FBI's profiling team, states, "We don't get hung up on why the killer does the things he does. What we're interested in is that he does it, and that he does it in a way that leads us to him."[25] Geberth discusses the utility of psychological profiling.

Psychological profiling is usually productive in crimes where an unknown subject has demonstrated some form of psychopathology in his crime. For example,

☐ sadistic torture in sexual assaults
☐ evisceration
☐ postmortem slashing and cutting
☐ motiveless fire setting
☐ lust and mutilation murders

☐ ritualistic crimes

☐ rapes

Practically speaking, in any crime where available evidence indicates a mental, emotional, or personality aberration by an unknown perpetrator, the psychological profile can be instrumental in providing the investigator with information which narrows down the leads. It is the behavior of the perpetrator as evidenced in the crime scene and not the offense per se that determines the degree of suitability of case profiling.[26]

The results or evaluations of psychological profiling found in the literature have not been conclusive. Godwin is very critical of profiling, characterizing it as dull, tedious, and of little use to the police.

> They play a blindman's bluff, groping in all directions in the hope of touching a sleeve. Occasionally they do, but not firmly enough to seize it, for the behaviorists producing [profiles] must necessarily deal in generalities and types. But policemen can't arrest a type. They require hard data: names, faces, fingerprints, locations, times, dates. None of which the psychiatrists can offer.[27]

Dr. John Liebert, a Bellevue, Washington, psychiatrist and consultant to Seattle's Green River Task Force, is distrustful of the psychological profiles put together by police agencies and the FBI and urges law enforcement personnel involved in a serial murder investigation to utilize the services of a psychiatric consultant. Liebert warns against phenomenological generalizations about a murderer: "Superficial behavioral scientific profiling that rigidly reduces serial murder to a few observable parameters can lead an investigation astray."[28]

Levin and Fox characterize psychological profiles as vague and general and thus basically useless in identifying a killer.

> The FBI's own recent evaluation of its profiling efforts, in our minds, underscores the limitations of this approach. A survey of 192 users of these profiles indicated, first, that less than half the crimes for which the profiles had been solicited were eventually solved. Further, in only 17 percent of these 88 solved cases did the profile help directly to identify the subject.[29]

Nonetheless, Levin and Fox also point out that

> profiles are not expected, at least in most instances, to solve a case, but simply to provide an additional set of clues in cases found by local police to be unsolvable. Indeed in over three-fourths of the solved cases, the profile did at least help focus the investigation.[30]

The FBI itself urges caution in perceiving profiling as an automatic solution to a difficult case. Hazelwood, Kessler, Depue, and Douglas state,

> Profiles have led directly to the solution of a case, but this is the exception rather than the rule, and to expect this will lead to failure in most cases. Rather, a profile will provide assistance to the investigator by focusing the investigation towards suspects possessing the characteristics described.[31]

Geberth also notes that the psychological profile "can be a valuable tool in identifying and pinpointing suspects; however, it must be noted that the profile has its limitations. It should be utilized in conjunction with the sound investigative techniques ordinarily employed at the scene of a homicide."[32]

Most homicide investigators appear to be convinced of the potential value of the psychological profile. The Behavioral Science Unit of the FBI is currently attempting an artificial intelligence software program to enhance this investigative tool's effectiveness. Also, private vendors have recently developed software programs for personal computers with an application for psychological profiling, referred to as computer-oriented profiling.

Centralized Investigative Network

VICAP

Control—meaning to identify, locate, and apprehend—is currently law enforcement's only viable strategy in responding to the phenomenon of serial murder. Identification of a serial pattern or modus operandi usually requires information from different jurisdictional sources. Once that information is collated at the central point and the probability of serial events is identified, the collator can redistribute the combined information to the original sources. Those discrete investigative agencies can then coordinate their investigative action. The collator's role is to ensure that valuable information is not missed.[33]

Such an investigative network, or system, is currently operational on both the national and the state level in the United States and on a national level in Great Britain and, to some extent, in Canada. The U.S. network is referred to as the Violent Criminal Apprehension Program (VICAP) and is located at the FBI National Academy in Quantico, Virginia. The Behavioral Science Unit at the academy is the central site for this system and functions as the collator.[34]

The VICAP concept was first operationalized during a multijurisdictional investigation of the killing of young children in Oakland County, Michigan, in 1976 and 1977.[35] A systematic approach coordinated the collection and distribution of case information to a team of investigators from different law enforcement jurisdictions in the county. Further development of the concept came in the form of a technical assistance task plan submitted to the Integrated Criminal Apprehension Program (ICAP) in September 1981. That plan included this description:

> VI-CAP [the acronym carried a hyphen until 1984], a product of ICAP, is a process designed to integrate and analyze, on a nationwide basis, all aspects of the investigation of a series of similar-pattern deaths by violence, regardless of the location or number of police agencies involved.[36]

The plan also provided this statement of the problem:

> Research of almost every multiple-murder investigation indicates an absolute need for a centralized information center and crime analysis function as a nationwide all-agency resource .... there is no question that on a number of occasions multiple killers could

have been apprehended much sooner if the several agencies involved in the investigation could have pooled and correlated their information.[37]

Between November 1981 and May 1982 four VI-CAP planning sessions were held, but funds for further planning efforts were then suspended because of the demise of the Law Enforcement Assistance Administration. Approximately one year later Sam Houston State University received a grant that included planning, developing, and implementing a National Center for the Analysis of Violent Crime (NCAVC), which would incorporate the VI-CAP system. A series of workshop meetings followed to develop and revise various reporting forms and conceptualize the model for the center. Then, in March 1984 the FBI received approximately $3.3 million to support the organizational development of NCAVC for two years.

VICAP currently operates as a major component of NCAVC, funded as a part of the regular FBI budget. As intended, the program is a centralized data information center and crime analysis system to collect, collate, and analyze all aspects of the investigation of similar-pattern, multiple murders on a nationwide basis, regardless of the location or number of police agencies involved. According to Brooks et al., VICAP provides "the information necessary to initiate a coordinated multi-agency investigation."[38] Cases that meet the VICAP criteria are these:

☐ solved or unsolved homicides or attempted homicides, especially those that involve an abduction; are apparently random, motiveless, or sexually oriented; or are known or suspected to be part of a series

☐ missing persons, with circumstances indicating a strong possibility of foul play and a still-missing victim

☐ unidentified dead bodies for which the manner of death is known or suspected to be homicide[39]

Levin and Fox argue that the value of VICAP is predicated in part on the presumption that serial murderers roam the country: "Traveling serial killers like Bundy, Lucas and Wilder are in the minority to those like Williams, Gacy, Corll, Buono, and Berkowitz who 'stay at home' and at their jobs, killing on a part-time basis." However, that conclusion is based on a data set of forty-two offenders involved in thirty-three acts of multiple murder, only ten of which were committed serially.[40]

The success of VICAP will not be known for some time. It is dependent on a number of factors, not the least of which is local law enforcement cooperation in completing a fifteen-page form for each unsolved case and transmitting it to the FBI. The concept, however, appears to be moving in the right direction of establishing a data base from which to identify serial murders. Darrach and Norris note that the United States has had a national system for reporting and tracing stolen cars for more than twenty years but that no national computerized clearinghouse exists for reporting unsolved homicides.[41] When VICAP develops the appropriate data base, the hope is that the identification of patterns will stimulate the necessary interagency communication and sharing of information that is currently almost nonexistent.

HALT

By the mid-1980s a number of states had initiated efforts to develop statewide analysis capabilities similar to those of VICAP. The first statewide system to become fully operational was the Homicide Assessment and Lead Tracking System (HALT), which began in 1986 in New York. To date, HALT is far from realizing its full potential but has become a model for other states to follow in terms of design, function, and cooperative relationship with VICAP. The HALT program was designed to provide a systematic and timely investigative tool for law enforcement agencies across the state. Through computer analysis of case incident information supplied by police agencies, HALT is able to determine when similar crime patterns exist in two or more jurisdictions. When such patterns are identified, the appropriate local agencies are notified.

HALT has been developed to be compatible with VICAP but is not simply a conduit to that federal program. The HALT system is value-added, providing communication linkages within the state, investigative support services, and a source center to refer law enforcement agencies to specific services or to provide the appropriate applied research information. HALT is considered a valuable resource in addressing the problem of violent serial crime in New York.

INTERPOL

Even though little information is currently available on the extent to which serial murder is an international phenomenon, one special international network should not be excluded from this discussion. INTERPOL, the International Criminal Police Organization, is an international networking and communication system responding to the transnational character of serial crime. INTERPOL is primarily a criminal information exchange service that provides its members with studies and reports on individuals and groups involved in crime on an international scale. "The purpose of INTERPOL is to facilitate, coordinate, and encourage international police cooperation as a means for embattling crime."[42]

INTERPOL is becoming an increasingly important tool for criminal investigation in the United States because it satisfies investigative leads that go beyond the borders of this country. Currently, each of the fifty states is setting up a point of contact within its own police system for all requests involving international matters. Although INTERPOL was not specifically designed to respond to serial murder, the in-place system of this organization is uniquely qualified to assist the investigation of a serial murder with transnational characteristics. Illinois was the first to establish a state liaison, and as the other states follow suit, INTERPOL will become better known to the law enforcement community as a tool for international information and assistance.

Other Responses to Serial Murder

In addition to the computer software applications referred to earlier, there is other software being developed to assist law enforcement agencies in responding to serial murder. One such program is the Dr. Watson Care Management System, which operates on a personal computer and was recently implemented by the regional police force in Brampton, Ontario. This system, similar in some ways to the HALT system, was implemented in early 1988 and has been utilized in several lengthy homicide investigations. Thus far, the system has been given very positive evaluations.[43]

In addition, a number of agencies investigating serial murders have attempted to conduct geographical analysis for pattern identification. However, only one forensic geographer has specifically researched this area and developed an analysis methodology. The late Milton B. Newton was in the process of developing a geoforensic analysis of localized serial murder when he was killed in an automobile accident in Mexico in 1988. Dr. Newton had presented a preliminary analysis of his research in October 1985. His latest and final research used an ethnographic method in post hoc analysis to locate geographically the site where many murders had actually taken place.[44] Newton's techniques could easily be used in an ongoing serial murder investigation, and this author hopes that other forensic geographers will continue Newton's research.

One final approach to serial murder took place in January 1982, when Clifford Robert Olson pleaded guilty in a Vancouver, British Columbia, courtroom to the rape and murder of eleven young boys and girls. Olson's pleas were entered in exchange for a promise by Canadian authorities to establish a $90,000 trust fund for Olson's wife and son. The story of this controversial arrangement received a great deal of coverage in Canada and the United States and prompted intense negative reaction from the public.[45] The outcry may prevent the recurrence of such an unusual event, but it is certainly worthy of note.

All of the law enforcement responses discussed here share a common focus: to reduce "linkage blindness" in a serial murder investigation and thus to increase multijurisdictional communication and networking. *Linkage blindness* is defined by the author as the absence of shared or coordinated investigative information and the lack of adequate networking among law enforcement agencies. The success of future serial murder investigations will be determined by the extent to which such shortsightedness or cross-jurisdictional myopia is reduced.[46]

Notes

[1] B.L. Danto, J. Bruhns, and H. Kutcher, eds., *The Human Side of Homicide* (New York: Columbia University Press, 1982), 7.

[2] R. Atkinson, "Killing Puzzle," *Washington Post,* 20 Feb. 1984, sec. A., p. 14.

[3] W. Wilbanks, *Murder in Miami* (Lanham, MD: University Press of America, 1984).

[4] R. Lindsey, "Officials Cite a Rise in Serial Killers Who Roam U.S. for Victims," *New York Times,* 21 Jan. 1984, 1; S.B. Garland, "Serial Killings Demand New Ways to Analyze Unsolved Homicides," *Houston Post,* 12 Aug. 1984, 1; J. Levin and J.A. Fox, *Mass Murder* (New York: Plenum, 1985), 232; Garland, "Serial Killings," 1.

[5] For a discussion of regional conferences dealing with unsolved murders, see T. Gest, "On the Trail of America's 'Serial Killers,' " *U.S. News & World Report,* 30 Apr. 1984, 53; R. Lindsey, "Officials Cite a Rise"; Regional Organized Crime Information Center, *ROCIC Bulletin,* Jan. 1985, 13.

[6] B. Prince, letter to author, 21 May 1985.

[7] "Red Haired Victims Found Along Highways," *Tennessean,* 25 Apr. 1984, 1.

[8] "State Police to Take Charge of Co-ed Murder Investigation," *Detroit News,* 30 July 1969, 1.

[9] J. Levin and J.A. Fox, *Mass Murder,* 168–69.

[10] C. Dettlinger and J. Prugh, *The List* (Atlanta: Philmay Enterprises, 1983), 68; J. Levin and J.A. Fox, *Mass Murder.*

[11] J. Levin and J.A. Fox, *Mass Murder,* 171.

[12] B. Darrach and J. Norris, "An American Tragedy," *Life,* July 1984, 64.

[13] P.R. Brooks et al., *Multi-Agency Investigation Team Manual* (Washington, DC: U.S. Department of Justice, 1988).

[14] Ibid., 1, 7, 23, 27, 49.

[15] P.R. Brooks, *The Investigation Consultant Team: A New Approach for Law Enforcement Cooperation* (Washington, DC: Police Executive Research Forum, 1982).

[16] Ibid., iii.

[17] Ibid., 6.

[18] R.R. Hazelwood and J.E. Douglas, "The Lust Murderer," *FBI Law Enforcement Bulletin,* Apr. 1980, 5.

[19] M. Reiser, "Crime-Specific Psychological Consultation," *The Police Chief,* Mar. 1982, 53.

[20] For a discussion of the origins of criminal profiling, see R.L. Ault and J.T. Reece, "A Psychological Assessment of Crime: Profiling," *FBI Law Enforcement Bulletin,* Mar. 1980, 23; A.J. Pinnizzotto, "Forensic Psychology: Criminal Personality Profiling," *Journal of Police Science and Administration* 12, no. 1 (1984): 32; V.J. Geberth, *Practical Homicide Investigation* (New York: Elsevier, 1983), 399.

[21] B. Porter, "Mind Hunters: Tracking Down Killers with the FBI's Psychological Profiling Team," *Psychology Today,* Apr. 1983, 55–60.

[22] R. Kessler, "Crime Profiles: FBI Behavioral Science Unit Paints Psychological Portraits of Killers," *Washington Post,* 20 Feb. 1984, sec. A, p. 16.

[23] R.K. Kessler et al., "Criminal Professional Research in Homicide," in *Rape and Sexual Assault: A Resource Handbook,* ed. A.W. Burgess (New York: Garland, 1985), 3; R.K. Kessler et al., "Criminal Profiling Research on Homicide" (Unpublished research report, 1982), 3.

[24] "FBI Develops Profile to Change Face of Sex Probes," *Law Enforcement News,* 22 Dec. 1980, 7.

[25] B. Porter, "Mind Hunters," 56.

[26] V.J. Geberth, *Practical Homicide Investigation,* 400–401.

[27] J. Godwin, *Murder USA: The Ways We Kill Each Other* (New York: Ballantine, 1978), 276.

[28] K. McCarthy, "Their Deadly Bent May Be Set in Cradle," *Los Angeles Times,* 7 July 1984; J.A. Liebert, "Contributions of Psychiatric Consultation in the Investigation of Serial Murder," *International Journal of Offender Therapy and Comparative Criminology* 29 (Dec. 1985): 199.

[29] J. Levin and J.A. Fox, *Mass Murder,* 176.

[30] Ibid.

[31] R.R. Hazelwood et al., "Criminal Personality Profiling: An Overview," in *Practical Aspects of Rape Investigation: A Multidisciplinary Approach,* ed. R.R. Hazelwood and A. W. Burgess (New York: Elsevier, 1987), 147.

[32] V.J. Geberth, *Practical Homicide Investigation,* 399.

[33] M.A.P. Wilmer, *Crime and Information Theory,* 32.

[34] Federal Bureau of Investigation, *Violent Criminal Apprehension Program: Conceptual Model* (Unpublished working document, July 1983), 1–4.

[35] J. Levin and J.A. Fox, *Mass Murder*; T. McIntyre, *Wolf in Sheep's Clothing: The Search for a Child Killer* (Detroit: Wayne State University Press, 1988).

[36] P.R. Brooks et al., *Multi-Agency Investigation,* 1.

[37] Ibid., 2.

[38] P.R. Brooks et al., *Multi-Agency Investigation,* 41.

[39] J.B. Howlett, K.A. Hanfland, and R.K. Kessler, "The Violent Criminal Apprehension Program VICAP: A Progress Report," *FBI Law Enforcement Bulletin* 55, no. 12 (1986): 15–16.

[40] J. Levin and J.A. Fox, *Mass Murder,* 4, 183.

[41] B. Darrach and J. Norris, "An American Tragedy."

[42] Interpol General Secretariat, "The I.C.P.O.—Interpol," *International Review of Criminal Policy* 34 (1978): 94.

[43] M.S. Trussler, letter to author, 27 Jan. 1989; "Police Track Serial Killer with Commercial DBMS," *Government Computer News,* 5 Dec. 1986, 78.

[44] M.B. Newton and B.C. Newton, "Geoforensic Analysis of Localized Serial Crime" (Paper presented at the annual meeting of the southwest division of the Association of American Geographers, Denton, Texas, 18 Oct. 1985); M.B. Newton and E.A. Swope, "Geoforensic Analysis of Localized Serial Murder: The Hillside Stranglers Located" (Unpublished manuscript).

[45] *Criminal Justice Ethics* (Summer/Fall 1983): 47–55.

[46] S.A. Egger, "A Working Definition of Serial Murder and the Reduction of Linkage Blindness," *Journal of Police Science and Administration* 12, no. 3 (1984): 348–57; idem, "Serial Murder and the Law Enforcement Response" (Unpublished Ph.D. diss., College of Criminal Justice, Sam Houston State University, 1985).

CASE STUDY
Genetic Fingerprinting:
The Narborough Murders

James N. Gilbert
Kearney State College

The November 1983 discovery of a murdered fifteen-year-old girl in the English village of Narborough ultimately had an enormous impact on international criminal investigation. Before the four-year murder inquiry was completed, a scientific discovery was applied that not only solved a double criminal homicide but completely revolutionized forensic identification. That great breakthrough in crime detection was the mapping of genetic DNA fragments, so-called genetic fingerprinting, and it had the same sensational impact on criminal investigation that the original discovery of fingerprints had.

At first the murder of Lynda Mann was barely noticed outside the three-village area known as Leicestershire, but it set into motion one of the largest homicide investigations in English history. A squad of more than 150 detectives was formed shortly after the killing and exhaustively investigated every possible lead and suspect. So thorough was the inquiry that every male between the ages of thirteen and thirty-four living in the murder area was noted and in many cases questioned. Nonetheless, the police could not locate the killer.

Then, in July 1986 fifteen-year-old Dawn Ashworth, also of the Leicestershire community complex, was found brutally raped and strangled. The modus operandi indicated the same killer and alerted the authorities to the presence of a serial murderer. This time more than two hundred criminal investigators were called out from across the country to apprehend a killer who had managed to terrorize a sizable portion of England. All leads again proved to be useless until one suspect was finally developed. A seventeen-year-old hospital kitchen porter was linked to the murder through circumstantial evidence and was promptly arrested. The suspect quickly confessed, giving a detailed and convincing statement of the second murder but adamantly refusing knowledge of the first, despite the firm conviction of the police that both victims had been murdered by the same perpetrator. Fortunately, the resolution of that impasse was to be found only a short distance away at Leicester University.

Dr. Alec Jeffreys, a university scientist who had been working in the field of genetic research since the early 1980s, had recently discovered a process of human identification based on the DNA molecule. In everyone's DNA chain there are breaks, often referred to as stutters, which appear in a repetitive pattern throughout the DNA molecule. Dr. Jeffreys found that he could isolate portions of a molecule containing the stutters and could then produce an X-ray-like picture of the DNA fragment. The resulting film showed an image much like that of a bar code found on grocery items. A DNA bar code is unique to every individual except identical twins and is thus considered a genetic fingerprint. According to mathematicians, the probability of two unrelated individuals having the same DNA fingerprint is one in one trillion.

Whether the suspect's father or the British police first initiated contact with Dr. Jeffreys is still disputed, but the scientist was already known for his work in a paternity lawsuit in which his DNA technique established the identity of the father. In the Narborough murders Jeffreys first analyzed a semen sample from the body of Lynda Mann and then analyzed a similar sample from the Dawn Ashworth crime scene. The technique yielded a perfectly clear bar code image that was identical for both murders. Then, from a blood sample of the arrested suspect, Jeffreys obtained a DNA fingerprint for comparison purposes. Not only did the kitchen porter's DNA fingerprint not match that of the murder he denied, but it also failed to match that of the murder to which he confessed. The suspect was promptly released.

Certain of only one fact—that the same person had killed both teenagers—investigators decided to single out the perpetrator through genetic fingerprinting. Accordingly, in January 1987 all male residents seventeen to thirty-four years of age who lived in the three villages were asked to submit blood samples. More than 4,500 samples were examined before the police finally, in September 1987, arrested a local baker, Colin Pitchfork, and charged him with the murders. Pitchfork had had a long history of indecent exposure and sexual assault, and informant information had alerted the police to the fact that Pitchfork had cheated on his blood examination by persuading a co-worker to submit a blood sample for him. When the suspect's blood was legitimately tested, an identical match appeared for the DNA fingerprints found at both murder scenes. Pitchfork was subsequently convicted of both murders, based solely on his DNA fingerprint and the resulting confession it produced.

Thus, the Narborough murder investigations ushered in a new, effective, means of criminal identification that has already solved hundreds of felony cases that might otherwise have gone unsolved. Of course, criminal identification using biochemical examination is not new. Such techniques began with the discovery of blood typing in 1900 and progressed to the more recent analysis of specific body enzymes and proteins. However, the genetic fingerprint has made earlier identification procedures appear elementary and crude by comparison. Whereas former methods gave a one-in-one-thousand chance of a matching error, the DNA method gives a virtually unassailable one-in-four-trillion.

It should be noted that DNA fingerprints can be obtained only from certain types of cells that are present in specific physiological matter. Examples of such sources include whole blood, semen, hair roots, skin samples, tissues/organs, bone marrow, and dental pulp. DNA material will probably not be found in human material such as saliva, urine, feces, hair without roots, and dead skin.

Even though DNA fingerprinting is forever linked to criminal investigations, its utility is not limited to that area. The technique will certainly be used frequently in kinship civil trials in which child-support and immigration disputes are being contested. In addition, a DNA fingerprint can provide a means of identifying human remains. Yet it is the criminal identification application that will have the greatest impact on society. Many violent crimes in which blood is shed or other human trace evidence is left at the scene will now be solved. And a suspect's innocence may now be dramatically demonstrated. Thus, even though the murder of two teenagers can never be considered positive, it prompted a fortunate merger of investigative need and scientific technology that may help to deter such horrible crimes in the future.

Sources: Joseph Wambaugh, *The Blooding* (New York: William Morrow, 1989); Anastasia Toufexis, "Convicted by Their Genes," *Time,* 31 Oct. 1988, 74; "Forensic Questions & Answers, DNA Fingerprinting," promotional brochure (Germantown, MD: Cellmark Diagnostics, 1988).

17
Preparing for Court

Sidney C. Snellenburg
Virginia Polytechnic Institute & State University

P reparation for court should begin when a case is assigned to an investigator; in other words, each case should be treated as if it will be prosecuted in court. Careful and effective procedures help prevent a case from being dismissed and put the investigator in a much stronger position to influence how the case is handled.

Case Management

The vast majority of crimes are not reported to police departments, yet the volume of cases reported in most jurisdictions far exceeds the resources available to law enforcement agencies. Samuel Walker argues that "crime in America appears to have stabilized at a permanently high level."[1] Obviously then, not every case can be investigated. A 1975 study by the Rand Corporation concluded that "serious crimes are invariably investigated, [but] many reported felonies receive no more than superficial attention from the investigators. Most minor crimes are not investigated."[2] Different departments approach this problem in different ways.

An integral part of case management is attention to field note taking and the formal reports of investigators. Unlike the world of TV cop shows, documentation is critically important. Even though unglamorous and time-consuming, field notes and subsequent case reports form the foundation of any criminal charge. An investigator at a crime scene can easily assume that the lack of time justifies only a cursory attempt to document facts, statements, and so on. However, in criminal cases the court allows the defense "to review materials used by the officer during testimony."[3]

Illegible, inadequate, and/or inaccurate notes and reports can result in case dismissal for lack of a proper factual foundation.

It is important to understand the significance of having a case investigated. Because no one can be absolutely certain which case will be prosecuted or which case will go to trial, every case should be handled in the same way, according to established policies and procedures. It is easy to become frustrated with the prosecutor's office and/or the court; but if that frustration results in poor documentation, it creates a vicious cycle. Sloppy documentation leads to cases being dismissed or plea-bargained, which further frustrates investigators. This cycle can be broken, but investigators must deal with the reality of the criminal justice system.

Developing a Relationship with the Prosecutor

In most jurisdictions the prosecutor is by far the most important actor in the criminal justice system—that is, the most important in terms of power. Cox and Wade provide important insight in this regard:

> The prosecutor is first and foremost a political figure. In most cases, he runs for election with the support of one of the major political parties. As [George F.] Cole points out, prosecutors are "political actors of consequence" because they are generally elected with party support, they have patronage jobs at their disposal, and they exercise considerable discretion. Prosecutors are tied both to the internal politics of the criminal justice network and to local, state, or national organizations. Since the discretionary powers of the prosecutor are considerable, he or she may be persuaded to take political advantage of the criminal justice position. So, charges may be dropped to avoid the possibility of losing difficult cases (and, thereby, political support), disclosures of wrongdoing by political opponents may be made at opportune moments, and decisions about the types of crime to be prosecuted may be made for strictly political reasons.[4]

What are the implications of this reality for investigators? Investigators must accommodate local prosecutors. In other words, investigators must recognize that prosecutors have their own agendas, their own personal approaches to the use of discretion. David Neubauer identifies three major components of a prosecutor's discretion: (1) legal judgment, which may be seen in a determination that there is insufficient evidence to prosecute a case; (2) policy priorities, which may lead to aggressive prosecution of only certain types of cases—for example, violent crimes; and (3) personal philosophies, which may result in areas of emphasis, such as child molestation.[5]

Typically, there are also significant differences in the actual operation of prosecutors' offices. In a densely populated urban area, a prosecutor's staff will not only be significantly larger than that found in a rural jurisdiction, but is also likely to be more highly specialized. Howard Abadinsky refers to the approach in urban areas as horizontal prosecution and that in less populous jurisdictions as vertical prosecution.[6] The effect of this distinction is that investigators in more populous jurisdictions may need to develop a rapport with numerous deputy prosecutors.

Why should such importance be attached to the relationship between investigators and prosecutors? First, in most instances a prosecutor simply doesn't have time to do an in-depth analysis of the strengths and weaknesses of every case. As a matter of fact, in large metropolitan jurisdictions, it is not unusual for the prosecuting attorney to first see all but the most serious felony cases only minutes before the defendant appears before a judge for disposition.

Furthermore, deputy prosecutors tend not to have much experience. They tend to work first in traffic court and then advance to prosecuting misdemeanors and/or less serious felonies. Generally, only the most talented deputy prosecutors are involved with serious felony cases. The length of time that a deputy prosecutor remains in office varies, of course, but most tend to leave their positions as soon as they have gained sufficient exposure to be attractive to a private law firm. It should also be noted, however, that the caseloads of most deputy prosecutors are excessively high, and their compensation tends to be low in comparison to other areas of law. Even in less populated jurisdictions the prosecutor may be only part-time, frequently maintaining a civil practice full-time on the side.

How does all of this relate to the need for investigators to develop a good working relationship with prosecutors? In all facets of life, we tend not to be overly concerned with people that we don't know. Prosecutors also tend to be cynical (often with good reason) when it comes to the quality of an investigation. If a prosecutor learns over time that a particular investigator presents consistently high-quality cases, that prosecutor will tend to be more receptive to an investigator's input concerning the most appropriate disposition of a case.

Probable Cause Hearings

Investigators are more often involved with probable cause hearings than with actual trials. Probable cause hearings may be conducted in one of two ways, depending on the jurisdiction. An investigator may be required to testify under oath before a judge (which is almost always the case when a search warrant is being requested), or a judge may simply find that probable cause does or does not exist based on a written and signed probable cause affidavit. Among the varied definitions of probable cause, this is perhaps the best:

> *Probable cause* is more than bare suspicion; it exists when the facts and circumstances within the officers' knowledge and of which they have reasonably trustworthy information are sufficient in themselves to a person of reasonable caution in the belief that an offense has been or is being committed. In searches and seizures (as contrasted with arrests), the issue of probable cause focuses on whether the property to be seized is connected with criminal activity and whether it can be found in the place to be searched.[7]

In almost every jurisdiction the probable cause affidavit is a standardized form. All the investigator has to do is fill in the blanks, providing the details sufficient for a judge to believe that a particular person committed a particular crime (for an arrest warrant) or that a particular thing will be found in a particular place (for a search warrant). Proof beyond a reasonable doubt is not required for a warrant.

It would seem appropriate here to emphasize a fundamental point related to search or seizure. "The general rule is that a search or seizure is valid under the Fourth Amendment only if made with a warrant. Searches without warrant may be valid, but they are the exception rather than the rule."[8] The good faith exception to the exclusionary rule (stating that evidence illegally obtained cannot be used in court) is quite specific in its application. First, in *Leon,* which established the exception, the officers involved had sought and received a search warrant, so it was not a warrantless search.[9] The district court concluded that the affidavit on which the search warrant was issued was "insufficient to establish probable cause,"[10] but the government's argument for a good-faith exception to the exclusionary rule was subsequently adopted. Justice White, writing for the majority, reemphasized the superiority of a search warrant over a warrantless search.

> Because a search warrant "provides the detached scrutiny of a neutral magistrate, which is a more reliable safeguard against improper searches than the hurried judgment of a law enforcement officer 'engaged in the often competitive enterprise of ferreting out crime,' " we have expressed a strong preference for warrants and declared that "in a doubtful or marginal case a search under a warrant may be sustainable where without one it would fail."[11]

Investigators should learn to prepare probable cause affidavits for their own cases. They are an invaluable aid in understanding the perspective used by a prosecutor in evaluating a criminal case. They also show the prosecutor involved that the investigator has a fundamental understanding of the elements of the crime required to prosecute a case. And that understanding should help focus the investigator's time and effort in the most beneficial manner. Furthermore, the probable cause affidavit itself is an important tool in plea bargains. The affidavit can be used to establish a factual foundation when a formal plea bargain is accepted by a judge, thereby relieving the investigator of the need to be present for this largely perfunctory task.

Presenting the Case

Once an investigation has been completed, the investigator presents the case to the prosecutor. Perhaps the most frustrating experience for a prosecutor is to have an investigator present a verbal review of a case with only limited documentation. The prosecutor will be at a disadvantage because of the inadequate factual foundation and will need to integrate the facts into a meaningful legal perspective—a laborious and time-consuming task.

To avoid such a situation, the investigator should organize each case properly before it is presented to the prosecutor. All of the pertinent records and reports need to be made available; and an information, the legal indictment form, should be prepared for the prosecutor's signature wherever applicable.

(Pursuant to *Hurtado,* "state felony charges may be prosecuted by indictment or formal information, and twenty-two states authorize both methods of prosecution."[12]) In addition, two sets of photocopies of all documentation should be prepared—one of which is for the defense. Otherwise, the defense may call the investigator as a defense witness.

> It is sometimes to the advantage of the defense to call a police officer as a defense witness at a preliminary hearing in order to gain discovery of the police investigation if no other avenue of discovery is available. The evidence produced at a preliminary hearing is not binding, at trial, upon either side. It can be and is used as grounds for impeachment, however, when a witness deviates at trial from his testimony at the preliminary hearing, or when he is legally unavailable to testify at trial.[13]

It should be noted that "the state of the law governing discovery is constantly changing, but the trend appears to be in favor of broadening the right of discovery for both the defense and the prosecution."[14] In addition, the Court has held "that the suppression by the prosecution of evidence favorable to an accused upon request violates due process where the evidence is material either to guilt or to punishment, irrespective of the good faith or bad faith of the prosecution."[15] If the defense receives photocopies of the state's documentation and sees the strength of the case, the defense will be much more likely to negotiate with the prosecutor in a way that favors the investigator's point of view.

Plea Bargains

Plea bargains are not a new phenomenon. Malcolm Feeley's research suggests that the guilty plea was common throughout most of the nineteenth century. "Furthermore, another pattern emerged in the late 1800s: the practice of changing initial pleas of not guilty, which were accompanied by the prosecutor's decision to drop one charge or more in a multiple charge case. In 1873 this practice accounted for roughly one-half of guilty pleas."[16]

Plea bargains have come under attack through the years for a variety of reasons. "As recently as the 1920s the legal profession was largely united in its opposition to plea bargaining. As America's dependency on pleas of guilty increased, however, attitudes changed."[17] Then, in 1973 the National Advisory Commission on Criminal Justice Standards and Goals recommended the abolishment of plea bargaining by 1978, and the State of Alaska did, for all practical purposes, ban plea bargaining in 1975.[18] In a study of the impact of Alaska's ban, Rubinstein and White conclude: "The attorney general's experiment was successful in that he substantially changed a deeply ingrained pattern and practice. Nevertheless, in our opinion, the shift of responsibility for sentencing from lawyers to judges did nothing to improve the quality of justice in the state of Alaska."[19]

At this point plea bargaining has become so entrenched in the criminal justice system that it would be realistically impossible to prohibit the practice nationally. A cursory review of Supreme Court decisions relative to plea bargains makes the Court's position clear. In 1969 the Court handed down the *Boykin* decision, which incorporated some of the language of *Carnley* (which involved the waiver of the right to counsel) in establishing that a guilty plea must be ascertained by the trial judge to be intelligent and voluntary on the part of the defendant.[20] The next year the defendant's argument in *Brady* was that when "the fear of death is shown to have been a factor in the plea," the plea should be found to be invalid.[21] In deciding that the defendant's plea was not invalid, the Court adopted the lower court's standard:

> A plea of guilty entered by one fully aware of the direct consequences, including the actual value of any commitments made to him by the court, prosecutor, or his own counsel, must stand unless induced by threats (or promises to discontinue improper harassment), misrepresentation (including unfulfilled or unfulfillable promises), or perhaps by promises that are by their nature improper as having no proper relationship to the prosecutor's business (e.g., bribes).[22]

Justice White concluded, "Although Brady's plea of guilty may well have been motivated in part by a desire to avoid a possible death penalty, we are convinced that his plea was voluntarily and intelligently made and we have no reason to doubt that his solemn admission of guilt was truthful."[23]

A subsequent decision, *Santobello,* is interesting from two points of view. First, the Court endorsed plea bargains. Chief Justice Burger, writing for the majority, stated, "The disposition of criminal charges by agreement between the prosecutor and the accused, sometimes loosely called 'plea bargaining,' is an essential component of the administration of justice. Properly administered, it is to be encouraged."[24] Secondly, the Court held that once an agreement between a prosecutor and a defendant has been entered into, the prosecution cannot subsequently fail to honor all of the terms of the agreement.[25]

Nonetheless, one could argue that the Court's most obvious support for plea bargains can be found in two other decisions. In 1970 the Court handed down its decision in *North Carolina v. Alford.* In that case the defendant argued that "he had not committed the murder but that he was pleading guilty because he faced the threat of the death penalty if he did not do so."[26] Justice White, writing for the majority, held that even though "most pleas of guilty consist of both a waiver of trial and an express admission of guilt, the latter element is not a constitutional requisite to the imposition of criminal penalty. . . . When his plea is viewed in light of the evidence against him, which substantially negated his claim of innocence and which further provided a means by which the judge could test whether the plea was being intelligently entered, its validity cannot be seriously questioned."[27]

Finally, the support of the Court for plea bargaining became undeniable in a decision handed down in 1978. In *Bordenkircher* a prosecutor had threatened to reindict a defendant on a more serious charge if the defendant refused to plead guilty to the original less serious charge.[28] Justice Stewart, writing for the majority, argued that "the course of conduct engaged in by the prosecutor in this case, which no more than openly presented the defendant with the unpleasant alternatives of foregoing trial or facing charges on which he was plainly subject to prosecution, did not violate the Due Process Clause of the Fourteenth Amendment."[29]

Some of the significant actors in the criminal justice system—prosecutors, defense attorneys, and judges—have come to rely on the plea bargaining process. If one accepts the assumption that the majority of prosecutors and defense attorneys are either inexperienced or unskilled, the appeal of plea bargains for those two types becomes easier to understand. The fact that relatively few prosecuting attorneys have any trial experience leads them to be wary of the pitfalls of trials; there are no guarantees of winning. But a plea bargain is a guaranteed win in the minds of some; certainly it doesn't have the appearance of a loss. The defense attorney, on the other hand, recognizes the strong probability that the defendant will receive a more harsh sentence if found guilty at trial than the client would have received with a plea bargain.

Prosecutors never knowingly enter into a sentencing agreement that a judge would find to be inappropriate. Most prosecuting attorneys take great pains to interpret a judge's prior sentencing history and then demand a more harsh sentence in a plea bargain if the judge hearing the case is conservative. Just the opposite is true if a more liberal judge is on the bench. Nevertheless, the defense attorney will be perceived as negotiating a better outcome than would otherwise result if the case were to go to trial, and that represents a win for the defense. The third group, judges, tend to be supportive of plea bargains on the grounds of efficiency. The generally accepted argument is that if all (or even a significant number) of plea-bargained cases went to trial, the court system would be overwhelmed and unable to process with existing resources the mounting backlog of cases.

Another factor that supports more lenient sentences and/or probation is the overcrowding of our penal facilities. Prison inmate populations have exploded in the last decade: "Between 1930 and 1984 the State prison population more than tripled. . . . About two-thirds of this increase, however, occurred between 1975 and 1984."[30] The 1984 prison census found that although living space had been increased by about 29 percent between 1979 and 1984, the prison inmate population had increased by 45 percent during that same time frame.[31] Similar surveys show that between 1978 and 1983, inmate population in jails increased 41 percent while the number of beds increased only 11 percent.[32]

Jail and prison overcrowding has placed significant demands on the courts' time and attention. Currently, "thirty-six states, the District of Columbia, Puerto Rico, and the Virgin Islands are operating under court orders because of violations of the constitutional rights of prisoners. . . . Each of these orders has been issued in connection with total conditions of confinement and/or overcrowding. . . . In addition, legal challenges to major prisons are presently pending in five other states."[33] Andy Hall points out that "judges make more decisions affecting jail population than anyone else; this often makes them leaders in seeking jail-crowding solutions."[34] Those solutions may not always be the most desirable from a law enforcement perspective, but as long as such problems exist in corrections, many of the offenders that should be incarcerated simply won't be.

Testifying

Investigators are called on to give depositions and to testify at probable cause hearings (for search or arrest warrants) and at trials. Defendants are not required to testify because of the Fifth Amendment protection against self-incrimination. The investigators involved in a case, however, must always testify because of the Sixth Amendment right of a defendant to face his or her accusers. In this connection we need to recognize that "most evidence in criminal trials is testimonial."[35] Thus, the investigator whose case is being tried is the most important witness in a trial—not because the investigator's testimony is the most critical but because the investigator's demeanor sets the tone for the case, particularly in the eyes of the jury. An investigator must be viewed as credible, and that credibility is established by the investigator's demeanor under cross-examination.

Sometimes an investigator's demeanor is influenced by irrelevant circumstances. For example, investigators frequently have to wait for prosecutors or for judges or both. Probable cause hearings, for instance, are often squeezed between preliminary hearings, sentencing hearings, or misdemeanor cases. Waiting is the rule. Investigators who are impatient may allow their frustration to affect their demeanor. And even though there is no jury involved in a probable cause hearing, a judge could find an inappropriate demeanor to be suggestive of an ill-prepared investigator or an ill-founded case.

One situation involving testimony that is especially important for investigators to understand is the deposition. Depositions are an important tool for some defense attorneys—retained attorneys, that is. The reason that public defenders don't depose prosecution witnesses is very simple—a lack of money. Depositions are generally very expensive, but they can be very useful. Defense attorneys tend to depose state witnesses to learn what their testimony will be so that they can plan a defense and can also use the depositions to destroy witness credibility at trial if testimony and depositions vary.

There is one cardinal rule that every investigator should follow: Never give a deposition in the absence of a prosecutor. A deposition is conducted in the same way that testimony is elicited at trial. That is, objections for the record can be made, requiring a judge's ruling. Obviously, that can't happen if no prosecutor is present, and the prosecutor may then be at a disadvantage at trial. An investigator may not recognize a defense strategy, and a competent defense attorney may be able to make the investigator look very foolish in court.

Although most investigators do not go to trial frequently, there is one tactic that should always be utilized when a case does go to trial. The investigator should have the prosecutor make a motion to have the investigator stipulated to the prosecutor's table on the grounds that the investigator will be helping the prosecutor with the case. In the absence of extraordinary circumstances, this motion will always be granted, even when the defense has already succeeded with a motion to have all of the witnesses separated. During trial, of course, communication between the prosecutor and the investigator is by notes. The prosecutor may verbally ask the investigator a question, but the investigator should never verbally ask the prosecutor a question because it could cause the prosecutor to lose a train of thought or misunderstand testimony.

Witnesses

Witnesses are fundamentally important to any criminal case, and some witnesses are more important than others. Some state witnesses—such as the investigator in charge of the case, police lab technicians, and so on—routinely testify on behalf of the state. Lay witnesses, on the other hand, are likely never to have testified at a trial before, and their cooperation will vary greatly. Some witnesses may be concerned about being harassed later by the defendant or friends of the defendant. Others may simply not want to get involved. Some, particularly victims or members of a victim's family, may be anxious (sometimes too anxious) to testify. In any event, the investigator in charge of a case must maintain contact with all of the witnesses involved in the case until it has been resolved through a plea bargain or at trial.

One of the most used—and perhaps abused—motions made in court is the motion for a continuance. In most instances, such a motion is granted, unless it is too obviously a delaying tactic. More often than not a motion to continue a case is just that—a delaying tactic on the part of the defense. Witnesses can move; they can die; and they can forget. Nonetheless, motions for continuance are the norm in most cases. However, the impact on witnesses is often not recognized.

Subpoenas are sent out about ten days before trial, and every time a continuance is granted and a new trial date is set, the regeneration of subpoenas is set in motion. In most jurisdictions subpoenas are prepared by identifying the defendant (e.g., State v. John Doe), date of the trial, and a time (e.g., 9:00 A.M.). Other information may appear on the subpoena, but the point is that most witnesses feel obligated to appear at the time and place stated on the face of the subpoena. If and when they do, they will likely become frustrated waiting—just like the investigators.

There are a variety of problems with issuing subpoenas in this way. First, in some jurisdictions judges hear motions for continuance even up to and including the scheduled time of the trial. This practice has become less frequent but still does occur. Secondly, it is likely that the defense and the prosecution will agree to a plea bargain at the time of the trial or shortly before. And even though subpoenas have already been issued, witnesses are not apt to be notified. If they show up unnecessarily, they may become irate about wasting their time and effort. Many may also have lost a day's pay, or at least a portion of it.

Another problem revolves around the actual appearance of witnesses in court. There are three different ways that an individual can be compelled by the court to testify at a criminal trial. A subpoena ad testificandum requires an individual not in custody to testify; a subpoena duces tecum requires an individual, usually the keeper of the records, to bring documents, records, and so on; and finally, a writ of habeas corpus ad testificandum can be issued to whoever has custody of an individual to bring that person to court to testify. Technically, a witness can be held in contempt for failing to appear as ordered by the court.

Witnesses who fail to respond to a subpoena may be cited and punished for contempt of court. Continued refusal to appear as a witness may result in the issuance of a body attachment or arrest warrant, ordering an appropriate court or peace officer to bring the reluctant witness to court. Out-of-state witnesses can be compelled to appear and testify. Flight to avoid testifying as a witness in a felony trial is punishable as a federal offense.[36]

In reality, if a witness doesn't show up, judges are not likely even to issue a contempt citation in misdemeanor or nonserious felony cases. It is simply a waste of time for everyone involved. In another situation, perhaps a relatively serious felony case (but not as serious as murder, rape, or kidnap), a witness may be willing or even anxious to testify but may have moved several states away. In most jurisdictions the prosecutor's office has a limited amount of money for such circumstances. An annual amount of, say, $2,500 with an average cost of $500 to bring a witness back doesn't provide for many out-of-state witnesses.

Any answers to these problems will probably be provided by investigators involved with individual cases. Working with witnesses is almost exclusively their job. Investigators should coordinate the witnesses' appearance times through the prosecutors in charge. In addition, prosecutors almost always know ahead of time whether the defense will seek a continuance; investigators, then, can let the state's witnesses know whether to take off from work. Considerate treatment of witnesses encourages their cooperation.

Thus, the involvement of investigators should not end when their cases are presented to the prosecutors. Investigators have continuing opportunities to influence the disposition of their cases, and professional investigators should be properly prepared to participate in every stage of the courtroom process.

Notes

[1] Samuel Walker, *Sense and Nonsense About Crime: A Policy Guide* (Monterey, CA: Brooks/Cole Publishing, 1985), 3.

[2] Richard N. Holden, *Modern Police Management* (Englewood Cliffs, NJ: Prentice-Hall, 1986), 160.

[3] James N. Gilbert, *Criminal Investigation,* 2d ed. (Columbus, OH: Merrill, 1986), 67.

[4] Steven M. Cox and John E. Wade, *The Criminal Justice Network: An Introduction* (Dubuque, IA: William C. Brown Publishers, 1985), 38–9.

[5] David W. Neubauer, *America's Courts and the Criminal Justice System,* 2d ed. (Monterey, CA: Brooks/Cole Publishing, 1984), 89–90.

[6] Howard Abadinsky, *Law and Justice* (Chicago: Nelson-Hall, 1988), 123–4.

[7] Rolando V. del Carmen, *Criminal Procedure for Law Enforcement Personnel* (Pacific Grove, CA: Brooks/Cole Publishing, 1987), 139.

[8] Ibid.

[9] United States v. Leon, 104 S. Ct. 3405 (1984).

[10]   Ibid., 3410–11.

[11]   Ibid., 3416–17.

[12]   Hurtado v. California, 4 S. Ct. 111 (1884); Ronald L. Carson, *Criminal Justice Procedure,* 2d ed. (Cincinnati: Anderson, 1978), 89.

[13]   Paul B. Weston and Kenneth M. Wells, *Criminal Evidence for Police,* 3d ed. (Englewood Cliffs, NJ: Prentice-Hall, 1986), 50.

[14]   John N. Ferdico, *Criminal Procedure for the Criminal Justice Professional,* 3d ed. (St. Paul: West, 1985), 36–7.

[15]   Rollin M. Perkins and Ronald N. Boyce, *Cases and Materials on Criminal Law and Procedure,* 6th ed. (Mineola, NY: Foundation Press, 1984), 1067.

[16]   Malcolm M. Feeley, "Plea Bargaining and the Structure of the Criminal Process," ed. George F. Cole in *Criminal Justice: Law & Politics,* 4th ed. (Monterey, CA: Brooks/Cole Publishing, 1984), 398.

[17]   Albert Alschuler, "The Prosecutor's Role in Plea Bargaining," *University of Chicago Law Review* 36 (1968): 50.

[18]   National Advisory Commission on Criminal Justice Standards and Goals, *Courts* (Washington, DC: U. S. Government Printing Office, 1973), 46–50.

[19]   Michael L. Rubinstein and Teresa J. White, "Plea Bargaining: Can Alaska Live Without It?" in *Criminal Justice: Law & Politics,* 185.

[20]   See Frank W. Miller et al., *Cases and Materials on Criminal Justice Administration,* 2d ed. (Mineola, NY: Foundation Press, 1982) for a discussion of these Supreme Court decisions: Bordenkircher v. Hayes, 434 U.S. 357 (1978); Boykin v. Alabama, 395 U.S. 238 (1969); Brady v. Maryland, 373 U.S. 83 (1963); Brady v. United States, 397 U.S. 742 (1970); Carnley v. Cochran 369 U.S. 506 (1962); Hurtado v. California 4 S. Ct. 111 (1884); North Carolina v. Alford, 400 U.S. 25 (1970); Santobello v. New York, 404 U.S. 257 (1971); United States v. Jackson 390 U.S. 579 (1968); and United States v. Leon 104 S. Ct. 3405 (1984).

[21]   Ibid., 876.

[22]   Ibid., 880.

[23]   Ibid., 882.

[24]   Ibid., 911.

[25]   Ibid.

[26]   Ibid., 901.

[27]   Ibid., 902.

[28]   Ibid., 888.

[29]   Ibid., 890.

[30]   Christopher A. Innes, "Population Density in State Prisons" (Washington, DC: U.S. Department of Justice, Bureau of Justice Statistics, 1986), 1. In state prisons the inmate population increased from 263,553 in 1979 to 381,955 in 1984 (Ibid., 4).

[31]   Ibid.

[32]   Charles B. DeWitt, "New Construction Methods for Correctional Facilities" (Washington, DC: U.S. Department of Justice, National Institute of Justice, 1986), 2–3.

[33] Alvin J. Bronstein, "The National Prison Project News Release," (Washington, DC: American Civil Liberties Union Foundation, 1987), 1–2.

[34] Andy Hall, "Systemwide Strategies to Alleviate Jail Crowding," (Washington, DC: U.S. Department of Justice, National Institute of Justice, 1987), 3.

[35] Paul B. Weston and Kenneth M. Wells, *Criminal Evidence for Police,* 2d ed. (Englewood Cliffs, NJ: Prentice-Hall, 1976), 53..

[36] Ibid., 30.

18

Futures Research: Implications for Criminal Investigations

William L. Tafoya
Federal Bureau of Investigation

During the last half-century American law enforcement has become increasingly sophisticated in its ability to capture, record, and report crime figures. Daily these data are scrupulously collected by more than 16,000 municipal, county, and state agencies and are routinely reported to the Federal Bureau of Investigation (FBI). Since 1930 these figures have been compiled as a summary-based system, annually published by the FBI in *Crime in the United States* and commonly referred to as the uniform crime reports (UCR).

Although not without its shortcomings, the UCR provides a useful measure of the prevalence and incidence of crime.[1] Darrel W. Stephens, a former police chief and now executive director of the Police Executive Research Forum (PERF), believes that the UCR program, recently converted to an incident-based reporting system, will address a myriad of hitherto unanswered questions about victims, criminals, crimes, and crime sites.[2] Such data may constitute the only useful means of identifying long-range trends in major crimes and the crime rate.[3]

Small annual fluctuations in crime are often given little notice. However, with the current UCR data for a number of American cities, even unsophisticated statistical measures demonstrate that many crimes may not only double but also quadruple in a period of twenty years. Those who dismiss such observations make a serious mistake.

Tomorrow's crisis may well be today's minor problem overlooked.[4] Nonetheless, as recently as the beginning of the 1980s, the police were giving seemingly little thought to the nature or extent of crime in the year 2000 or beyond.

Substantial advances have been made in law enforcement, yet some observers contend that the same problems besetting the police at the beginning of the century continue to erode their effectiveness today. Others suggest that the situation—particularly administratively—is even worse.[5] Is this simply a matter of localized resistance to change? Or do the causes extend beyond the local and regional boundaries?

The Legacy of Future Shock

Two decades have passed since the term *future shock* was first introduced.[6] Most people worldwide are now familiar with it, but what is it? Future shock is a dizzying disorientation that springs from the premature arrival of the future. It occurs when a greatly accelerated rate of change takes place in society and a new culture is superimposed on an old one. Toffler further defines *future shock* as "the distress, both physical and psychological, that arises from an overload of the human organism's physical adaptive systems and its decision-making processes."[7] Simply stated, it is the human reaction and inadequate adaptation to overwhelming change.

Historically, humankind has been able to cope with change because it has been gradual and has extended over long periods of time. During this century, however, and especially since the end of World War II, the perplexing rapidity of change has confounded society and underscored the need for long-range planning.[8] The ten-year period beginning in the mid-1960s was a particularly unsettling era for law enforcement. It was the beginning of the drug scene and a time of protest against the war in Vietnam as well as enchantment with flower power gurus.

From a police perspective the courts and prisons during that period seemed to have revolving doors. From the lower courts to the U. S. Supreme Court, criminal justice appeared to be working at cross purposes with law enforcement at the precise moment when blue ribbon panels were extolling the virtues of the systems approach. Few within the police, the courts, or corrections agencies seemed to know what working systematically meant. However, hardened criminals and youthful miscreants alike seemed intuitively to understand. The streetwise seemed easily able to manipulate the system, conning probation and parole officers while continuing to commit serious crimes.[9]

An endless stream of committees and four presidential commissions explored the problem of crime on the streets, but a large number of police officers perceived public hostility toward law enforcement and thus found their jobs especially difficult and stressful during that era. There was relief that people were finally comprehending what law enforcement was up against and recognizing that police officers could not do it all.[10] But at the same time that awareness did little to enhance police self-esteem.

Early visionaries like August Vollmer and O. W. Wilson championed the military model and bureaucratization, which they believed to be the key to problems of the past and the hallmark of police professionalization. Certain that familiarity breeds corruption, police administrators went to great lengths to ensure autonomy and impersonal policing. In addition, strict command and control provided stability and consistence of operations. However, many today wonder whether those models of policing have outlasted their usefulness and may, in fact, have led to overbureaucratization.[11]

In particular, the influx of young, socially sophisticated, inquisitive, and usually highly educated men and women into policing suggests a need for reduced bureaucratic hierarchy and less autocratic managerial styles.[12]

The way in which police executives and managers assess the need for change is vitally important. Irresponsible attempts to halt change will produce consequences as destructive as reckless efforts to advance change. As a profession, policing has relied too heavily on experience and not enough on innovation. Divergent new approaches to traditional methods of policing must evolve from educational objectives that are future oriented.[13] Thus far, the single endeavor specifically designed around a future orientation is the California Commission on Peace Officers' Standards and Training (POST) Command College. This program encourages future leaders to develop a questioning attitude and a willingness to experiment.

The key to success in the future is flexibility. Given a turbulent technological and social environment, law enforcement education and training programs must promote and not merely expose personnel to novelty. Success in the future calls for a high degree of tolerance for chaos, ambiguity, and mistakes.

Management of change requires the conversion of what could be into what may be in pursuit of what should be. And determining what should be calls for the discipline of futures research.[14]

Forecasting is the purest form of futures research.[15] One analogy likens forecasting to the illumination from the headlights of an automobile being driven on a winding road through a nighttime snowstorm in an unfamiliar locale. A bit of what lies ahead is revealed, although not clearly enough so that the driver can advance without trepidation. Enough of the darkness is uncovered to avoid disaster and enable the driver to proceed to the intended destination.[16]

A prediction is not synonymous with a forecast. The former often suggests guesswork and is used with that connotation here. It is a statement about what will happen, usually to an individual. A forecast, on the other hand, is never about individuals. It is a statement about what may be changed and what should be brought about. It suggests what may occur if. . . .[17]

Views of the Future

Throughout recorded history there is evidence of curiosity about the future. Three general public perspectives predominate, representing a continuum along which most people's attitudes vary. A preference for one or another of these views will tend to shape one's opinion of the relevance of forecasting and the need for proactive measures.

The apocalyptic view holds that what lies ahead for humankind is a cataclysmic end. Negativism and fanaticism characterize this outlook, as well as a belief that nothing will change what is destined. Iranian religious literature, for example, abounds with such symbolism.[18] Modern fatalists retreat from responsible action and thought, believing that nothing matters but the present. Punk rockers epitomize this perspective.[19]

The teleologic view, characterized by positivism and faith, holds that what lies ahead for some of humankind is redemption. However, one's destiny is guided by compliance with certain proscribed behavior, which will be judged by the absolute power in the universe. Thus, the modern determinist strives to lead an exemplary life in the hope of receiving eternal salvation. The Protestant ethic and Catholic doctrine pervade this perspective, which is guided by abstinence and obedience, as well as tenets of the past. This is the predominant view in Western societies.[20]

The prophetic view, characterized by purposeful, reasoned optimism, holds that one's future is neither doomed nor determined. Individuals direct their own destinies, controlling their own actions, influencing their own environment, and deciding what legacy they will bequeath to future generations. This unconditional openness requires well-regulated innovation and a continuous reappraisal of one's assumptions. This is the world of the modern futurist, the inventor of tomorrow.[21]

Futures Research: The Discipline

Since the dawn of antiquity, people have been fascinated with images of the future. In Greek mythology Apollo, the god of prophecy, is said to have sought counsel from the oracle at Delphi early in the Hellenic period, sometime between the third and the first century B.C.[22]

Futures research, however, is a distinctly modern phenomenon, developed by scholars and scientists seeking to address social ills in original and novel ways. The precepts of the social and physical sciences are based on historical fact, scientific methods, and human values. To this formula, futures research adds vision, creativity, and innovation. These crucial ingredients set futures research apart from traditional disciplines.[23]

Historical Development of Futures Research

As early as 1902 the British science fiction writer H. G. Wells suggested that the future should be a field of serious study. In 1907 American sociologist S. Colum Gilfillan was the first to propose a name, mellontology, for the study of the future. In 1944 political scientist Ossip Flechtheim, a refugee from Nazi Germany, coined the word *futurology* to describe the scientific study of the future. Neither descriptor gained popular recognition. Today, the two most frequently used references to the futures movement are *futuristics* and *futures research*.

Two events generated by Army/Air Force General Henry H. "Hap" Arnold, a military defense planner, contributed significantly to the futures movement. In 1944 Arnold instigated the first forecast of future technological capabilities and military armaments. Two years later he persuaded the Douglas Aircraft Corporation to study the potential for airborne intercontinental warfare. As a result, Project RAND (an acronym for Research and Development) was established and, with funding from the Ford Foundation, became independent in 1948. The RAND Corporation thus became an organization unlike any other in the world—the first think tank.[24]

Two subsequent events at RAND added further credence to the futures movement. The first was the 1953 development of the Delphi technique, a sophisticated forecasting methodology introduced by Olaf Helmer and Norman Dalkey. The second was the publication of a paper entitled "The Epistemology of the Inexact Sciences" by Olaf Helmer and Nicholas Rescher (1959). This vitally important paper provided the philosophical underpinnings for the emerging discipline of futures research, an outgrowth of operations research and the systems approach.[25]

In 1961 the nation's second think tank, the Hudson Institute, was founded in Croton-on-Hudson, New York, by a physicist and former RAND research analyst, Herman Kahn. That same year Richard L. Meier began addressing the subject of the future in his resources planning classes in the School of Natural Resources at the University of Michigan and subsequently in his city planning and architecture classes at the University of California at Berkeley.

The first association of futurists, Mankind 2000, was formed in London by historian Robert Jungk in 1965. In 1966 at the New York City New School for Social Research, Alvin Toffler taught the first course dealing exclusively with the future; it was entitled "Social Change and the Future." That same year the World Future Society was founded in Washington, DC, under the leadership of journalist Edward Cornish. Thereafter, the International Futuribles Association was formed in Paris, the Club of Rome in Italy, and the Institute for the Future in Menlo Park, California. More courses appeared in more universities, then a futures study program at the University of Massachusetts at Amherst, and finally the first full-fledged future studies graduate degree program in 1974 at the University of Houston at Clear Lake City. As the discipline of futures research has evolved, consensus has developed around certain principles, premises, and priorities.

Principles

Concurrence has been reached regarding three convictions: (1) the unity or interconnectedness of reality, (2) the crucial importance of time, and (3) the significance of ideas. Futurists do not view the world as a hodgepodge of unconnected entities acting in random fashion, coincidentally interacting purposefully and meaningfully. Rather, they envision a holistic universe, a megasystem whose components interact. Futurists are systems oriented.[26]

Furthermore, futurists are not preoccupied with immediate concerns, although they do not discount them. Futurists tend to focus on time frames of five years and beyond, believing that in most organizations a time lag of three to five years occurs between the making of a decision and its impact on the organization. Futurists also believe that virtually anything can be changed in society's organizations, given a lead time of two decades. Futurists subscribe to six time frames:

- ☐ Immediate: present to 2 years
- ☐ Short-term: 2 to 5 years
- ☐ Mid-level: 5 to 10 years
- ☐ Long-range: 10 to 20 years

☐ Extended: 20 to 50 years

☐ Distant: 50 years and beyond

Finally, futurists do not cling to the status quo, the tried and true beliefs of the past. The inevitability of change is central to their thinking. Consequently, they explore divergent ways of dealing with old problems and unprecedented ways of anticipating new problems. Convinced that ideas can move mountains, futurists are extremely interested in the methodical development of ideas.[27]

Premises

Consensus has also solidified around three postulates: (1) the future is not predetermined, (2) the future is not predictable, and (3) future outcomes can be influenced by individual choice. In regard to the second premise, the word *prediction* is used in traditional disciplines, such as mathematics and statistics, to describe the existence or nonexistence of a relationship between variables. One predicts from an independent to a dependent variable. Aptitude tests, for example, are used to predict future achievement; intelligence tests have for many years been used to predict learning ability.[28]

No serious futurist believes that the future can be predicted; fragmentary data about the past and the present would have to be coupled with an incomplete understanding of the processes of change and an uncertain anticipation of the direction or influence of individual choice. Whereas uncertainty can be minimized in the physical sciences, social and behavioral scientists do not enjoy that same luxury with economic, social, or political systems.

In addition, futurists believe that individual choice can influence future outcomes. Even though there are no guarantees that the exercise of choice will produce the desired result, it will have some effect on the outcome.[29]

Priorities

Futurists accept these three goals for futures research: (1) form perceptions of the future (the possible), (2) study likely alternatives (the probable), and (3) make choices to bring about particular events (the preferable). If future outcomes are to be influenced, perceptions of the future must be formed. Fresh new images must be generated, identifying the opportunities as well as the risks. This goal is image driven and requires breaking the fetters of one's imagination. This is the vital, creative goal of futures research.

Once new images have been generated, likely alternatives must be studied. The probable paths to the future must be analyzed qualitatively as well as quantitatively. This process, which is analytically driven, usually requires estimating the probability of events and trends and evaluating the consequences of certain choices. This is the systematic and scientific goal of futures research.

In order to bring about particular events, it is necessary to make choices among alternatives. This process is characterized as value driven; it determines the preferred paths to the future. This is the managerial, decision-making goal of futures research.[30]

Thus, the future is best anticipated in an imaginative, analytical, and value-conscious manner. In addition, criminal investigators should receive training in the scientific method and the use of forecasting techniques. Even though statistical precision is difficult or impossible to achieve in behavioral studies, a rough idea is better than no idea. The principles of the scientific method and forecasting "are not merely the tools of 'scientific research'; they are powerful instruments for dealing rationally with the problems of everyday existence. Ignorance of them constitutes a form of functional illiteracy."[31] Today's criminal investigator must look ahead and must understand what is being examined.

Forecasting Methodologies

The tools for looking ahead are many and varied. Criminal investigators need not master their use but should know enough about forecasting methodologies to be able to ask pertinent questions of the technician who is skilled in using such techniques. For example, one should have some familiarity with the strengths and weaknesses of several forecasting methods. One should also understand which method is best suited to a particular type of analysis. And an understanding of the issues of reliability and validity is essential.[32]

When forecasting, criminal investigators should follow a rule of threes. That is, data should be analyzed by three different methods. Disparate results would suggest that something may not have been properly considered. On the other hand, three sets of results that are on target should enhance the level of confidence in the forecast.

In a research effort commissioned by the U. S. Army Corps of Engineers, the Center for the Study of Social Policy at SRI International (then the Stanford Research Institute) of Menlo Park, California, evaluated some 150 forecasting methods. In 1975 the first of a three-volume series, *Handbook of Forecasting Techniques,* was published, outlining twelve methodologies. The second volume describes thirty-one techniques; the third lists seventy-three methods.[33] The books present a synopsis of each forecasting method, assess its limitations, and address issues that are important to criminal investigators and other decision makers, such as confidence levels, time and cost required to undertake an analysis, and appropriate alternative methods. This study appears to be the most comprehensive to date.[34]

Futures Research Methods

The five forecasting methodologies discussed here could be useful to criminal investigators. They are among the premier methods in the futures research field and are widely used today in a great variety of applications.[35]

Scenarios. The word *scenario* is widely used, frequently incorrectly. In its simplest form a scenario is a story. In a research sense, however, a scenario encompasses four essential characteristics: it is hypothetical, summarized, multifaceted, and factually based. A scenario must be based on fact; it should be a carefully researched, realistic representation of a sequence of events. The very best scenarios are not one-dimensional. Rather, they depict at least three conceivable outcomes: the best case, the worst case, and the most likely case of the forecast alternative futures.

No scenario will materialize exactly as portrayed. Its utility lies in the fact that it offers an opportunity to evaluate a present state of affairs in terms of what may occur, given certain assumptions and parameters. It is important that all of the suppositions and limitations inherent in the presentation be outlined. The most valuable scenarios are those that present possible, probable, and preferable futures. Scenarios are ideal for use by criminal investigators because the method lends itself to complex situations, such as serial murder or rape.

Delphi Technique. The Delphi technique is a structured group process that maximizes the likelihood of reaching consensus and identifying disagreement. Essentially, this method involves anonymous structured exchanges between members of a panel of experts, who are furnished with controlled feedback and statistical group response between iterations (rounds) of propositions posed by a moderator (facilitator) using a series of mailed questionnaires.[36]

The key to Delphi's success rests with its ability to bypass the negative consequences of group dynamics typically present in conventional committee meetings—such factors as the pressure to agree with the majority, deference to authority, the influence of articulate or dominant individuals, and so on. It is the method of choice in situations that are long range, cross-disciplinary, lacking in theoretical foundation, or extremely complex or when it is impractical to bring together the experts. Thus, it is a means of last resort.

The potential applications of the Delphi technique for long-range planning in law enforcement are varied. It could serve as a forecasting probe (to estimate the year and probability of certain occurrences); a strategy probe (to assess alternatives); or a preference probe (to identify what should be). It could also serve as a dynamic device that might be the basis for public policy planning. For criminal investigators it could serve as a means of coming to consensus when widely differing views have been expressed and are impeding further progress on a case.[37]

For law enforcement the strength of the method results from its precision and ability to circumvent impediments to decision making in conventional group settings. Its weakness results from the necessity to use experts and the length of time required to conduct a conventional Delphi study, typically six to eighteen months. Several variations of the original Delphi technique have emerged since the mid-1960s. Those that seem to have the most direct and immediate applicability for law enforcement are the mini-Delphi and the Delphi conference.

The mini-Delphi lends itself to situations in which experts are unavailable, face-to-face interaction of participants is desirable, and/or time is limited. In such cases some, but not all, of the desirable anonymity of the Delphi technique is lost. With the mini-Delphi each participant independently and anonymously records an estimate on a 3-by-5 card. Those cards are collected and collated by the facilitator, who arranges the estimates in descending order. If the group is large (fifty or more), quartiles and a median should be calculated. The results are then displayed in a manner that permits all participants to see the range of responses. A chalkboard or flip chart serves this purpose well. The facilitator then initiates a brief verbal exchange among participants, permitting different points of view to be expressed and hopefully drawing the group closer to consensus. Thereafter, each participant once again independently and anonymously records an estimate on another index card. Those cards are then collected, quartiles are calculated, and the median is taken as the group's estimate. The entire process can be completed in about thirty minutes and requires only knowledgeable individuals, rather than experts, as panelists.

Delphi conferencing, or D-net, is the application of computer technology to the Delphi technique, an adaptation that is elegant in its simplicity. For several years microcomputer enthusiasts have been exchanging views and opinions via computer bulletin boards. Such forums for discussion and debate require only the addition of response anonymity and statistical calculation of group responses to constitute a Delphi conference. Such an adaptation maximizes the strengths of the Delphi technique and eliminates at least one of its weaknesses, the time required to complete a Delphi study. Because the exchanges are not dependent on the postal service and are not hampered by distance, a full-fledged D-net can be undertaken in a fraction of the time necessary to complete a conventional Delphi study.[38]

Cross-Impact Matrix. The cross-impact matrix (CIM) is a means by which the probability of one forecast event can be adjusted as a function of its potential interaction with all other forecast events. This is a particularly useful feature inasmuch as the forecasts that emerge with other methods are frequently one dimensional, that is, they view events in isolation and ignore factors that might be mutually reinforcing or mutually exclusive.[39] CIM is especially useful in refining forecasts made with the Delphi technique and can serve as an aid in building models, or formulas. An example of CIM is illustrated in Figure 18–1.

Relevance Trees. Relevance trees present a hierarchical structuring of detailed relationships. This method is used to analyze situations in which distinct levels of complexity can be identified in a hierarchy.[40] The process directs attention to the critical nodes and branches of the relevance tree and highlights the most cost-effective pathways to completion of a project. This methodology is similar to other systems approaches—for example, morphological analysis—but is most like the program evaluation and review technique (PERT).[41] Relevance trees, originally termed PATTERN (Planning Assistance Through Technical Evaluation of Relevance Numbers), continue to be widely used by the military and defense industry complex. An example of a relevance tree is illustrated in Figure 18–2.

Technology Assessment. With a variety of forecasting and analytical tools, technology assessment anticipates and evaluates the potential impact on society of emerging technological developments. *Technology: Processes of Assessment and Choice* was the National Academy of Sciences (1969) report to the House Committee on Science and Astronautics that is considered by many to have legitimized technology assessment. Movement within Congress followed shortly thereafter, undoubtedly sparked by public outcry over the potential dangers that new technologies posed to human

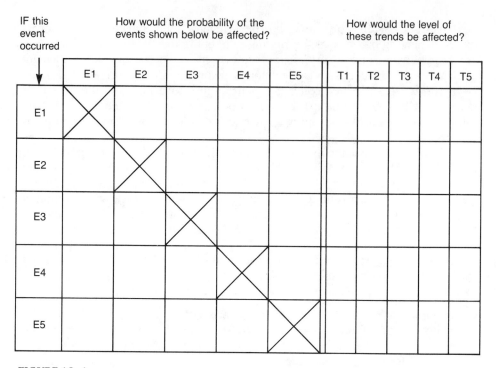

FIGURE 18–1

Cross-impact matrix.

Source: Adapted from the cross-impact matrix presented in *California Peace Officer* (March 1987), p. 26.

life and ecological systems. In 1972 legislative action resulted in the creation of the Office of Technology Assessment (OTA) as an analytical arm of Congress. Private industry was subsequently required to submit to the OTA detailed environmental impact statements prior to the introduction of new technology.[42]

Technology assessment, or more specifically the reports of OTA, should be of keen interest to law enforcement personnel. Criminal investigators, for example, might well benefit from the findings presented in one of the more recent OTA publications, *Science, Technology, and the Constitution.*[43]

Additional Methods

Other more conventional techniques also lend themselves to forecasting.

Qualitative Methodologies. These normative procedures also have a foundation in a systems approach. Essentially, they begin with future needs and work backward to the performance requirements necessary to meet those needs.[44] Such methods are particularly well suited to decision making that revolves around multifaceted, sporadic, and/or irregular activities, as is frequently the case in complex criminal investigations. Five techniques are discussed here that could be useful to criminal investigators.

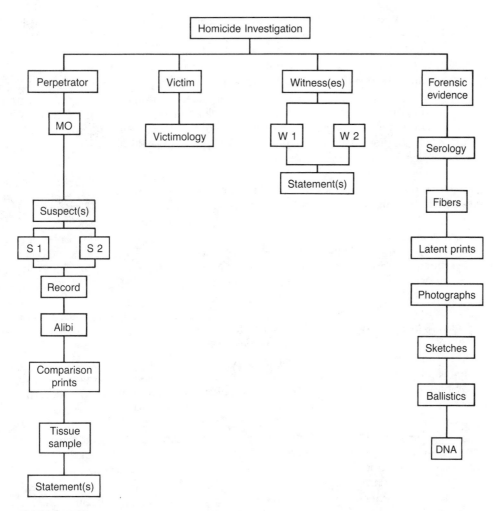

FIGURE 18–2
Relevance tree.

Brainstorming is designed to evoke creativity in individuals and groups by focusing on the spontaneous generation of ideas. Primarily because it is easy to use, brainstorming is perhaps the best known and most widely used of various problem-solving techniques. Its underlying assumption is that critical judgment inhibits—and may prevent—the expression of unorthodox and novel ideas in a group setting.[45] Thus, the process forbids the premature judgment of ideas and encourages a freewheeling atmosphere (the wilder the idea, the better) with a quantity of ideas, any of which may be combined or improved upon. The technique's primary utility for detectives is that it requires little time, is relatively cost free, and is easy to follow.

Brainstorming lends itself to criminal investigations in which leads and/or fresh, new ideas have been exhausted.

Morphological analysis involves studying the form and structure of an entity. A systematic juxtaposing of the elements of a situation is undertaken in order to evaluate all of the possible solutions to a specific problem. Relevance trees, a similar methodology, are designed to identify hierarchical relationships. Morphological analysis, on the other hand, breaks down a problem into its parallel parts, which are then examined individually.[46] The technique's utility for criminal investigators occurs when the pieces of the puzzle do not seem to fit together; it forces the whole to be broken down into its component parts.

A *mission flow diagram,* also referred to as mission taxonomy, is used to analyze sequential processes. The product or output of the method is a series of flow graphics. With this technique all of the alternative routes in a process are diagramed in order to identify critical stages and risks as well as to determine associated costs for each stage. As the flow becomes apparent, it is possible to add new routes and identify the corresponding critical steps, risks, and costs. Once difficulties and costs have been determined, performance requirements can be calculated for the mission or activity.[47] Mission flow diagraming is similar to PERT charting. An example of a mission flow diagram is illustrated in Figure 18–3.

Inherent in the *mixed-scanning* methodology is the perspective that most decision makers are one of two types. Incrementalists, who make up the vast majority, are task oriented and tend to focus on near-term accomplishments. Preoccupied with immediate needs and short-range objectives, they seem unable to grasp the big picture. In addition, incrementalists seem unable to deal effectively with the complex nature of the interactions of elements (other than their own) within the system in which they operate. Even if they are able to articulate the concept, incrementalists do not comprehend the significance of synergy.[48]

Rationalists, the second type of decision maker, are project oriented and tend to focus on long-range achievements. Concerned with future needs and ultimate goals, they are guided by the big picture. Although quite comfortable with the multitude of systems interactions and stimulated by complexity, rationalists seem unable to deal effectively with individual elements; they are exasperated by the minutia required to make the systems function.

Incrementalists believe that their environment and the events that impact them are utterly chaotic; they reject the rationalist perspective as unrealistic and undesirable. Rationalists, on the other hand, believe in a systems approach. Consequently, they reject the incrementalist perspective as staggering "through history like a drunk putting one disjointed foot after another."[49]

Mixed scanning incorporates the best of both rationalist and incrementalist approaches. It explores long-range alternatives to help overcome the status-quo nature of incrementalism, and it limits details to reduce the unrealistic aspects of rationalism.[50] Mixed scanning can be thought of as a weather plane flying in the general direction of a hurricane. It uses its radar systems to scan the environment to assess the long-range implications. Then, flying into the eye of the hurricane, the crew uses direct contact observation to evaluate immediate conditions. Analysis of

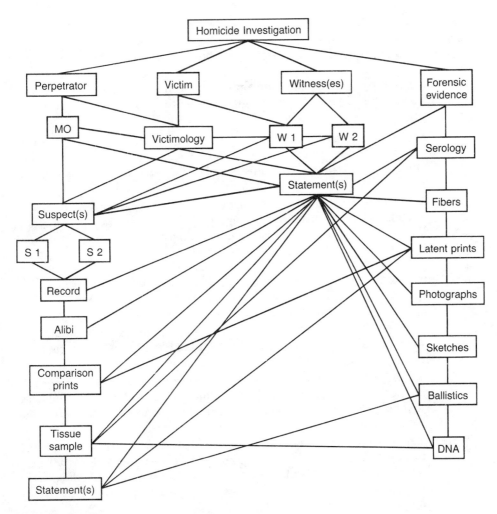

FIGURE 18–3
Mission flow diagram.

both sets of data permits a reliable forecast concerning which land masses should be evacuated and so on. Mixed scanning is little used in criminal investigations but seems particularly well suited to complex investigations.

The *nominal group technique (NGT)* encompasses elements of both brainstorming and the Delphi technique in an effort to identify in a relatively short period of time the best way to deal with a specific issue.[51] The process, however, is the key to the method's real value. It provides the decision maker with a high degree of confidence that the ideas suggested represent real, rather than fabricated or forced, consensus of the management or investigative team. Such consensus is highly unusual in conventional small-group settings because of hierarchical structures and the negative dynamics that frequently surface in typical face-to-face meetings.

The NGT procedure is relatively straightforward. The problem to be addressed is first recorded so that it is clearly visible to all of the participants; a chalkboard or flip chart serves this purpose quite well. The question posed must be clear, concise, and focused on a single issue. At that point a six-step process begins.

☐ *Step 1: Idea generation phase.* All participants silently and independently record their own suggestions on a sheet of paper. This is the most important part of the process, for this is where the burst of ideas occurs. Ten minutes is an ideal time period for this phase.

☐ *Step 2: Round-robin phase.* The facilitator asks each participant, in turn, to articulate one idea at a time. As suggestions are offered, they are recorded for all to see. A participant is permitted to pass during any iteration and then rejoin the process as new ideas occur (as in brainstorming). In a group of ten, fifty to sixty ideas are typically suggested in a span of thirty to forty minutes.

☐ *Step 3: Expurgation phase.* Ideas are clarified, and duplicates are eliminated. The facilitator's role is to ensure that participants withhold judgment about the issues (as in brainstorming) and concentrate instead on eliminating redundancy. An original list of fifty ideas might be reduced to forty in this process. This phase requires ten to twenty minutes.

☐ *Step 4: Serial discussion phase.* Participants are encouraged to comment on the merits of each idea. By calling on different participants, the facilitator can ensure full and nearly equal participation and can mitigate defensiveness. This phase requires twenty to thirty minutes.

☐ *Step 5: Truncation phase.* Participants are asked to selectively reduce the list by half. That is, they are asked to record the ideas they believe will best resolve the issue under consideration. Group consensus thus reduces a list of forty ideas to twenty. This phase generally requires ten to twenty minutes.

☐ *Step 6: Prioritization phase.* Participants are asked once more to reduce the list by half and to rank-order the ideas that remain. A truncated list of twenty is thus converted to the ten best ideas that the group believes are the most likely to successfully resolve the issue under consideration. This phase usually takes no more than ten to fifteen minutes. For a group familiar with the process, the entire procedure might be completed in ninety minutes, although two to four hours is a more realistic estimate for most groups not conversant with NGT.

An adaptation of the classic procedure just outlined can provide a higher degree of anonymity and, as a consequence, more reliable results. It should also produce more meaningful recommendations. During the idea generation phase, truncation phase, and prioritization phase, ideas or selections are recorded on

3-by-5 cards that are then collected so that no one, including the facilitator, knows how anyone else voted on a particular suggestion. In addition, the verbalization of suggestions—the round-robin phase—is eliminated, thus increasing the anonymity and enhancing confidence in the process. This increased anonymity, a hallmark of the Delphi technique, permits participants to focus on the logic of the ideas suggested rather than on the personality or style of the individuals offering the ideas.

The NGT method should be highly desirable for criminal investigators and other law enforcement decision makers. Like the mini-Delphi, this technique requires little time to complete, does not require the use of experts, and suggests a higher degree of reliability than conventional decision making offers.

Quantitative Methodologies. These methods are especially well suited to the analysis of regularly occurring, patterned activities, such as fraud, burglary, auto theft, and rape. Five statistical procedures are discussed here that could be useful to criminal investigators.

With *multiple regression* a linear algebraic relationship is defined among several variables, and an equation is then solved that predicts the value of dependent variables. A powerful analytic tool with wide applicability to varied experimental and nonexperimental problems, multiple regression can deal with continuous and categorical variables. It can be used for the same purposes that the more sophisticated analysis of variance (ANOVA) is used,[52] but it has some of the same limitations that the less sophisticated extrapolation has.[53] Nonetheless, it is precisely because multiple regression is so straightforward and accommodating that it can serve as a valuable forecasting tool for criminal investigators.

When variables or relationships are not deterministic in situations where one or more critical variables in a decision model are probabilistic, an approximate quantitative solution may be appropriate.[54] Many law enforcement forecasts, such as a future number of motor vehicle accidents, do not lend themselves to analysis by techniques such as multiple regression. In such cases a variance-reduction method, such as *Monte Carlo,* would be the procedure of choice. This technique has been used effectively in cost-benefit studies. However, simulating all or part of a complex system, such as an entire police department or the criminal investigation division, may be the method's most important application. It also offers many other law enforcement planning possibilities.

Until recently the use of Monte Carlo in probability distributions, sampling, and random number generation seemed to make it impractical for all but the largest law enforcement organizations, those with their own Fortran programming capabilities and minicomputer or mainframe systems. Today, however, random number generation is available in software programs written in Fortran or Pascal that run on microcomputers.

A *Markov chain* is a mathematical model that describes a process in which a set of states moves through a sequence of steps, obeying probabilistic rather than deterministic laws.[55] This technique is used to analyze the current movement of a variable in order to predict the future movement of that variable and has been found to be particularly valuable in describing social processes. The Markovian principle has been used successfully, for example, to delineate organizational growth and personnel administration matters. It could be used in law enforcement to project future staffing needs, promotional potential, shift assignments, restructuring of elements within the organization or unit, and so on. Most of these issues are given little advance attention in law enforcement, almost none in a probabilistic manner.

The *Bayesian approach* enables the planner or criminal investigator to utilize actual, realistic variables in anticipating the unexpected. Bayesian statistics is perhaps the best mathematical approach to problem solving in which uncertainty is a major factor. It is particularly valuable because it lends itself to small sample sizes and analysis of situations for which no prior experience exists. Ironically, it is also amenable to situations in which expectations have been established, such as most criminal investigative situations.[56] In law enforcement disciplinary matters, for example, data are seldom available in advance to support objective decision making. Consequently, subjective decisions are frequently made, based on inaccurate and unsubstantiated interpretations. With Bayesian statistics it would be possible to establish probability weights and factor in certain contingencies that would reduce the need for such subjective decisions.

The *Box-Jenkins method* of autoregressive integrated moving averages (ARIMA) fits somewhere between multiple regression analysis and computer simulation in terms of its utility as a forecasting technique. It is a great deal more sophisticated than multiple regression but is less powerful than computer simulation because it can forecast only one variable. The procedure is designed to handle complex time-series data in which there is no apparent pattern. Unlike other quantitative techniques, the Box-Jenkins method does not require a clear definition of the trend, yet it is extremely accurate, providing the most likely value as an upper and lower bound of the probability range. However, one of the principal drawbacks of the procedure is that it does not work well with fewer than fifty to one hundred cases.[57]

Potential law enforcement applications might include an estimation of the number of calls for service in a given area for a specific time frame. Criminal investigators could use the method to forecast certain crimes and then compare the results with estimates based on multiple regression and Monte Carlo analyses.

Computer Technology.   There are other methods that encompass both quantitative and qualitative components and lend themselves to forecasting. These long-standing and reliable procedures have been greatly enhanced by computer technology, particularly color and graphics capabilities. Three techniques are discussed here that could be useful to criminal investigators.

A *model* can be static (with no motion or flexible parts) or dynamic (capable of movement). In its simplest terms a model is a miniature replica of a real-world entity. It permits examination and modification of entities too large or too valuable to risk damaging.

One application of modeling useful to criminal investigators and crime analysts is pin maps, which approximate the location of certain crimes. Different colored pins may represent different crimes, days of the week, times of the day, and so on. Mock-ups and miniature cities have been used in the past to represent locations where a raid is planned or to develop a strategy to deal with informant information about an upcoming crime. It is now possible to generate computer models for both of these situations and many more.[58]

A *simulation* evolves from the addition of motion to a model. The value of simulation is that it permits subjecting a prototype to conditions that would be either too costly or too dangerous to attempt experimentally under real-world conditions. On a computer it is possible to test an unlimited number of model variations in an infinite number of environments with a zero-tolerance risk factor.

One example of an early law enforcement simulation is the "Shoot, Don't Shoot" firearms training film. A more sophisticated contemporary version utilizes interactive video and a laser fitted to a handgun that emits a pulse of light instead of a bullet. The trainee reacts to various computer-controlled video scenarios, which permit both instructor and trainee to assess shooting technique and judgment.

Another example of a computer simulation useful to criminal investigators is image-aging. Years ago, composite drawings were developed to approximate the facial features of a suspect or a victim. Such sketches can now be computer generated, and one product, called Face Software, even superimposes the image of an older face over that of a young child. By simulating the aging process to suggest what a child might look like years later, this program shows great promise in child abduction cases.[59]

A *game* results from the addition of human interaction and competition to simulation. Two or more such interactions—efforts to outperform or surpass another using equivalent means—constitute a game. Games permit the blending of several methodologies and enable decision makers to experience the consequences of their choices in a hands-on environment. Future, a game developed at the RAND Corporation, exemplifies the use of the Delphi technique and the cross-impact matrix method.[60] Examples of computer games that might be useful to criminal investigators are "Where in the World Is Carmen Sandiego?" and "Crime Adventure."[61]

A simple illustration shows the natural flow from a model to a simulation to a game. When the many parts of a kit are removed from a box and carefully assembled, the result may be a model airplane. As it rests on a surface, it is a static model. When it is picked up and moved through various maneuvers, it becomes a dynamic model because motion has been added and a simulation because the action of flight is being mimicked. When two individuals each pick up similar model airplanes and attempt to outmaneuver one another, human interaction and competition have been added to the simulation, resulting in a game. Given state-of-the-art computer color and graphics technology, imagination becomes one's only limitation.

At each step the criminal investigator refines the original model and finds justification for progressing and escalating the planned activity or entity. For decision makers this procedure should reflect a well thought-out, cost-conscious presentation worthy of serious consideration.

Conclusions

While speaking about law enforcement management, Gordon E. Misner, professor of criminal justice at the University of Illinois at Chicago, stated,

> Frankly, I think it is somewhat ludicrous to talk in terms of executive leadership—in today's "high tech" era—without addressing the issue of the future. To do so is to repeat old mistakes of creating obsolescence. In my judgment, one of the "growth areas" in management training is specifically going to focus on ways in which to anticipate the future, thereby giving some precision to strategic planning.[62]

Criminal investigators, too, should consider these words of wisdom. The failure of law enforcement to be anticipatory is a function of the reactionary nature of policing; the law must be violated before the police can enforce it. But reactive policing is not the way it must be.

Criminal investigators—detectives—have long reveled in the public perceptions that they are the elite of law enforcement. However, that myth has been challenged, and the time may be at hand to "put up or shut up."[63] Futures research offers both the philosophy and the tools to analyze, forecast, and plan in ways rarely seen in American policing. It is possible now to do more than meticulously capture, record, and report crime data. Guided by insight, imagination, and innovation, success awaits criminal investigators willing to attempt creative new approaches to dealing with crime and criminals.

In 546 B.C., ill-prepared to do battle with the armies of Cyrus of Persia, Croesus, the king of Lydia, sought the counsel of the oracle at Delphi. The oracle advised Croesus that the stronger army would win. Confident that the gods favored him, Croesus attacked the forces of Cyrus and was summarily defeated by the Persians.

This now-famous Delphic foretelling may prove to be prophetic for law enforcement. Indeed, the better prepared will win the war on crime. Unfortunately, too many criminal investigators are oblivious to what lies ahead and are committed to the belief that the forces of good and justice will prevail because they always have in the past. However, the present battle with street gangs and cocaine and crack dealers may be an ominous foreshadowing of the pernicious and multifaceted nature of crime to come. Law enforcement is having difficulty coping with crime now and shows little inclination to modify its approaches in the future. Who will risk stepping out of the darkness of the cave and walking into the light of day?

Notes

[1] See James Q. Wilson and Richard J. Herrnstein, *Crime and Human Nature* (New York: Simon and Schuster, 1985) for a cogent, concise, and balanced view of the pros and cons of the utility of the uniform crime report (UCR) as opposed to the National Crime Survey (NCS) data.

[2] William Spelman, "Beyond Bean Counting: New Approaches for Managing Crime Data" (Washington, DC: Police Executive Research Forum, January 1988), iii.

[3] James Q. Wilson and Richard J. Herrnstein, *Crime and Human Nature,* 32.

[4] Edward Cornish, *The Study of the Future* (Washington, DC: World Future Society, 1977), 98–99.

[5] See Wayne A. Kerstetter, "The Police in 1984," *Journal of Criminal Justice* 7, no. 1 (Spring 1979): 1; Jack L. Kuykendall and Peter C. Unsinger, *Community Police Administration* (Chicago: Nelson-Hall, 1975), 13; Thomas A. Reppetto, *The Blue Parade* (New York: Free Press, 1978), 11; Joseph J. Senna and Larry J. Siegel, *Introduction to Criminal Justice,* 3d ed. (St. Paul: West, 1984), 151; William A. Geller, ed. *Police Leadership in America: Crisis and Opportunity* (New York: Praeger, 1985), xx; John E. Angell, "Organizing Police for the Future: An Update of the Democratic Model," *Criminal Justice Review* 1, no. 2 (Fall 1976): 49; Anthony V. Bouza, "The Future of Policing: One Man's Opinion," *PMA News* 1, no. 3 (1983): 4; James F. Newman, review of *On Thermonuclear War,* by Herman Kahn, *Scientific American* 204, no. 3 (March 1961): 27.

[6] Alvin Toffler, "The Future as a Way of Life," *Horizon* 7, no. 3 (Summer 1965): 109.

[7] Alvin Toffler, *Future Shock* (New York: Random House, 1970), 13, 290.

[8] Edward Cornish, *The Study of the Future,* 4; idem, "From Future Shock to Anticipatory Democracy," *The Futurist* 10, no. 2 (April 1976): 105.

[9] William L. Tafoya, "Project Intercept: The Los Angeles Experience," *Journal of Criminal Justice* 2, no. 1 (Spring 1974): 56.

[10] David J. Bordua and Albert J. Reiss, Jr., "Command, Control, and Charisma: Reflections on Police Bureaucracy," *American Journal of Sociology* 72, no. 1 (July 1966): 74.

[11] Egon Bittner, "The Functions of the Police in Modern Society," (Chevy Chase, MD: National Institute of Mental Health, 1970; Cambridge, MA: Oelgeschlager, Gunn & Hain, 1980), 143; Herman Goldstein, *Policing a Free Society* (Cambridge, MA: Ballinger, 1977), 136; Academy of Criminal Justice Sciences, "Police Officers Won't Tolerate Autocratic Management Style," *ACJS Today,* January 1984, 6; Jerome H. Skolnick and David H. Bayley, *The New Blue Line: Police Innovation in Six American Cities* (New York: Free Press, 1986), 227; Gerald E. Caiden, *Police Revitalization* (Lexington, MA: Lexington Books, 1977), 12; Thomas A. Reppetto, *The Blue Parade,* 244; William F. Walsh, "Patrol Officer Arrest Rates: A Study of the Social Organization of Police Work," *Justice Quarterly* 3, no. 3 (September 1986): 271–90.

[12] Lawrence W. Sherman, *The Quality of Police Education* (San Francisco: Jossey-Bass Publishers, 1978), 199; John C. LeDoux et al., "A Study of Factors Influencing the Continuing Education of Law Enforcement Officers" (Quantico, VA: FBI Academy, July 1982), 21.

[13] William L. Tafoya, "Needs Assessment: Key to Organizational Change," *Journal of Police Science and Administration* 11, no. 3 (September 1983): 309; Alvin Toffler, *Future Shock,* 356, 381.

[14] Alvin Toffler, *Future Shock,* 407.

[15] Edward Cornish, *The Study of the Future,* 106.

[16] Terry W. Rothermel, "Forecasting Revisited," *Harvard Business Review* 60, no. 2 (March-April 1982): 146.

[17] Earl C. Joseph, "An Introduction to Studying the Future," in *Futurism in Education: Methodologies,* ed. Stephen B. Hencley and James R. Yates (Berkeley, CA: McCutchan, 1974): 9–10.

[18] Edward Cornish, *The Study of the Future,* 53.

[19] Eric Hoffer, "Imitation and Fanaticism," in *The Ordeal of Change* (New York: Harper & Row, 1963), 18–22; John Lofland, *Doomsday Cult* (Englewood Cliffs, NJ: Prentice-Hall, 1966).

[20] Charles Y. Glock and Rodney Stark, "Religiosity," in *Religion and Society in Tension* (Chicago: Rand McNally, 1965), 18–38.

[21] Edward Cornish, *The Study of the Future,* 53–54.

[22] Thomas Dempsey, *The Delphi Oracle: Its Early History, Influence, and Fall* (Oxford, England: Blackwell, 1918; New York: Benjamin Blum, 1972), 35.

[23] Edward Cornish, *The Study of the Future,* 51; Alvin Toffler, *The Futurists,* 4.

[24] Peter W. Greenwood, Jan M. Chaiken, and Joan Petersilia, *The Criminal Investigation Process* (Santa Monica: Rand Corporation, 1975).

[25] Norman C. Dalkey and Olaf Helmer, "An Experimental Application of the Delphi Method to the Use of Experts," *Management Science* 9, no. 3 (April 1963): 458–67; Olaf Helmer and Nicholas Rescher, "On the Epistemology of the Inexact Sciences," *Management Science* 6, no. 1 (October 1959): 25–52.

[26] Edward Cornish, *The Study of the Future,* 97.

[27] Ibid., 99–102.

[28] Fred N. Kerlinger, *Foundations of Behavioral Research,* 2d ed. (New York: Holt, Rinehart and Winston, 1973), 459–60.

[29] Roy Amara, "The Futures Field: Searching for Definitions and Boundaries," *The Futurist* 15, no. 1 (February 1981): 25.

[30] Ibid., 26.

[31] Alvin Toffler, "The Future as a Way of Life," 115.

[32] Reliability and validity are too important to treat superficially, yet space does not permit a thorough discussion here. The reader is directed to Edward G. Carmines and Richard A. Zeller, *Reliability and Validity Assessment* (Beverly Hills, CA: Sage, 1979) and Jerome Kirk and Marc L. Miller, *Reliability and Validity in Qualitative Research* (Beverly Hills, CA: Sage, 1986).

[33] Stanford Research Institute, *Handbook of Forecasting Techniques* (Fort Belvoir, VA: U.S. Army Corps of Engineers, 1975), NTIS# AD–AO19 280/7; idem, *Handbook of Forecasting Techniques: Description of 31 Techniques* (Fort Belvoir, VA: U.S. Army Corps of Engineers, 1977), NTIS# AD–AO44 810/0; idem, *Handbook of Forecasting Techniques: List of 73 Techniques* (Fort Belvoir, VA: U.S. Army Corps of Engineers, 1977), NTIS# AD–AO44 809/2.

[34] These documents are available from the National Technical Information Service, U.S. Department of Commerce, 5285 Port Royal Road, Springfield, VA 22161.

[35] An excellent discussion of forecasting methodologies from a criminal justice perspective is presented in John K. Hudzik and Gary W. Cordner, *Planning in Criminal Justice Organizations and Systems* (New York: Macmillan, 1983), 165–82.

[36] Harold A. Linstone, "The Delphi Technique," in *Handbook of Futures Research*, 273–300; Harold A. Linstone and Murray Turoff, eds. *The Delphi Method: Techniques and Applications* (Reading, MA: Addison-Wesley, 1975).

[37] An excellent assessment of the Delphi technique from a criminal justice perspective is found in Timothy J. Flanagan and Michael R. Buckman, *The Delphi Technique: A Tool for Criminal Justice Planners* (Albany, NY: State University of New York at Albany, School of Criminal Justice, November 1976).

[38] The Police Executive Research Forum's (PERF) METAPOL computer system—although not, strictly speaking, Delphi conferencing—incorporates most of the features commonly associated with that technique.

[39] Delayne Hudspeth, "The Cross Impact Matrix," in *Futurism in Education: Methodologies*, ed. Stephen F. Hencley and James R. Yates (Berkeley, CA: McCutchan, 1974), 115; Olaf Helmer, *Looking Forward*, 159.

[40] Joseph P. Martino, *Technological Forecasting for Decision Making*, 2d ed. (New York: Elsevier, 1983), 159.

[41] J.H. McGrath, "Relevance Trees," in *Futurism in Education: Methodologies*, 78. PERT calls for three estimates: the optimistic time reflects the expectation that everything will occur on schedule. The pessimistic time assumes that nothing will go right. The most likely time expects things to be neither perfect nor chaotic. An excellent police-related discussion is Peter C. Unsinger, "PERT and a Planning Problem," in *Effective Police Administration: A Behavioral Approach*, ed. Harry W. More (San Jose, CA: Justice Systems Development, 1975), 192–98.

[42] Among those addressing technology assessment are Vary T. Coates and Joseph F. Coates, "Technological Assessment and Education," in *Futurism in Education: Methodologies*, 235; Joshua Menkes, "The Role of Technology Assessment in the Decision Making Process," *Futures Research Quarterly* 1, no. 3 (Fall 1985): 5; and Harry Jones and Brian Twiss, *Forecasting Technology for Planning Decisions*, 43.

[43] U.S. Congress, Office of Technology Assessment, *Science, Technology, and the Constitution: Background Paper* (Washington, DC: U.S. Government Printing Office, 1987).

[44] Robert U. Ayres, *Technological Forecasting*, 33; William G. Sullivan and W. Wayne Claycombe, *Fundamentals of Forecasting* (Reston, VA: Reston Publishing, 1977), 193; Harry Jones and Brian C. Twiss, *Forecasting Technology for Planning Decisions*, 55; Joseph P. Martino, *Technological Forecasting for Decision Making*, 159.

[45] Herbert G. Hicks, *The Management of Organizations: A Systems and Human Resources Approach*, 2d ed. (New York: McGraw-Hill, 1972), 219; James L. Adams, *Conceptual Blockbusting: A Guide to Better Ideas*, 3d ed. (Reading, MA: Addison-Wesley, 1986), 135.

[46] Joseph P. Martino, *Technological Forecasting for Decision Making*, 164.

[47] Ibid., 165–66.

[48] F. Buckminster Fuller, *Operating Manual for Spaceship Earth* (Carbondale, IL: Southern Illinois University Press, 1969), 70.

[49] Amitai Etzioni, "Mixed-Scanning: A 'Third' Approach to Decision Making," *Public Administration Review* 27, no. 5 (December 1967): 387.

[50] Ibid., 385.

[51] Andre L. Delbecq, Andrew H. Van de Ven, and David H. Gustafson, *Group Techniques for Program Planning* (Glenview, IL: Scott, Foresman, 1975).

[52] Fred N. Kerlinger and Elazar J. Pedhazur, *Multiple Regression in Behavioral Research* (New York: Holt, Rinehart and Winston, 1973), 3.

[53] An extrapolation is an estimate of a value that lies beyond the range of the baseline data evidenced in a trend. This method assumes that the trend will continue in the same direction and at the same pace. These are safe short-term assumptions for variables that tend to be stable, such as population growth or the number of miles driven by police patrol vehicles. However, these assumptions are questionable at best for sociological variables, such as crime, that tend to fluctuate quite dramatically. Discussion of this topic can be found in any elementary statistics text, often under the heading "Regression Analysis."

[54] David W. Miller and Martin K. Starr, *Executive Decisions and Operations Research* (Englewood Cliffs, NJ: Prentice-Hall, 1960), 273–80.

[55] James F. McNamara, "Markov Chain Theory and Technological Forecasting," in *Futurism in Education: Methodologies,* 303.

[56] William L. Hays, *Statistics for the Social Sciences,* 2d ed. (New York: Holt, Rinehart and Winston 1973), 809–12.

[57] Stanford Research Institute, *Description of 31 Techniques,* 28–29; Thomas D. Cook and Donald T. Campbell, *Quasi-Experimentation: Design and Analysis Issues for Field Settings* (Boston: Houghton Mifflin, 1979), 235.

[58] See Paul Gray and William R. Heitzman, "A Detective Allocation Model," *Journal of Criminal Justice* 4, no. 4 (Winter 1976): 341–46. See also Lawrence E. Cohen, "Modeling Crime Trends: A Criminal Opportunity Perspective," *Journal of Research in Crime and Delinquency* 18, no. 1 (January 1981): 138–64.

[59] Leigh Rivenbark, "Graphics Software Helps FBI Face Identification Challenges," *Federal Computer Week* 2, no. 3 (18 Jan. 1988): 9. See also Jonathan F. Bard, "The Use of Simulation in Criminal Justice Policy Evaluation," *Journal of Criminal Justice* 6, no. 2 (Summer 1978): 99–116.

[60] Olaf Helmer and Theodore J. Gordon, "Report on a Long-Range Forecasting Study."

[61] See Larry J. Siegel, Dennis C. Sullivan, and Jack R. Greene, "Decision Games Applied to Police Decision Making: An Exploratory Study of Information Usage," *Journal of Criminal Justice* 2, no. 2 (Summer 1974): 131–46.

[62] Gordon E. Misner, Letter to author, 1 Dec. 1987.

[63] Peter W. Greenwood, Jan M. Chaiken, and Joan Petersilia, *The Criminal Investigation Process;* Jack L. Kuykendall, "The Municipal Police Detective: An Historical Analysis," *Criminology* 24, no. 1 (February 1986): 175–201.